ERIKA VON BARAVALLE (Ed.)

# Rudolf Steiner's Laying of the Foundation Stone
## on September 20, 1913

The building from the southeast

ERIKA VON BARAVALLE (Ed.)

# Rudolf Steiner's Laying of the Foundation Stone on September 20, 1913

*In the Presence of the Stars*

ALKION
PRESS

*In Memory of Fritz Götte*

Original German Publication in 2013 by Verlag des Ita Wegman Instituts:
*Rudolf Steiners Grundsteinlegung am 20. September 1913: Im Angesicht der Sterne.*
Ita Wegman Institut
für anthroposophische Grundlagenforschung
Pfeffingerweg 1A, CH-4144 Arlesheim

Printed with the support of the Fern Hill Fund
ISBN:
Hardback: 979-8-9874429-1-3
Paperback: 979-8-9874429-2-0

Title: Rudolf Steiner's Laying of the Foundation Stone on September 20, 1913: In the Presence of the Stars

Editor: Erika von Baravalle

Translation revised by Patti Corozine
Layout and Design: Ella Manor Lapointe
Cover motif: Photo of the Foundation Stone, September 20, 1913
Frontispiece: The building from the southeast

# CONTENTS

# An Acknowledgement

I met Erika von Baravalle for the first time in 1996. She was standing in a neighbor's driveway, admiring and contemplating the architectural aspects of her house on Juraweg, a stone's throw from the Goetheanum in Dornach. As a result of this encounter, I became her multi-tasked helper for a number of years. Her house had been designed by her late husband, Albert von Baravalle, and was a treasure trove of sorts. On the ground floor, the scale model of the first Goetheanum rested on a beautifully handcrafted wooden table. A few feet away, within a curtained space, a simulated model of the large cupola was suspended from the ceiling under which a person could comfortably sit. Nearby was the "red room" with its vibrant scarlet walls on which hung the seven planetary seals, each on a disc of indigo blue with its symbol drawn in gold paint. The interior of the house was of artistic simplicity oriented towards practical needs.

During this time, Erika—in addition to writing numerous essays — also had many speaking engagements and therefore travelled widely.

In 2011, I left Dornach and returned to the United States in 2013. Although I phoned her periodically, I was only made aware of the publication of her book by a mutual acquaintance. When asked, she readily agreed to send me a copy and asked only that I try to have it translated and published in English. Early attempts did not bear fruit. Time passed until the necessary cosmic configuration became manifest and all became possible. With this being said, I would like to acknowledge and thank the following individuals who—wittingly or unwittingly—contributed towards the publication of this book.

Hans Schumm, Gary Lamb, Eric G. Müller, Thomas O'Keefe, Andy Shaw, Gopi Krishna Vijaya on behalf of the Foundation of Cultural Renewal. A note of thanks to Ines, Christiane Marks, Roswitha Smith, along with Brittany and Wayne at the Yancey County Library in Burnsville, NC.

Erika was an individual of singular artistic temperament. One can have a feeling of deep gratitude for her inspiration, perseverance, and the manner in which she crafted her book.

Celo, North Carolina, Holy Nights, 2023
*Patti Corozine*

# Foreword to the 2013 German Edition

When one wants to get a concrete mental picture of the laying of the foundation stone in Dornach in 1913, various eyewitness accounts and later articles can serve this purpose. For these, we owe our thanks to Fritz Götte, the long-time editor of the *Mitteilungen aus der Anthroposophischen Arbeit in Deutschland* [Communications from the anthroposophical work in Germany]. These texts are now [in 2013] only available in old journals. In 1953, on the fortieth anniversary of the laying of the foundation stone, Fritz Götte wrote an essay that provided the basis for an understanding of the development of the Anthroposophical Society from 1913 to 1923. This stimulated a wave of further accounts, which he published in 1953, 1956, and 1963. Considered from the various aspects of different disciplines, these essays offer accounts of the world-historic significance of Rudolf Steiner's deed. With the present book—thanks to the kind permission of the editors of the *Mitteilungen aus der Anthroposophischen Arbeit in Deutschland* [Communications from the anthroposophical work in Germany), to whom we hereby express our sincere gratitude—these accounts can now be made accessible to a wider circle of readers. The wording of the articles has not been altered; however, the editorial introductions and cross-references within contemporary periodicals have not been included; the spelling has been standardized and adapted to the current rules; spelling or grammatical errors have been corrected.

Götte's ingenious interpretation of the threefold building impulse—building in one's own soul, on the Earth, and within the community—cannot be appreciated highly enough.[1] Yet this may have led him to relate the act of the Christmas Conference solely to the building of the anthroposophical community and not, in like manner, to the Second Goetheanum. Actually, the relationship between the foundation stone and the community is self-evident. Every laying of a foundation stone for a building for the enactment of the mysteries would be meaningless if it did not also apply to a community, which not only accompanies the act of building but is also responsible in the future for a meaningful use of what has been built.

For the second building, Rudolf Steiner did not design a new physical foundation stone because the building was intended to have the same function as the first one. He left the stone in its place. Instead, he created a comprehensive mantra, which contained all of anthroposophy.

In her preface to the 1935 *Second Edition of Rudolf Steiner's Wahrspruchworten (True-wrought-words)*, when the stanzas beginning with the call "Human Soul" were first published, Marie Steiner connected the mantra with the planned second building by a reference to "the words of the laying of the spiritual foundation stone of the Second Goetheanum spoken by Rudolf Steiner himself at the Christmas Conference in 1923/24."

In order to understand this comment, we must learn to read the new style of architecture. Important approaches in this direction are found in the lifelong, ground-laying research of the architect Albert von Baravalle. Through many years of study, I learned to understand how this building is not only an intensified continuation of the first one but also realizes a goal that Rudolf Steiner set himself from the beginning with his buildings in Dornach, namely: to be able to address all human beings worldwide with a gesture that is both inviting and leaves them free. This gives rise to further aspects of the laying of the foundation stone.

The [German edition of this] book was planned for September 20, 2003, the 90th anniversary of the laying of the foundation stone of the First Goetheanum. Unexpectedly, the work dragged on until Pentecost 2013. This points us to Rudolf Steiner's Pentecost lectures in 1908 and 1910, published under the title *Pfingsten: das Fest der freien Individualität* [Pentecost: The festival of the free individuality]. These lectures can serve to trace the multi-layered Mystery of the foundation stone. Ultimately, this

Mystery concerns the newly consecrated human soul that rises to receive the fiery tongue of the Spirit of Truth. This is the purpose of building and community.

That the book can now appear on the 100th anniversary we owe to the cooperation of the following friends: Peter Selg as director of the *Ita Wegman Institut für anthroposophische Grundlagenforschung* (Ita Wegman Institute for Basic Research into Anthroposophy), Felicitas Graf and Walter Schneider from the *Verlag des Ita Wegman Instituts* (publishing house of the Ita Wegman Institute), Clara Steinemann from the *Vorstand der Anthroposophischen Gesellschaft in der Schweiz* (Executive Council of the Anthroposophical Society in Switzerland), architect Henrik Hilbig, EngD as advisor and technical helper, Ingrid Everwijn and Christine Yokoyama as helpers with the writing, and Roeland Everwijn as photographer of the crystals.

Dornach, Pentecost 2013
*Erika von Baravalle*

*Fig. 1: Rudolf Steiner at the building site in Dornach, 1913.*

# Preliminaries

There are some moments in Rudolf Steiner's life that make one sit up and take notice. For example, a few evenings before the laying of the foundation stone on September 20, 1913, a significant scene took place on the Dornach hill, which only two people were called by destiny to experience: Wilhelm Schrack, who later described it in writing, and Carl Schmid-Curtius, who would then direct the building work on the First Goetheanum for the first year. They witnessed how Rudolf Steiner determined the place on the Earth for the foundation stone. The master builder—dressed as usual in black, with Wellington boots, coat, and a walking stick in his hand—paced back and forth a little ways above them. As he did so, he looked alternately at the heavens and the Earth, occasionally taking a closer look at something with the stick, until suddenly he thrust it into the Earth, announcing loudly, "This is the spot!" What a fascinating symbol of his lifelong work! Only two pairs of human eyes could observe the process, which, nevertheless, at the same time drew the eyes of innumerable angels and elemental beings.

And then, at the laying of the foundation stone itself, there were other sensory impressions that provoked meaningful premonitions in many of those present. They heard Rudolf Steiner's sonorous voice rising up from below in the excavation pit and perceived the heartfelt words with which he addressed all nine hierarchies one after the other—asking blessings for the act of consecration. The answer came from the stars as a "golden rain" that ever since has been upon the hill. Thus, Rudolf Steiner kindled a new dialogue between the human being and the angelic world.

His whole work ultimately consists of heavenly gifts. Gifts, however, want to be received. Rudolf Steiner found the first recipients in the Theosophical Society in 1902. Since his lectures "Über den verlorenen und wiederzuerrichtenden Tempel" [On the lost and to-be-rebuilt temple] in 1952 and the Munich Congress in 1907,[3] the art of building—which has belonged to all Mystery sites since time immemorial—had been his earnest endeavor. This, however, requires a community that not only wants to receive but also to collaborate and to carry further. Such people came together in Munich to establish a building for theater and performance and theater in the Rosicrucian style of art. This took some time. Meanwhile, in Malsch near Karlsruhe, a model for a Rosicrucian Temple of Initiation was created, according to the main elements presented by Rudolf Steiner in 1907 for the decoration of a rented concert hall.

In Malsch, [during Holy Week] 1909, he performed for the first time a laying of a foundation stone, in the already-erected, inconspicuous building whose exterior betrayed nothing of its interior. For this purpose, esoteric disciples from the Theosophical Society gathered together. Despite the stark simplicity of the foundation stone—which consisted of a flask containing a document—Rudolf Steiner spoke words that expressed the deepest meaning of this act of consecration, words that he never formulated in this way again:

> In pain has our Mother Earth solidified. Our mission is to spiritualize her once again, to redeem her, by remaking her—through the power of our hands—into a spirit-filled work of art. May this stone be a first foundation stone for the redemption and transformation of our planet Earth; and may the power of this stone be multiplied a thousandfold.

> *Unter Schmerzen hat unsere Mutter Erde sich verfestigt. Unsere Mission ist es, sie wieder zu vergeistigen, zu erlösen, indem wir sie durch die Kraft unserer Hände umarbeiten zu einem geisterfüllten Kunstwerk. Möge dieser Stein zugleich ein erster Grundstein zur Erlösung und Umwandelung unseres Erdenplaneten sein und möge die Kraft dieses Steines sich vertausendfältigen.*

The plan was that the room was to be hidden underground, but it could not be realized as a building at that time. Later, it was implemented in the cellar of the Stuttgart branch.

In 1913, a group broke away from the Theosophical Society as an independent "Anthroposophical Society." Now Rudolf Steiner could hope for a larger, truly understanding audience, and he found free ground in Dornach for the building for the enactment of the mysteries initially planned for Munich. The wooden building of the First Goetheanum gave many people the opportunity to lend a helping hand and also to give their work as a gift. Thus, they could try to develop social capacities, all the while experiencing the adversaries lurking everywhere around their activities.

From the beginning, these adversaries had been in opposition to Rudolf Steiner's wish to inscribe anthroposophy into the Earth in the form of a building. The authorities of Munich did not grant a building permit. In February 1913, the decision was made to erect the building in Dornach. Rudolf Steiner, who [at that point] was not a member of the Building Association (Bauverein) or the Anthroposophical Society, left the determination of the building material to the members. They chose wood, after the timber merchant Joseph van Leer offered the immense quantity needed as a donation. Rudolf Steiner, who had conceived the building in concrete,[4] let it happen (probably also in the hope of being able to complete the building more quickly in this way, given his premonitions of an impending war). The First World War began in August 1914. During construction, many people from warring nations worked together, but things were not as peaceful as they seemed from the outside.

Every year during his addresses commemorating the laying of the foundation stone in 1913, Rudolf Steiner urged fellowship. He spoke of a "vow" (Gelöbnis) to the spirit of anthroposophy; and, after all, participation in the laying of the foundation stone had already signified the making of this vow. Already after one year, he even had to dismiss the leading architect [Carl Schmid-Curtius]; and through the years it has been remembered how he said during a discussion in 1915: "Outside, people are talking about the blind faith in authority of the anthroposophists! In reality, all I have to do is say something and the opposite happens."[5] But Rudolf Steiner held his ground; and, in 1920, he participated in the provisional opening of the unique total-work-of-art (*Gesamtkunstwerk*), which was not quite completed. Further on, there were many problems that weighed on his hopeful soul. On Sylvester Night [New Year's Eve] 1922, the miraculous work was completely destroyed by arson. Rudolf Steiner's admonitions to be vigilant had also not been heeded.

This truly wise teacher continued to work; forgiving everything, he reconnected with his dedicated students in the Christmas Conference. Thus, he was still able to make a model for the Second Goetheanum and reveal Michael's wisdom in abundance. Wonder after wonder occurred, and, after his death, the new building was erected by an enthusiastic team of architects, and inaugurated at Michaelmas 1928 with roughly 2000 participants. Today, "Michael's Castle," with its exterior architecture made of "forms awakening karma-vision," still stands in the landscape as a legacy pointing far into the future.

And still, again and again, from then until now, dark clouds gather over the hill. Michael's students ask themselves: Was it all in vain? But as they proceed along the stony paths over the hill, suddenly it shimmers like gold upon the ground. They are amazed. ... Then a ray of sunlight reaches the building of Michael. During his last address, on the eve of Michaelmas 1924, Rudolf Steiner gave another special treasure: the mantra of the "Michael Imagination." This the master builder also wove into the etheric aura of the hill. "Michael's radiant garment" embraces its followers: protectively, encouragingly, nourishing with the fire of enthusiasm.

*Erika von Baravalle*

Endnotes

1    See also Erika von Baravalle, "Der dreifache Bauimpuls" [The threefold building impulse], 1–3.

2    Rudolf Steiner, "Concerning the Lost Temple and How It Is to Be Restored," *The Temple Legend*, lectures in Berlin on May 15, 22, 29, & June 5, 1905, pp. 121–180. CW 33

3    Rudolf Steiner, Occult Seals and Symbols, CW 284 *Rosicrucianism Renewed*.

4    Cf. Alexander Strakosch, *Lebenswege mit Rudolf Steiner* [Life-paths with Rudolf Steiner].

5    Reported by Adelheid Petersen. See Gerhard Wehr, *Rudolf Steiner* (München: Hugendubel, 2005); cf. "Dornach in den Jahren 1914/15" [Dornach in the years 1914/15], in Erika Beltle and Kurt Vierl, eds., *Errinerungen an Rudolf Steiner*, 188f.

# I.
# The Significance of the Laying of the Foundation Stone in 1913

Essays by Erika von Baravalle

# The Mystery of the Laying of the Foundation Stone

*On the 90th Anniversary of the Laying of the Foundation Stone of the
First Goetheanum Building on September 20, 1913*

Ninety years ago, the Mystery of the laying of the foundation stone of the First Goetheanum on the Dornach Hill took place. So, may it once again light up in the consciousness of many people, because it is—together with the second part, the laying of the Foundation Stone during the Christmas Conference in 1923—the most significant event of Rudolf Steiner's activity. After it was initially shrouded in silence for a long time (for understandable reasons), Fritz Götte wrote a two-part essay in the 1953 Michaelmas and Christmas issues of *Mitteilungen aus der Anthroposophischen Arbeit in Deutschland* [Communications from the anthroposophical work in Germany],[6] in which he traces the deeper connections in Rudolf Steiner's work and characterizes the concept of the "threefold building impulse." This refers to our tasks of building in our own higher 'I', building within the human community, and the very real physical building activity, which he presents in their mutual interdependence. A special light is also shed on the laying of the Foundation Stone in 1923, which is so often one-sidedly regarded as a consequence of the Goetheanum fire. He quotes Rudolf Steiner, who on September 20, 1916, in remembrance of the laying of the foundation stone in 1913, spoke the following words:

> But in many of our souls there lives an honest, gen-
> uine will; and this honest, genuine will—if it is true
> to itself—will add understanding to the honesty of the
> will; and then—in all our souls—the other foundation
> stone will be able to form. This other foundation stone
> would like to carry spiritually into the world, in various
> and manifold ways, that which we ourselves wanted to
> establish, for the sake of our ideal, upon the physical

23

foundation stone which, three years ago, we sacredly entrusted to the Earth, here on this hill.

From this indication, given seven years before the Christmas Conference of 1923, it is clear that Rudolf Steiner had probably prepared from the beginning, along with the Mystery act of laying the foundation stone in 1913, a further deed, which was then first implemented with the Christmas Conference. This [further deed] could be envisioned—with the [First Goetheanum] building continuing to exist—as relating to the inauguration of the Goetheanum as a Mystery building, which was supposed to take place only after the completion of the sculptural group and its placement within the small cupola in the east.[7]

Götte marks the significance of the 1913 event as follows: The event took place

> not at an arbitrary position on the planet, but at a place that [Rudolf Steiner] had previously investigated physically and spiritually down to its foundations. The whole surrounding landscape and the history of humankind in the stream of time spoke in unison with this act on the Dornach hill. . . . The Anthroposophical Movement had arrived at the decisive act at this historical moment. It connected itself with the "condensed kingdom of the elements." From this moment and from this place began the immediate work of redemption by anthroposophy on the Earth. As an extension of the many aspects of the spiritual background of this laying of the foundation stone that have been shown by Rudolf Grosse and Sergei Prokofieff, we would like to turn attention to some aspects of its very concrete occurrence on and in the Earth.[8]

As an extension of the many aspects of the spiritual background of this laying of the foundation stone that have been shown by Rudolf Grosse and Sergei Prokofieff, we would like to turn attention to some aspects of its very concrete occurrence on and in the Earth.[9, 10]

The date of the laying of the foundation stone can be brought into various relationships with Rudolf Steiner's work. Here we mention only two facts that have hardly been noticed until now. First, archaeological research discovered roughly fifty years ago that the [Greater] Mysteries of Eleusis were enacted on September 20 and 21. Secondly, Hella Wiesberger has pointed out that Marie Steiner took office in the Theosophical Society on September 20, 1902, which was the prerequisite for Rudolf Steiner to work within it. The constellation on the evening of the laying of the foundation stone has been described in more detail by Elisabeth Vreede in 1935 and Walther Bühler in 1953.

There is an eyewitness account from Wilhelm Schrack concerning the orientation for the laying of the foundation stone on the Dornach hilltop:

> When I paid a visit to the Dornach hill one evening, I met the architect Schmid-Curtius from Stuttgart there. Soon, Rudolf Steiner came armed with Wellington boots, a coat, and a walking stick. About seventy meters away from us, Rudolf Steiner then walked in an arc forward, sideways, and backward again, often raising his gaze to the stars, and he also stretched out his stick to the stars several times. Thereupon, Rudolf Steiner lightly inscribed a small circle on the earth with the stick, almost constantly looking up to the stars, stopped briefly, and suddenly thrust the stick into the soil and shouted, "This is the spot."[11]

In the following days, the pit of six meters in diameter and 1.75 meters in depth was dug through arduous manual work by many participants.

More detailed indications about the composition of the foundation stone are available from the master locksmith Max Benzinger. The foundation stone, manufactured in Munich, was a construction made from copper in the form of two dodecahedrons welded together, a larger one with the length of 63 cm and a smaller one with the length of 54 cm. A dodecahedral pyrite stone was suspended in each body, a smaller stone in the larger body, a larger one in the smaller body. Copper has a relationship with Venus, the star of love; pyrite is comprised of sulfur and iron. The foundation stone was sunk into the soil in a protectively closed concrete container as a symbol of the human soul, "in the condensed kingdom of the elements." Rudolf Steiner placed special value on the exact orientation of the foundation stone axis along the east-west direction.

In the interior of the foundation stone lay the document of 130 cm in length and 90 cm in width, which had to be rolled [vertically, from top to bottom]. As a result, the cardinal points on the parchment [aligned with] the geographical ones, and [the lines of text would be read across from west to east and down from north to south].

The foundation stone document consisted of a bull calf skin inscribed by Rudolf Steiner (Fig. 4). In an enclosed egg shape, he drew a double dodecahedron with the initials of the Rosicrucian verse; in the middle line, the "C" for "Christo," which was always written out in the context of the occult seals, was left out as "too holy."[12] Alongside it, on the left and on the right, Rudolf Steiner placed the syllables "Anthropos." Three fine, mutually interweaving, manifold, and variously bowed lines entwine the dodecahedral figure with an enfolding and nurturing gesture. At the ends, the lines are marked by the initial letters of the nine hierarchies. A sketch that Rudolf Steiner made of this has since appeared in print.[13] Even without the confining egg shape around it, the eurythmically swinging lines make an incomparable impression. Words can hardly express the loving, freeing gesture. By observing the alignments, one can learn something about the relationship of the hierarchies to their "problem child," the human being, whose entelechy carries within itself the potential for the tenth hierarchy. Even Rudolf Steiner's numerous verbal descriptions are not able to express this. If one allows the sketch to work upon oneself for a longer time, one can surmise what an outcry of joy went through the world of the elemental beings as Rudolf Steiner placed this message within their fold. In the present world situation this touches us all the more deeply. And it can be consoling to know that such an encounter between heavenly and earthly forces once took place at a definite location on Earth and works on further.

From the text under the drawing, two things are to be emphasized: Rudolf Steiner has written in the sketch "You Symbol of the Force ..." which he later changed, according to tradition, into "This Symbol of the Force." Such an intimate relationship is expressed in the personal form of address! In the numbers 3, 5, 7, 12, one can discover the whole of anthroposophy.

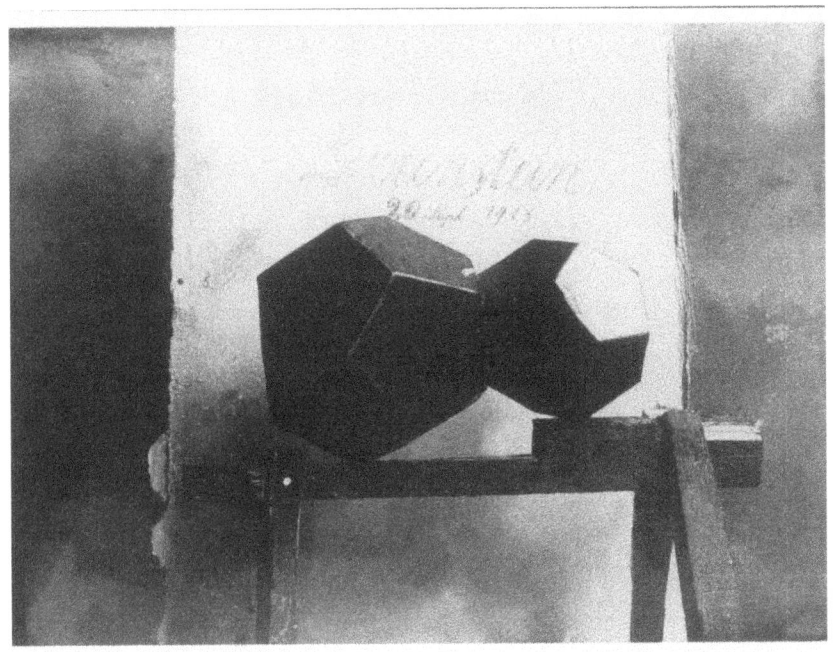

*Fig. 2: The foundation stone dodecahedra.*

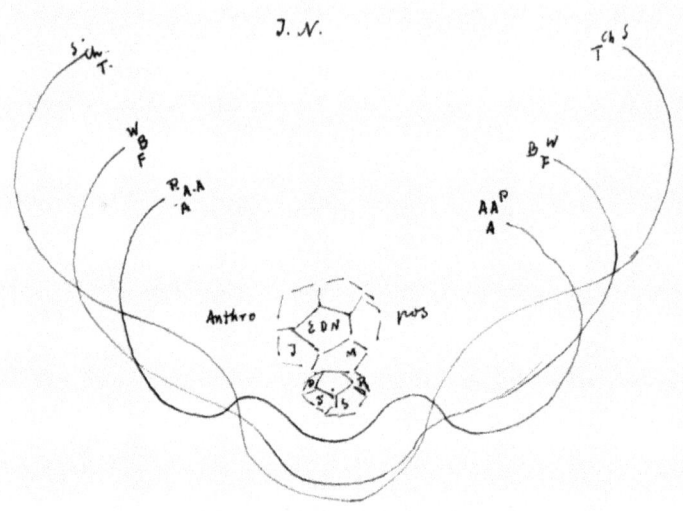

Fig. 3: Rudolf Steiner's sketch for the certificate.
© Rudolf Steiner Archive, Dornach.

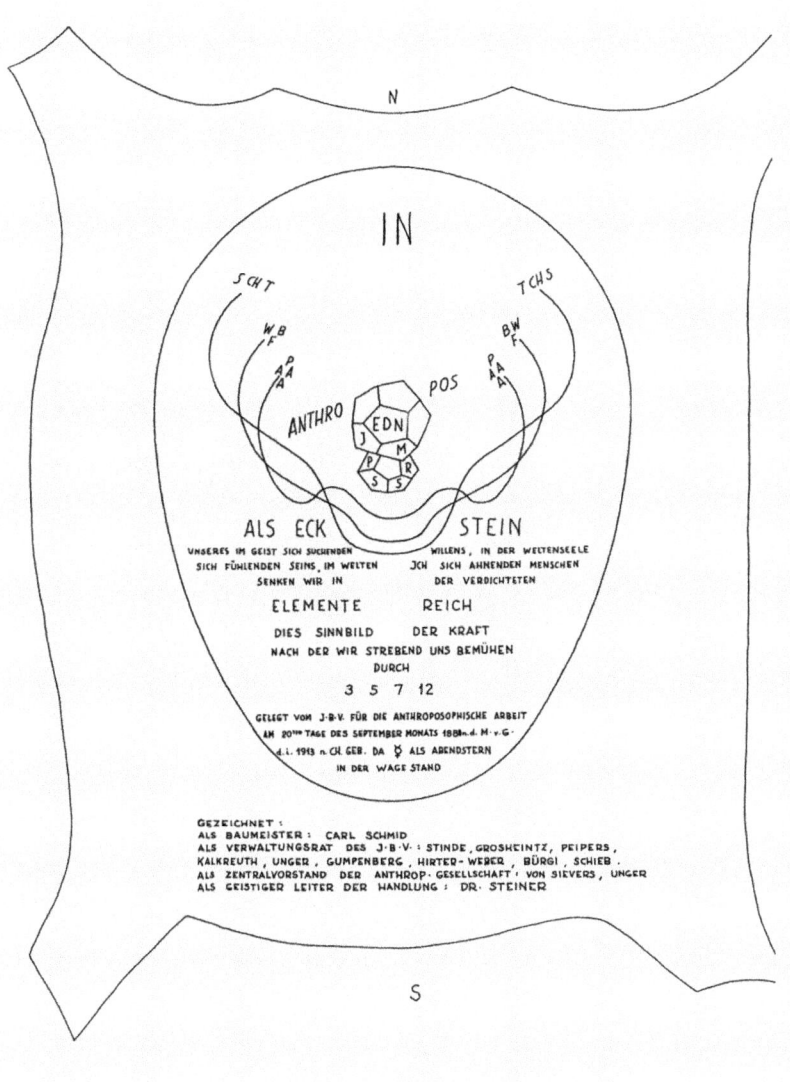

*Fig. 4: Drawing by Albert von Baravalle.*

29

Endnotes

6      See in this volume "First Publication of Essays," Fritz Götte, "From the Laying of the Foundation Stone in 1913 . . . ," parts 1 & 2.

7      The opening of the building with the First University School Course (*Hochschulkurse*) in September 1920 had a merely provisional character.

8      See in this volume Fritz Götte, "From the Laying of the Foundation Stone . . . , Part I."

9      Rudolf Grosse, *The Christmas Foundation Meeting*, Dornach 1976

10      Sergei Prokofief *Rudolf Steiner and the Founding of the New Mysteries*, Dornach 1986 and *The Twelve Holy Nights and the Spiritual Hierarchies*, Stuttgart 1982

11      See in this volume "First Publication of Essays," Wilhelm Schrack, "Letter to Jürgen von Grone."

12      See Rudolf Steiner, Occult Seals and columns,1907; and in the buildings that followed Malsch 1909 and Stuttgart 1911

13      Rudolf Steiner, *Mantric Sayings*, CW 238.

# "It Will Be Ensheathed!"

*Rudolf Steiner's Address, Given during the Act of Consecration*

The act of consecration—the laying of the foundation stone —occurred on Saturday, September 20, 1913 on the Dornach hill.

Let us first bring before ourselves the external situation in order to form as concrete a mental picture as possible. We shall do this on the basis of three eyewitness accounts, which essentially correspond, but diverge in some details.

It was a rainy, autumnal day. The ground was very soggy when the seventy or so—invited and uninvited—participants arrived at the building site in the evening. A protective covering was stretched over the pit. Nearby, a woodpile was lit for illumination, and torches were placed around the pit, for it was already noticeably dark. It was now raining lightly and only after the end of Rudolf Steiner's second address did the announced thunderstorm fully discharge itself. The historic act lasted from 7:00 to 8:30 p.m.

The words that Rudolf Steiner first spoke [during the act] have so far [in 2013] only been published in Rudolf Grosse's book about the Christmas Conference. Herewith, we are now in the fortunate position to make the text available to all readers.

\* \* \*

We begin our work. – (Turning to the [west, north, east, and south], and, for each direction, calling out a name:)

You Seraphim, you Cherubim, you steerers of the world, and you, who like streaks of lightning, take up the sheaths of the Cherubim through the spiritual streams, wedding them to the creative existence of the world, you high Thrones, you we call as protectors of our activity; and you, you Wisdoms (*Weisheiten*), who are all that is present in human beings prior to any manifestation of their being, and you, you Keepers (*Bewahrer*) of the eternal world-forces, and you, you Formers of our existence, who set the pattern of all being into the streams of existence: You we call as the protectors of our activities. And you, you Personalities of this spiritual stream, and you helpers, Archangeloi and Angeloi, who are for the Earth the messengers of the spiritual life of human beings, we call you all to be the protectors and those who will steer this our action. We are calling on you to come down onto the Human Soul, which we want to consecrate, insofar as it is up to us. We take a step towards the Human Soul that we want to consecrate for the work, which, according to our best knowledge of the time, is to be of service to it. As a symbol of the Human Soul, which consecrates itself to our great work, we have formed this stone. It is for us a symbol (*Sinnbild*) in its double twelve-memberedness of the striving Human Soul, sunk as microcosm into the macrocosm. Anthropos, the Human Being, as derived from the essential-being (*Wesenheiten*) of the divine-spiritual hierarchies. In such a way, this, our cornerstone (*Eckstein*), is the symbol of our own soul, which we integrate into what we have recognized as the right spiritual striving for the present time. So, we will place this stone, which is formed according to the world-pictures of the Human Soul, into the kingdom of the elements. Within this stone, two rocks are to be found, taken from the condensed kingdom of the elements, which best express how the macrocosmic forces collaborate in the condensed kingdom of the elements. This twelve-memberedness, we will place as the genuine sign of the Human Soul into the place above which will rise what is to become for us like a sign of our working, if we understand it rightly, my dear theosophical friends, on this evening. And with this stone we want to place into the Earth that which lies within our stone through which we have avowed to recognize as the authenticity of our spiritual life.

This certificate that within our stone which will be lowered down, bears the inscription:

*In the Name* of the Seraphim, the Cherubim, the Thrones, the Wisdoms, the Movers (*Beweger*), the Formers, the Personalities (the Archai), the Archangeloi, the Angeloi! There lives, as microcosm in the macrocosm, the human being, *Anthropos*, also represented here as a twice twelve-membered image, symbol of the spiritual world. And within this symbol the verse of Rosicrucianism, well known to you, my dear friends, expresses the sense of our striving: (*E.D.N. I.C.M. P.S.S.R.*) *Ex Deo nascimur. In Christo morimur. Per spiritum sanctum reviviscimus.*

As a formulation of our vow (*Angelobeformel*)—let us understand ourselves rightly—it appears on this stone, which, as a *cornerstone* (*Eckstein*), is an expression of the one who wants to seek themselves in the Spirit, who wants to feel themselves in the World Soul, who has a presentiment of themselves in the World-'I': the Human Being. This stone we sink into the condensed kingdom of the elements, this symbol of the force for which we are striving through 3, 5, 7, 12, laid by the Johannes Building Association in Dornach on the twentieth day of September 1880 after the Mystery of Golgotha, that is, 1913 after the birth of Christ, when Mercurius as the evening star stood in the Scales.

Architect:
Carl Schmid-Curtius

As the Administrative Board of the Johannes Building Association (*Johannesbau-Verein*):
[Sophie] Stinde
[Emil] Grosheintz
[Hermann] Linde
[Felix] Peipers
[Pauline Countess von] Kalckreuth

[Carl] Unger
[Emilie Baroness von] Gumppenberg
Mrs. [Lucie] Bürgi
Mrs. [Maria] Schieb
Mrs. [Marie] Hirter-Weber

As the Central Executive Council of the Anthroposophical Society:
[Marie] von Sivers
[Carl] Unger

and Dr. Steiner,
as the spiritual leader of the activity.

This document is incorporated into the symbol of the Human Soul, and then into the condensed kingdom of the elements.—(The document is incorporated into the copperplate container, and this is then soldered.)

The stone, as the symbol of our souls, is placed into the condensed kingdom of the elements. – (The stone is carried by Dr. Peipers, held by [four] men on long straps, and brought to the place where it shall rest. It is placed in such a way that the larger dodecahedron lies to the east and the smaller one to the west, that is, converse to the building, whose larger dome is aligned toward the west and whose smaller one is aligned toward the east.)

The stone as symbol (*Sinnbild*) of our soul is laid within the Earth; it may be taken as a true embodiment of spiritual truth (*Wahrzeichen*, lit. "true sign") of the striving towards knowledge, towards love, towards strong action, of the symbol of humankind. It shall be a sign of our souls, so that to us sounds forth evermore from the deepest sense of the World Word: *Ex Deo nascimur. In Christo morimur. Per spiritum sanctum reviviscimus.*

There, out of the symbol of the human soul shall emerge a sign of the human soul. Into the sign of the human soul, I consecrate you with these first hammer blows, those which shall be made on this our building of truth (*Wahrbau*).—(3, 5, 7 taps on the small, 12 taps on the large dodecahedron.)—The stone has thereby become a sign from the symbol. And now, we want to entrust it to the kingdom of the condensed elements, to the Earth, into which our soul has been sunk, to develop in the evolution of humankind that which is the Earth's mission. So the stone, from the sign, now becomes the sheathed one (*zum Verhüllten*), by our entrusting it to the Earth. The human soul rises up threefold to the three mysteries of existence: Symbols are they first, signs are they then, whilst the soul reads the eternal World word; still yet, the deepest depths of the World Mysteries—they become livingly bonded with the soul when this soul is able to give itself the sheath from the kingdom of the hierarchies.—So be sheathed! Become a sheathed one out of the symbol and the sign, so that you may be a firm cornerstone of our striving, of our searching, as we have recognized it to be right in the evolution of humankind. Thus, we want to make the stone, which is the sign of our soul, into the sheathed one.

* * *

The architect, Mr. Schmid-Curtius, and Englert, the engineer cover the stone with earth upon which Miss von Sivers has laid a bouquet of roses—twelve red and one white rose. Thereupon, Dr. Steiner reaches out his hands toward those present around the foundation stone, Dr. Peipers, Dr. Grosheintz, Miss von Sivers, [Miss Stinde,] the architect Schmid and the engineer Englert, holding them crosswise over each other. Then, all depart, Dr. Steiner being last, from the depths of the pit.

## Explanations Relating to the Ceremony

The text spoken as regards the activity is divided into ten sections.

*In the first section*, Rudolf Steiner calls all nine hierarchies, one after the other, to be protectors and steerers of the activity.

*In the second section*, he explains the meaning of the double pentagon-dodecahedral foundation stone as a symbol and sign of the human soul, the Anthropos. With it, the vow of those present to what is recognized as spiritually right shall also be sunk into the Earth.

*In the third through sixth sections*, he reads out the text, written by himself, on the foundation stone document with the names of those who signed it.

*In the seventh section*, he announces the first physical act of the event that is now to take place: he himself rolls up the certificate and slides it into the copper foundation stone lying ready. Now, Max Benzinger, who had created the vessel in Munich according to Rudolf Steiner's indications and then hung the two pyrite crystals within it in Dornach, solders the closing plate over the opening.

*In the eighth section*, Rudolf Steiner briefly announces the transportation of the foundation stone into the pit. Five chosen men ceremoniously carry it together down nine steps and lay it strictly east-west, so that the larger dodecahedron rests in the east, the smaller in the west—that is, contrariwise to the two Goetheanum domes. Then, Rudolf Steiner also steps down the steps, as did Marie von Sivers.

*In the ninth section*, Rudolf Steiner seals the accomplished sinking of the stone with characterizing words.

*The tenth section* brings the accompanying words to the high point of the act of consecration through Rudolf Steiner's tapping with a hammer on each of the two dodecahedrons. He explains the spiritual process more specifically. The foundation stone is at first a symbol of the human soul, in which—firmly bound together—the forces of the macrocosm and microcosm meet. This symbol, through the hammer blows, becomes a sign, a hieroglyph. With the embedding in the Earth, the sign becomes sheathed, is transformed into "the sheathed one." This is the deepest meaning of the event: outwardly resembling a burial, yet spiritually an act of birth. The archetype of the human being, the entelechy of the Anthropos, is entrusted to the Earth as an effective landmark (*Wahrzeichen*, lit. "true sign"). The meaning of the Earth's mission is the development of the force of Love in the sense of the Christ sacrifice, the ultimate goal of evolution being the transformation of the Earth through the human being into a star of love radiating out into the cosmos. This plan of the Gods can be fulfilled only in full free inner activity (*Freiheit*). The "formulation of our vow" with the wording "this symbol of the force for which we are striving to endeavor" refers to this. Ultimately, it is the force of LOVE.

After everyone had left the pit, Rudolf Steiner held the great address on the Macrocosmic Lord's Prayer, which has been printed in various contexts. Connecting to this, Marie Steiner wrote some words of remembrance on August 16, 1925, in which the earnestness and the greatness of the whole event comes to expression:

> . . . The large torches that illuminated the pit into which the stone was lowered continually let pieces of flame from their bodies fall into it: a scene of terrific, somber seriousness and unforeseen greatness. For the words of Rudolf Steiner sounded over the uproar of the elements, rang out clear, great, fateful, and mighty.
>
> We were a little heap of poor human beings. Among us a great one, such as history places only at very wide intervals at the turning points of time, who had subordinated his will to the will of the Spirit; who knew then that he was speaking at a time in which the evils were prevailing.[14]

Continuing our observations, we want to dedicate ourselves to the interconnections between the act of the laying of the foundation stone and the Goetheanum building and its environment, as well as its effects on the development of the Anthroposophical Movement.

Endnotes

14      Marie Steiner quoted from Nelly Grosheintz-Laval. See "First Publication of Essays," Nelly Grosheintz-Laval, "Memories . . .," 107; previously published as Marie Steiner, "The Mystery Plays in Munich."

# The Dornach Hill as the Center
## of the Anthroposophical Movement

The act of consecration, the laying of the foundation stone, on the Dornach hill on September 20, 1913, was a unique event. Long-prepared in the spiritual world and in Rudolf Steiner's karma, it could be accomplished at the right time and in the right place, in a good karmic stream, thanks to the alertness and readiness for sacrifice on the part of his students. One year before the outbreak of the First World War, whose threatening clouds Rudolf Steiner had long seen coming, a "seed" for an oasis of peace was thus laid in the Earth: the foundation stone for a building that was to become a meeting center for human beings from all over the world, regardless of race and religion. The significance of the event points to the distant past as well as the distant future.

## *The condensed kingdom of the elements*

Since ancient times, sacred sites have been characterized by three main elements: (1) The Holy of Holies, (2) The Temple, (3) The Sacred Precinct. From the beginning of his work with the First Goetheanum, Rudolf Steiner had a vision for the whole hill and worked in a way that had many formative and transformative effects on the existing terrain.

For the building itself, he developed the idea of a double dome, according to which principle he also designed all the other buildings. They contain the polarity of turning outward and turning inward, exemplified in the large and small dome. Under the large dome lies the auditorium, with its protruding portals speaking to the outside and welcoming visitors; while the stage is completely concealed from the exterior, surrounded by a wide perimeter of functional rooms solely for workers and artists. Only its roof—the small dome—is visible to the public. In the two interlocking circles of the ground plan, one easily recognizes a relationship to the similarly dual structure of the foundation stone: a symbol for the lower and higher 'I' of the human being.

On the crest at the western end of the hill, next to the "Holy Road"—the wide entranceway to the western front of the building—a residential house for the donor of the building site was planned for construction, which began in 1915. At this time, Rudolf Steiner suggested the shape of a bean, which appears closed off (convex) on one side, and opens concavely on the other. Such a configuration can also be experienced on the hill itself: the north side is more of a delimiting slope; the south side graciously opens in a wide hollow. Rudolf Steiner gave this bowl-shaped terrain its peculiarly expressive character by the use of several different measures: by encircling it at the top with an arching row of walnut trees; widening it at the bottom with the narrow path leading up to the Felsli; and bordering it with a distinct edge by creating an embankment in the lower tail of the Felsli path. Thus, from there we experience the inviting gesture of this recess as it gently directs our gaze to the south side of the Goetheanum, quite different from the slope to the northwest where the building sits enthroned rather castle-like as a crowning outcrop on the hill.

During the laying of the foundation stone, "Mercurius as the evening star stood in the Scales" above the hollow. Again and again, we can remember this constellation by admiring the radiant beauty of this planet (today called [occult] Venus), which bends over this hollow, followed by other celestial bodies, as if in greeting as it sets. In such encounters of heaven and Earth, secret forces are stirred: blessings for the elemental world in and around the whole hill. If we try to get a picture of the being and tapestry of the hill, we will find wonderful clues in the natural conditions, of the rare butterflies in the biotope at the foot of the hill, and the cherry trees blossoming on the slope of the hollow, which, since 1914, have already been depicted on countless postcards showing the south side of the Goetheanum building. Since then, countless attentive hikers have been able to sense in this area the continuing effect of the macrocosmic-microcosmic dialogue opened by Rudolf Steiner on September 20, 1913.

*Fig. 5: The south portal, the large and the small dome.*

*Fig. 6: Reconstruction model 1:100 of the First Goetheanum
by Albert von Baravalle; top: view from southwest; bottom:
view from southeast.*

## The Building as a True Embodiment of Spiritual Truth

The deepest secret of the act of laying the foundation stone is contained in the word "sheathed" (*Verhüllen*). It means: to enclothe spiritual beings and forces within earthly substances. Even building, in the concrete architectural sense, can ultimately be understood as a kind of sheathing process. The task of the observer is then: to cognitively counteract the enveloping spiral of such events; to solve the secrets of design; and thus, to find the way back to the beings and forces.

This task was described pictorially and literally by Rudolf Steiner in the [triptych of the] southern rose window of the First Goetheanum. In the first window [on the left side when facing south], a person lying on a rock looks at the Goetheanum entrance portal, at the top of which is the building motif. Rudolf Steiner placed here the words: "I behold the building" (*Ich schaue den Bau*). In the third window [on the right side when facing south], the human being has risen and—like Orpheus playing the lyre—activates artistic powers. There, instead of the building motif, they are confronted with a human face. Rudolf Steiner added here the words: "And the building becomes the Human Being" (*Und der Bau wird Mensch*). On his black-and-white sketches for these windows, he wrote: "The threshold sheaths itself" (*Die Schwelle verhüllt sich*) and "The threshold reveals itself" (*Die Schwelle offenbart sich*) (Fig. 7 and 8).

In his lectures on the building, Rudolf Steiner recommends *learning to read* the building composition in detail, not mystifyingly with the intellect, but with an artistically sensing soul. Thus, every attentive perception can lead one across the threshold: By inwardly comprehending the organically oriented creative processes, we step into the spiritual world. Therefore, Rudolf Steiner speaks of individual forms (for example, the column capitals) as "signs" (*Zeichen*) as well as of the whole building as a true embodiment of spiritual truth (*Wahrzeichen*) to be erected: An embodiment for the "Anthropos"; an embodiment that contains the whole of verbally presented anthroposophy and more.

Let us take a closer look at one of the "signs" depicted on the rose window described above. This building motif looks out at the observer a total of twenty-nine times, in five variations, above all via the gateways and windows on the western wing above the terrace. Also, when entering the Great Hall, the motif again greets the student of the spirit in two further variations—on the stage arch and on the eastern vault of the small cupola. As revealed in the rose window, this motif is the archetype of the human being—its entelechy—which, again and again, speaks, as a kind of mirror image, to the beholder. What was written in letters above the entrance to the temple of Apollo in Delphi—the ancient mystery words, "Know thyself"—Rudolf Steiner translated as a hieroglyph into a five-membered sculpted form. This marks the indispensable fundamental experience for all further steps on the path to higher knowledge, as depicted in the second scene of the mystery drama *The Portal of Initiation*. Five times, from different sides, Johannes, the student of the spirit, hears the call, "O Human Being, know yourself!"

Delphi: the sacred site where Apollo conquered the dragon; where human beings from all the Greek tribes met peacefully to pay festive tribute to Apollo and receive spiritual instructions; this holy place can be seen as a kind of model for the meeting center initiated by Rudolf Steiner: Dornach, a new Delphi for humanity.

*Fig. 7: "The threshold sheaths itself." Rose window in the south, left side [facing south]. Sketch by Rudolf Steiner (from Rudolf Steiner, Die Goetheanum-Fenster, text vol., 38f.; images vol., 54).*

*Fig. 8: "The threshold reveals itself." Rose window in the south, right side [facing south]. Sketch by Rudolf Steiner (from Rudolf Steiner, Die Goetheanum-Fenster, text vol., 38f.; images vol., 55).*

*Fig. 9: View of the west portal of the First Goetheanum.*
*Watercolor by Albert von Baravalle, 1938.*

## The Vow

In the years following the laying of the foundation stone, Rudolf Steiner reminded the members in Dornach of this date with a commemorative address or a lecture (as often as he could), and supplemented his earlier remarks with new aspects. If one brings all of his remarks together, a picture gradually emerges which can help to trace the secrets of that macrocosmic-microcosmic dialogue. Unfortunately, the seven addresses and lectures—edited, little by little, by Marie Steiner (partly in beautiful bibliophilic individual editions)—have been out of print for a long time and have not yet been published in Steiner's collected works.[15] Rudolf Steiner's remarks are steps towards that spiritual construction of the anthroposophical movement which he had been speaking about since 1913 and to which he referred in an increasingly urgent manner in his addresses. In the face of the many opposing forces escalating in the world (not only the physical combat that broke out in the war), Rudolf Steiner urged his students toward fellowship, perseverance, and wakefulness. After the burning of the Goetheanum, his decision ripened in 1923 to join the General Anthroposophical Society directly as the leader at Christmas. He created a spiritual foundation stone, which he commended to the reception of the hearts of all present. The miracle of Rudolf Steiner's deed can seem like a magnificent treetop that gradually grew up over ten years from the roots of the foundation stone laid in 1913. In his opening speech on December 24, 1923, he mentions again the fertile "soil of Dornach":

> For everywhere, warmth can grace us from out of the *spiritual* content of the anthroposophical movement, warmth capable of enlivening innumerable seeds— held by the very soil of Dornach and what belongs to it—for the spiritual life of the future.

Shortly after the outbreak of the First World War, on August 13, 1914, Rudolf Steiner described the social task of those involved in the Goetheanum building:

> And if we could, for example, in our own ranks gathered here around our building—an expression of our spiri-

tual striving—if we could now strongly place into our hearts, into our conduct with one another, an example, a model picture, a model of the attitude of fellowship, then it would have to be this thought. [The thought of unshakable trust in the power and effectiveness of the spirit, explained in detail earlier—Baravalle's note.]

In these times, when everything seems to be shaken, let us strive to be a group that cherishes peace and harmony in every heart, so that everyone has the best thoughts about everyone, without envy, without discord.

Rudolf Steiner's intended goal with the building in Dornach, his intention of giving an impulse of peace whose effect would reach far into the world, this intention can only succeed under the conditions mentioned—a thoroughly unifying community of fellowship.

On September 19, 1914, on the eve of the commemorative day, Rudolf Steiner clearly described this goal:

We may celebrate the annual festival of a building, which, in the most eminent sense, is to serve to harmoniously unite human souls across the Earth. . . . Let us build on what spiritual science can give us. We will find in it the possibility—across all borders, from soul to soul—of finding our togetherness . . . .

On September 20, 1914, there followed the words from Rudolf Steiner that characterize the innermost essence of the Goetheanum building with all its forms:

My dear friends, today, as we stand once again before the unfinished building for which we laid the foundation stone a year ago, let us take within us the vow that we want to hold faithfully to what spiritual science can give us. . . . Let us take into ourselves the consciousness . . . [that] the Christ belongs to all human beings . . . . We then find the way to every human being and to the peaceful choirs of all higher hierarchies—and we find the way to the Christ. . . .

May it be fulfilled for our salvation: that in these forms one sees how the spirit—which has communicated itself to the Earth through the Mystery of Golgotha—

49

flows through our forms . . . so that permeating the soul is the consciousness . . . Not I, the Christ in me! May also this building . . . make the impression on the human souls who enter it: Not I, not my own is that which makes an impression on the eye through the external forms—but rather the Christ will speak, he who seeks an expression, a revelation through the Word of the higher hierarchies . . . . And this building is to be "the mouth"!

Endnotes

15    [Lecture summary: Basel, Feb. 3, Sept. 22, 1913; Dornach, Aug. 13, Sept. 19, 20, 1914; Sept. 20, 1916; Sept. 21, 1923.]
Rudolf Steiner, *Schicksalszeichen auf dem Entwicklungswege der Anthroposophischen Gesellschaft* [Signs of destiny on the path of development of the Anthroposophical Society], includes lectures in Basel on Feb. 3 and Sept. 22, 1913 and in Dornach on Aug. 13 and Sept. 19, 1914;
Rudolf Steiner, *Die Sehnsucht der Seelen nach Geist* [The longing of souls for spirit], includes lecture in Dornach on Sept. 20, 1914;
Rudolf Steiner, *Bauformen als Kultur- und Weltempfindungsgedanken* [Building forms as culture- and the world-sensing thoughts], includes lecture in Dornach on Sept. 20, 1916;
Rudolf Steiner, *Eine Erinnerung an die Grundsteinfeier zur Befestigung des Anthroposophischen Wesens* [A remembrance of the foundation stone celebration for the fortification of the being of anthroposophy], includes lecture in Dornach on Sept. 21, 1923.

# Resonance

We look back once again to the act of laying the foundation stone, to the sense-perceptible part of the ceremony, which Rudolf Steiner continually accompanied with words. Here was the consecrating of the human soul as the highest, most daring—though endangered by this freedom—creature of God. And, indeed, the consecration was carried out by the authority of a human being who knew how to judge and act purely as a spiritual human being. In his second address to all the people (invited and uninvited) at the top of the earthen pit, Rudolf Steiner spoke of the corrupting effects of the adversaries. But first, he called in prayer upon all nine hierarchies, from top to bottom, individually, to help.

Already the first budding lines form a prelude to that mighty hymn of the Christmas Conference, ten years later, with its threefold call "Human Soul!"[16] Herein is contained a presentation of the human being in its relationship to the macrocosm—to the Trinity, with all the hierarchies—given in all detail, as a summary of anthroposophy. It is an offering of the human being, Rudolf Steiner, out of his own most spiritual substance, behind which one can see, shining, the offering of the Thrones at the beginning of evolution.[17] And just as the spirits of the Archai (the Primal Spirits) were born out of the Thrones' substance of courage offered up to the Cherubim, so this offering can lead to a new "beginning turning point of time," if many people will actively take it up in the depths of their souls.

The event—the laying of the foundation stone, the copper double-dodecahedron, into the concrete container standing in the earthen pit—could be witnessed by only a few people down in the pit. One other took the initiative at the top of the pit to stenograph the wording, using a friend's back as a support. This was Rudolf Hahn, a Swiss man from Reinach, an esoteric student of Rudolf Steiner, to whom we also owe the original transmission of the text.

With the first call, Rudolf Steiner touches on secrets of the very highest creative caliber, as apparently nowhere else in his work. They are a small, precious jewel of his mantric art of building, completely unique.

> You Seraphim, you Cherubim, you who steer the
> course of the world
> and you—who like streaks of lightning through the
> spiritual streams,
> take up the sheaths of the Cherubim,
> wedding them to the creative existence of the world—
> you high Thrones,
> you we call as protectors of our activity . . .

> *Ihr Seraphim, Ihr Cherubim, Ihr Lenker der Welt,*
> *und [der] Ihr gleich Blitzen durch die geistigen Strö-*
> *mungen aufnehmet*
> *die Hüllen der Cherubim,*
> *sie vermählend zu schöpferischem Dasein der Welt,*
> *Ihr hohen Throne,*
> *Euch rufen wir als Schützer unserer Handlung . . . .*

The words "spiritual streams" point to a living network of veins in the cosmos, an interplay of many worlds. The term "like streaks of lightning" refers to the "sheaths" of the Cherubim, which Rudolf Steiner described in the thirteenth class lesson on [May 17], 1924 as "tools" (*Werkzeuge*) of the Cherubim. These are "wedded" by the Thrones "to the creative existence of the world." There the origin of all creatorship reveals itself. With these extremely brief formulations, in which the content for many an "occult science" is hidden, Rudolf Steiner provides an opening through which we can take a look into the ultimate mystery of the universe. Himself probably shuddering before this miracle, he calls the Thrones as he has never done for any other hierarchy before: "You high Thrones."

Only too gladly, one would like to be able to inwardly imagine the tone of his voice, described by some witnesses as unforgettable. After the so resolutely placed individual terms and concepts, which create for us a picture of the working together of the hierarchies, a solemn, celebratory crescendo with a fermata takes place here in the middle of the flow of the text.

Actually, the listeners would probably have needed some time to let the whole prelude sink in, but it was soon followed by the larger, tremendously serious second address on the "inverse Lord's Prayer." In much the same way, the first address was not dealt with in anthroposophical literature. Perhaps our aphoristic remarks can serve as a stimulus for further study of the complete text of the address: for spiritually, all these words resounded as well in the *presence of the stars.*

Endnotes

16      Rudolf Steiner, *Truth-Wrought Words*, CW 40
17      Rudolf Steiner, *Inner Experiences of Evolution CW 132*

# The Composition of the Foundation Stone

In Munich, during the summer of 1913, the locksmith Max Benzinger manufactured the foundation stone at Rudolf Steiner's request as a vessel of sheet copper, consisting of two differently sized pentagonal dodecahedrons, with the diameter dimensions 63 cm and 54 cm. This resulted in a rather weighty construction of roughly one meter in length, which was then ceremoniously carried down nine steps into the earthen pit by five men in Dornach.

## 1. The design: Two connected, differently sized, dodecahedral bodies

Rudolf Steiner chose *duality* (*Zweiheit*, literally, "twofoldedness") as an indicator of the lower 'I' and the higher 'I'—the aspects of the human being's essence—one part bound to the physical and one part oriented towards ideas and ideals. This stands in accord with the fundamental uniaxial symmetrical structure not only of the First Goetheanum but also of all the other buildings on the hill, including the Second Goetheanum.

The *pentagonal dodecahedron* points to the numbers five and twelve, which play a role in the microcosm and macrocosm. This relation to the human soul can be interpreted on many levels. Rudolf Steiner's main consideration for the choice of the pentagonal dodecahedron probably originates in his own occult research, which corresponds to old macrocosmically oriented traditions concerning the Platonic bodies.

We will attempt to approach the matter purely phenomenologically. We proceed from a naive question: Why did Rudolf

Steiner not choose a garnet stone as a symbol of the human soul? This luminous blood-red crystal, often mentioned as carbuncle in literature and which was even identified with the Grail stone, is also a dodecahedron, though, indeed, from rhombuses, not from pentagonal planes. In his address, while standing below in the pit, during the laying of the foundation stone, and within the circle of the seven participants, Rudolf Steiner calls the foundation stone a "symbol of the human soul" five times and also points two times to its twelvefoldedness. The fivefoldedness he does not mention.

The rhombic dodecahedron initially appears related to the pentagonal dodecahedron, although, with more exact observation, we actually see regular quadrilaterals—indeed, it can appear as a cube viewed in perspective. With the pentagonal dodecahedron we perceive other images: different aspects show a tendency towards circular and spherical shapes. The circle, as a symbol of the God-created universe, stands in contrast to the cube, the symbol of the Earth. In his address, Rudolf Steiner points to the macrocosm as the goal of human striving, as well as to the forces functioning in the natural crystal. And he describes the dodecahedral structure as formed "according to the world-pictures of the human soul." Thus, our hypothetical question is answered. The difference between both dodecahedra lies in the orientation to the macrocosmic, on the one hand, and to the microcosmic, on the other.

Longer observations of rhombic and pentagonal dodecahedra, both of individual stones and of groups, yield still more revealing phenomena. The edges of the rhombic planes protrude more than those of the pentagons, and the corners appear more pointed. In this way, the individual planes assert themselves more in the dodecahedral-complex. The pentagons nestle together in a friendly way, they seem to strive willingly towards a community, while the rhombuses demonstrate a juxtaposition. Thus, a stronger adhesive force prevails between the pentagons. It is striking that the most beautiful aspect of a rhombic solid emerges when we focus on *five* planes at the same time.

*Fig. 10 and 11: Rhombic dodecahedra of garnet.*

*Fig. 12 and 13: Pentagonal dodecahedra of pyrite.*

*Fig. 14 and 15: Rhombic dodecahedra.*

*Fig. 16 and 17: Pentagonal dodecahedra.*

## 2. The pyrite crystals in the copper vessel

Within the spacious structure of the foundation stone vessel there are found two small pyrite crystals with diameters of 2.5 cm and 3.5 cm. Over against the human-made double dodecahedron, a God-made dodecahedron should also be present—why? We can grasp the deepest sense of this measure if we study Rudolf Steiner's presentation of the emergence of crystals, given in 1924 in his last out-of-town lecture cycle in Torquay [England].[18] There he describes subtle mysteries of initiate consciousness. In order to perceive the act of creation of crystals, the occultist must first develop love for all beings of the world, otherwise they cannot hold themselves in the infinite void. But then, they become aware of cosmic streams from all sides, through whose encounters free-floating crystals emerge. The researcher inwardly experiences the miracle of the birth of essences. They may have a look into the workshop of God. Rudolf Steiner sketched the situation in a blackboard drawing (Fig. 18).

Cosmic mysteries are revealed when we face different crystal forms. Astonished, one understands: "And so it is that there are as many differently formed world-currents . . . as there are crystals from which the Earth is composed."

After a detailed verbal description of different shapes, he summarizes the inner experience conclusively: "We behold in the immeasurable, manifold forms of the crystals a revelation of a great fullness of beings, who come to life in mathematical-spatial designs in the crystals. In crystals, we look upon the gods." And then Rudolf Steiner gives us the task of integrating with divine-beingness when observing natural crystals: "Through anthroposophy, the human being should be able to take notice, in every unique crystal, of the weaving and ruling of a god in the universe. Then, the entire human soul will be filled with world-content, not only the head with thoughts."

It is an ultimately unfathomable wonder of the Earth that we find such heavenly messengers in its dark layers of crust, which reveal to us the geometrically forming, architectural force-streams of the universe. By letting those two natural pentagonal dodecahedrons be attached, freely suspended in the copper shells of the foundation stone, Rudolf Steiner symbolized the divine spark in the human soul, wherein the tenth hierarchy is established as a predisposition. It did not matter that most of the participants in the laying of the foundation stone did not see it. They could imagine it through Rudolf Steiner's words. They could, by later encounters with such stones, think of the two examples in the foundation stone and become conscious of the divine elements in their own souls. That this occurs again and again was Rudolf Steiner's wish with regard to the act of the laying the foundation stone. Annually, he held commemorative speeches,[19] through which he wanted to sharpen the consciousness of the participants concerning the significance of the event and to awaken a feeling of responsibility.

Still, there is yet another aspect needed to clarify the embedding of both pyrite crystals. Rudolf Steiner referenced this in response to the inquiring Ehrenfried Pfeiffer. Smiling, he said, "The pyrites hold both building cupolas." Does that not sound like a joke? Or magic? How could one explain this reference? The fact that physically small elements can influence great things is confirmed by many achievements of modern technology.

Already, sixteen years before his descriptions of the crystal-building streams of forces in Torquay, we find strikingly similar-sounding formulations from Rudolf Steiner. In a lecture in Berlin on May 13, 1908, he spoke about his encounter with the temples in Paestum:

> During the entire development of humankind, the architectural thought is best expressed in Greek architecture. It is born from out of the cosmic laws of space. . . . One thinks of God creating in space, His forces flooding space, as it were forming Himself a body, a garment. . . . Whoever understands space not as emptiness, but rather as being permeated by forces, whoever knows that there, in space, forces crystallize, and whoever senses these forces, feels that in the Greek temple something crystallized-out from the dynamic forces of the world.[20]

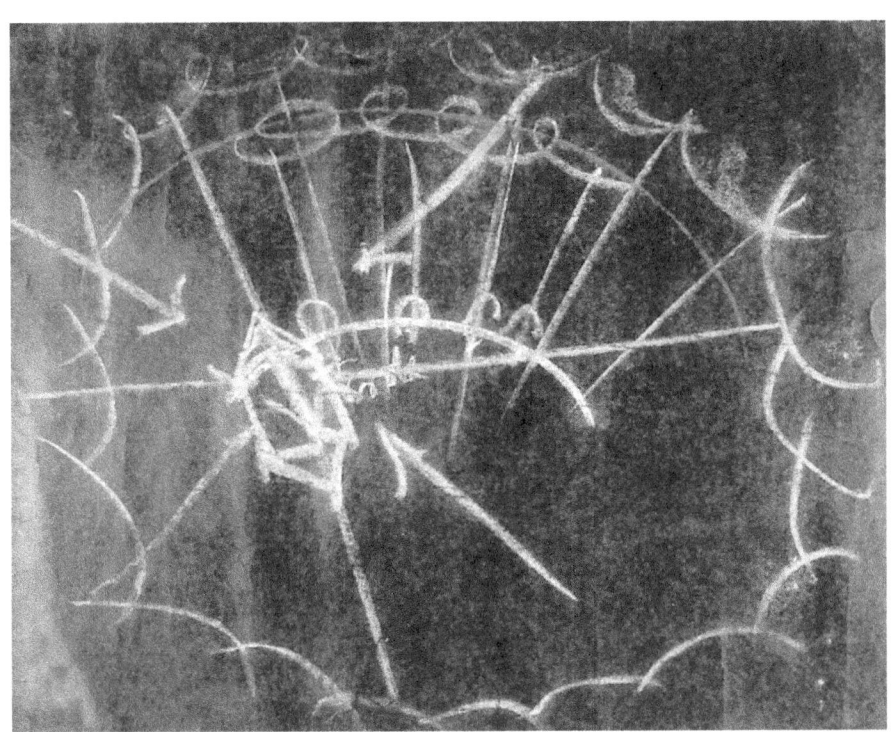

*Fig. 18: Rudolf Steiner: Blackboard drawing. Torquay, Aug. 13, 1924. From: Rudolf Steiner, Wandtafelzeichnungen zum Vortragswerk (Blackboard drawings from lecture work), vol. 15, p. 54.*

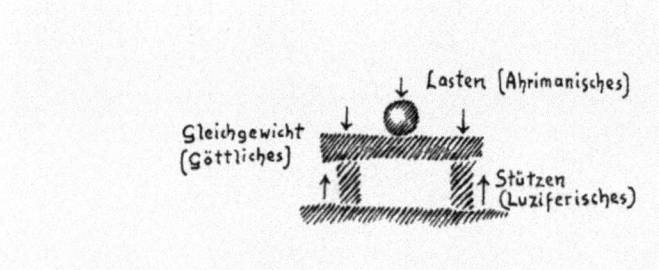

*Fig. 19. From: Rudolf Steiner, Art as Seen in the Light of Mystery Wisdom, lecture in Dornach on Jan. 2, 1915, p. 119.*

*(Lasten = weight/load (Ahrimanic); Stützen (Luciferic) = support; Gleichgewicht (Göttliches – balance (divine)*

To this day, at the so-called Temple of Poseidon in Paestum [Salerno, Italy], one can experience the forces that bear/carry and those that are pressing most impressively. Rudolf Steiner spoke again and again about this fundamental law of the art of building, also in relation to his own buildings. And he recommended to his lecture audiences to "crawl into" these forces directly with the sense of touch in order to develop a real architectural feeling. To this end, he made a blackboard drawing, which appears like a scheme of his sculptural group (Fig. 19).

With this, we arrive at a foundational theme of anthroposophy: the polarities of evil and their balancing-out. We can still ask whether such an equilibrium is not already inherent in the pyrite with its combination of the two substances iron and sulfur. Rudolf Steiner also mentions another aspect of pyrite in the Torquay lecture of Aug. 13, 1924:

> Let us take the example. . . : we look at a salt crystal and a pyrite crystal, a metal crystal. There one has the feeling, if one looks at the pyrite crystal: there you can build, that bears you. When one looks at the salt crystal, it appears as if one could fall through it, as if it does not bear you.[21]

So the pyrite even has a supporting effect on the soul of the researching clairvoyant—why not also on the building cupolas?

Considering the aspects mentioned, we can learn that crystals contain not only therapeutic but also static forces, so that we must consider them not as dead objects but as effective beings if we want to develop true mental pictures. We could perhaps even pose the question of whether the manifoldly formed crystals in the Earth do not also, in their totality, exercise an architecturally stimulating effect on humanity. In any case, the natural pyrites in the foundation stone play a significant, multilayered role. They are also messengers of the infinite fullness of living beings that populate the universe, to which Rudolf Steiner so often resolutely refers.[22]

## 3. The materials

*Pyrite*, the mineral which was chosen, is a compound of iron with sulfur. Iron can be interpreted as a symbol of the Earth's firmness; sulfur, as a symbol of the volatilizing tendency. Human life consists through and through in engagement with such polarities.

Why did Rudolf Steiner choose *copper*? It has a relationship with the planet Venus. He calls this the last stage of the Earth's sequence of metamorphosis, culminating in Love, whereby humanity is intended to become the tenth hierarchy. The foundation stone, as a symbol of the human soul, refers to the entelechy, the essence that carries its ultimate goal within itself—and in this way, it refers to the task of humanity.

## 4. The scroll

Rudolf Steiner elected to use the skin of a bull calf as its basis. He furnished this with a drawing and text by his own hand. At the ceremony, he rolled it up and slid it into the foundation stone. Rudolf Steiner brought the document to a close by putting together four numbers, which refer to different areas of anthroposophy:

> . . . this symbol of the force
> for which we are striving to endeavor
> through 3, 5, 7, 12 . . . .

And so, instead of closing with some words, Rudolf Steiner wrote down four Arabic numbers next to each other, without any letters. They stand there somewhat stiffly and reticent, peculiar signs for our brain to comprehend. This does not correspond to Rudolf Steiner's usual way of being. How are we to grasp it?

As a boy he already learned to love numbers. Geometry gave him an experience of happiness.[23] It became essential for him, as something vital, all his life. We can regard the ciphers, which initially seem prosaic to us, as seeds that, in order to flourish, require only some sensing and fantasy from out the wellspring of our soul, so as to then let sprout innumerable motifs from the ocean of anthroposophy. The most diverse themes of spiritual science are available to those who are eagerly striving. Rudolf Steiner liked to stimulate such growth processes through all his presentations, so also in this extremely concise form of numbers.

Many things can be discovered in it: The fundamental motif of Christian wisdom is the *Trinity*. In it is mirrored the human essence, as well. *Fivefoldness* marks the present epoch of humanity's evolution; it is also the number of crisis, even of evil. All temporal processes run in *sevenfold* rhythms, from the days of the week to the yearly biographical periods to the planetary stages of development. *Twelvefoldness* is already found in the ceremony of the laying of the foundation stone, when Marie Steiner laid twelve red roses and one white rose on the foundation stone, before Rudolf Steiner and subsequently, the others present each threw a spadeful of earth over it. Twelvefoldness originates in the fixed star world, in the zodiac, where there reign the macrocosmic laws of space. This already outlines a considerable part of anthroposophy.

We can also imagine the whole building of the First Goetheanum—then still only a conception—this unique home for theater and performance, which as a "form for experiencing" reveals the wisdom of anthroposophy that had initially been given as "forms for intellectualizing."[24] Its fundamental geometric form is a double-domed structure, whose cylindrical walls, artfully intertwining, bear the differently sized cupola vaults, the larger auditorium, and a smaller stage. Portals and windows are marked with a sculptural building motif carved in wood, which appears twenty-nine times in unified variations. On the other hand, the stage is enclosed all-around by storerooms and dressing rooms, so that only the dome is perceptible from the outside; its walls remain concealed.

Inside, one encounters a great abundance of carved forms, applied in relief, to walls and columns. The building motifs become augmented above the stage portal and in the east by two more variants. Column capital and pedestal forms are each developed into a seven-membered metamorphic series. On a five-meter-high architrave, one can read the course of humanity's development in continuous, musical motifs. To do this, one should feelingly enter into the movements of form, and not speculate about them intellectually.

Through patient, detailed observations, two general statements can crystallize. The variants of the building motifs, like a kind of mirror to self-knowledge, call out for a striving, in the sense of the human archetype, in every individuality. The series of columns and architraves stimulate work on the higher 'I', upon the entelechy, which contains in itself the goal of its development like in the kernel of a seed. Therein lies the real meaning of anthroposophy.

In the building, the four numbers appear most significantly in the following architectural elements: It is comprised of *three* fundamental materials—concrete, wood, and slate—the concrete in the foundation, the wood in the upper wall portions, and the slate in the roof. Both the portals and the windows are membered in *threes*.

*Fivefoldness* is in the five building sectors—two cupolas, two side wings, and the entry; furthermore, it is in the elements of the building motif—two wings, the central motif, and the two lower parts. It appears as a streaming five-pointed star (pentagram) in the east of the small cupola. All the columns are five-cornered there as well as in the large cupola. The [motif] on the stage still has a radiating pentagram as a kernel inside, as a symbol of the fact that from here the impulses and revelations are transmitted to the auditorium.

*Sevenfoldness* speaks from the twice-seven columns of the large cupola with their capital and pedestal motifs.

We find *twelvefoldness* as twice-six columns on the stage, which are aligned by the building principle of uniaxial symmetry.

Standing behind this are the ideas for the Rosicrucian Temple of 1907 in Munich and [1909] in the Malsch building with concrete representations of the twelve zodiac signs. For Malsch, Rudolf Steiner even specified twice-twelve symbols, which were to be painted on the ceiling above the twice-seven columns running in opposite directions. In the elliptical ground plan, Rudolf Steiner already inserted the law of uniaxial symmetry, which then governs the First Goetheanum.

*Twelvefoldness* is reminiscent of the twelve disciples of Christ as well as of the Round Table of King Arthur. In the [First] Goetheanum, it rules in the small cupola with its twelve columns and pedestals designed as thrones. Occasionally, Rudolf Steiner spoke of a "conference room for twelve," a purpose for which it could not at all serve because of the untimely fire. What force can still lie in *twelvefoldness* is shown by an indication Rudolf Steiner gave on December 18, 1920 in his Dornach cycle "The Bridge between World Spirituality and the Physicality of the Human Being":

> Yes, if a somber age were to dawn over the whole Earth, in which millions and millions of human beings would pass away solely by unspirituality. . . then, if there were only a dozen human beings with bright moral-spiritual enthusiasm, still, the Earth would shine, spiritually sunlike.[25]

If one brings together all the aspects mentioned above, one comes to the conclusion: The laying of the foundation stone in 1913 is in many respects the concrete preliminary stage to the "spiritual laying of the Foundation Stone" in 1923 at the Christmas Conference. Pictorially speaking, one can see it as the root of a tree whose top is formed by the Christmas Conference and whose trunk with its annual rings has grown from Rudolf Steiner's annual addresses. The theme of community building, which always creates the precondition for larger building projects, was Rudolf Steiner's main concern since the founding of the Anthroposophical Society in 1912, though despite all his declarations and admonitions, it had not been taken up earnestly enough. Nevertheless, during the Christmas Conference, he gained the assurance that in the meantime a process of awakening had developed in the circle of those present to such an extent that, on

January 1, 1924, he was able to give the first indications of his by-then-matured ideas for the new metamorphosis of the building motif with a drawing.[26]

Endnotes

18      Rudolf Steiner, *True and False Paths of Spiritual Research*, lecture in Torquay on Aug. 13, 1924, pp. 33–50. CW 243

19      Unfortunately, these have still not appeared in the complete works [GA/CW], although three of them (1914, 1916, and 1923) have already been published by Marie Steiner in somewhat bibliophilic individual editions. [The lectures have now all been published in the complete works; see endnote 15.]

20      Rudolf Steiner, *Good and Evil Spirits*, lecture in Berlin on May 13, 1908, pp. 117–18. CW 102

21      Rudolf Steiner, *True and False Paths of Spiritual Research*, lecture in Torquay on Aug. 13, 1924, p. 38. CW 243

22      CW 224, lecture in Dornach on April 13, 1923 and CW 110

23      Cf. Rudolf Steiner, *Autobiography*, CW 28

24      Rudolf Steiner, *Architecture as Peacework*, lecture on Oct. 24, 1914, p. 64. See further Rudolf Steiner, *Architecture as a Synthesis of the Arts* and other books with illustrations. Furthermore, there are good photos and pictures in various sizes. If one wants to explore the interplay of forms and colors in the Great Hall and on the stage, we recommend color prints of the watercolors in the size of approx. 50x50 cm, which Albert von Baravalle later created following exact reconstruction from his vivid memories.

25      Rudolf Steiner, *The Bridge Between Universal Spirituality and Human Physicality*, lecture in Dornach on Dec. 18, 1920, p. 148. CW 202

26      See the color photo in Rudolf Steiner, *Ways to a New Style in Architecture*. CW 286

# The Relationship of the Foundation Stone to the Second Goetheanum

1.  From the beginning, the foundation stone was also precon-
    sidered for a following building, because Rudolf Steiner
    knew that the planned building would endure for less than
    eighty years. This is what he revealed in an answer to the
    manufacturer Max Benzinger's question about the solder-
    ing material. Since a clairvoyant is not allowed to inves-
    tigate anything in their personal interest, Rudolf Steiner
    could not know the date of the destruction of the building.
    He by no means reckoned that this would already occur
    before the opening of the completed Mystery building.

    From the beginning up until the fire, Rudolf Steiner re-
    peatedly spoke of the incompleteness of this first attempt
    at building and added: "If I could build it again, I would
    design it completely differently." That he would then use
    concrete was for him self-evident, since that was how he
    had initially conceived of the Munich project. After the
    fire, following a meeting of the Building Association (*Bau-
    verein*) in the spring of 1923, he said to Pieter de Haan,
    then president of the Dutch National Society, "Surely, Mr.
    de Haan, you don't believe that I wanted to make the build-
    ing in wood!" However, after the choice of wooden mate-
    rials by the Building Association, he had adjusted to the
    advantages of such material, though, due to its particular
    structure, he did not find it ideal for organic forms.

2.  Rudolf Steiner considered the second building as being in a
    direct and cumulative continuity with the first. His remark
    that this one could only be a monument to the first referred
    to the immense manual work involved, not to the design.

From all his spoken and written expressions, it follows that he put the second building on the same level as the first in its relation to anthroposophy, i.e., also in relation to the foundation stone, which he therefore let lie in its place.

3. Rudolf Steiner proceeded with the design of the Second Goetheanum from the building motif of the First, from which its wooden character was redesigned into a concrete character.

4. Rudolf Steiner created the model from an inspiration of Michael as a "Michael castle" for students of Michael in concordance with fundamental Michaelic principles, which may be distinctly read therein. In his drawing of the building motif on Jan. 1, 1924, we find a part of a pentagon in the central motif.

5. In his model, the double-cupola principle is easily recognizable. The audience and stage sectors are separated by a distinct horizontal strip, and the [roof of the] latter is much lower than the former.

6. The task of the second building is essentially identical to that of the first, but expanded to include the mezzanine for matters of the Free School of Spiritual Science.

7. He wrote articles for both Basel newspapers in the fall of 1924 that point to the same function and also emphasize essential improvements from the first building, such as its relationship to the landscape.

# Foundation Stone, Building Site, and the Two Goetheanum Buildings

With anthroposophy, Rudolf Steiner showed humanity a way to recognize itself as an independent, free spiritual being. In his *Philosophy of Freedom*, he presented this way scientifically. By this path, the human being can experience itself again as a creature of the macrocosm, self-creative, as "God's image." Thus, the foundation stone was given the form of a pentagonal dodecahedron—an ancient symbol. The fact that Rudolf Steiner had it made from earthly material as a symbol and sign of the human soul, and then incorporated it into the Earth, gave his deed a larger-than-life effect, not only for the nascent building, but also for the entire hill.

In Munich—surrounded by tall buildings in the middle of the city—art-loving theosophists had planned a building in accordance with Rudolf Steiner's ideas. Inside, motifs of Rudolf Steiner's spiritual science were to be depicted in sculpted and painted forms. The whole building was planned in concrete, with columns made of lepidolite—a shimmering, rose-purple natural stone—as illustrated by Alexander Strakosch in his book *Lebenswege mit Rudolf Steiner* [Life-paths with Rudolf Steiner].[27]

When the city (later, a stronghold of Adolf Hitler) repeatedly refused a building permit, Rudolf Steiner brought another karmic thread into Switzerland, which later remained neutral in both world wars. He was offered a site without any building laws at the place where the Swiss freedom fighters had defeated the imperial army in 1499. A constellation of stars showed him the exact place for the foundation stone on the former battlefield.

His consciousness always spanned over the widest courses of time, so it could also build a bridge to the events on the so-called

"Blood Hill" (*Bluthügel*). On one side, it touched the compass of his idea to help lead the independent human soul of the human being towards the last step of becoming the tenth hierarchy. On the other side, it also touched the seed of modern democracies in the formation of the Swiss Confederation in 1291, which then created the precondition for independence in the event of 1499. On the occasion of the 500th anniversary in 1999, publications appeared that shed light on this important event directly on the threshold to modern times.[28]

Rudolf Steiner did not speak about it. However, eleven years after the laying of the foundation stone, in his Michael Letter of November 30, 1924, he described some aspects of the history of the fifteenth century.

An event where the influx of the spirit into earthly events reveals itself particularly brightly is the appearance and destiny of Joan of Arc (the Maid of Orleans, 1412–1431). . . . On the Earth, confusion prevails, which will prevent the Age of Consciousness. Michael must prepare his later mission from the spirit world. He can do it there, in human souls, where his impulses are taken up. The Maid has such a soul. He works also through many other souls, even when it is only possible to a lesser degree and is less visible for outer historical life.[29]

Could not the Dornach fighters also have heard this impulse? Here Rudolf Steiner found an event with which he was able to connect—as he always strove to do.

Now, the "House of the Word" was to be built there, whose language of forms could be understood by all human beings. Rudolf Steiner hoped to complete it before the already-seething political conflicts in Europe broke out. He knew, however, that this building would not last eighty years. The point was to make it appear at one time, as a kind of architectural reading book of his *Geheimwissenschaft* (Occult science), inscribed on the Earth—not just printed on the page with German letters, as in 1910. Even after its physical destruction, it would then continue to have an effect as the memory of a building of peace for people of the most diverse religions, races, and folk.

In the fall of 1914, concerning what had already been accomplished and predestined, he was able to proclaim:

> But, as I said, in this building is expressed in terms of a feeling of perception—not in terms of theoretical understanding—everything that we have taken in from spiritual science over the years, and much more.[30]

The double-domed building was visible from afar upon the Dornach hill. Thus, it had a demonstrative effect on the landscape with its geometric, circular architecture, which, like every circle, has an effect of inclusion and exclusion. Already in a private talk for members, he confessed his ideal of a building accessible to all the world:

> Oh, if only we could lead all, all human beings into such spaces! Do we deserve to have what we strive for as our most sacred enclosed in such an enclosure; where we have created something in this enclosure from which we exclude other human beings?[31]

It caused Rudolf Steiner grief that he was not able to fundamentally rework for the Dornach hill what was planned in the project for the Munich city center. Again and again from 1915 on, he excused the imperfection of this first attempt at building during guided tours, although he even carried out details himself. Even as late as 1922, he wrote to an architect:

> I was rushed, so that my thought of the building—for Munich—was transferred too quickly to the Dornach hill . . . . As a result, I feel that what has now been created is imperfect in many directions.[32]

After years of written and verbal opposition from the surrounding area, the wooden building was set on fire and nearly entirely destroyed on Sylvester Night [New Year's Eve] 1922/23. Following a meeting of the Building Association (*Bauverein*) concerning the fire in the spring of 1923, Rudolf Steiner said to Pieter de Haan, then president of the Dutch National Society, "Surely, Mr. de Haan, you don't believe that *I* wanted to make the building in wood!"[33] However, after the Building Association had chosen the wooden materials, he had come to appreciate its advantages (probably also because of the shorter construction time).

In designing the Second Goetheanum, he naturally returned to the concrete material. He proceeded from the building motif of the First Goetheanum, which he transformed from a wooden character to a concrete character. In March, out of an inspiration from Michael, he single-handedly created a large model as a "Michael Castle" (*Michaelsburg*) for Michael students (as reported by Ita Wegman in her letter "An die Mitglieder" [To the Members] of May 3, 1925 in the [*Nachrichten für Mitglieder* (News for members) supplement of the] weekly newssheet *Das Goetheanum*).[34] Once asked about the different nature of the building design, he smiled and said, "Yes, I have learned something."[35]

When viewed from the west, the building can be surveyed all the way to the side wings; its front does not act as a hindrance. An abundance of individual forms catches the eye on both sides until it meets the outer contour of the side wings and then loses itself in the forested slopes in the background. Even the oblique, longitudinal side-walls of the trapezoidal ground plan do not give the perception of being closed-off. Various vertical structural elements protrude as edges, columns, and wall-sections, forming three concave curvatures that are inviting like open gateways. All the way up to the variously shaped edges of the roof, the gaze can easily rise and experience the structure as a manifested *Philosophy of Freedom* (1894). Exactly thirty years after the creation of the thought for this building, Rudolf Steiner accomplished a metamorphosis into spacious, organic architectural forms. Now he was convinced that he had succeeded in addressing all human beings with it.

He wrote an essay about the project of the Second Goetheanum for the *Basler Nachrichten* (Basel News) of October 25/26, 1924, where he states:

> The opinion is present with the builder that something will be created which the general, unbiased taste, knowing or wanting to know nothing of anthroposophy, can definitely go along with.[36]

Ultimately, the future-oriented Michael Building became his final and most significant legacy.

Endnotes

27      Alexander Strakosch, *Lebenswege mit Rudolf Steiner: Errinerungen* [Life-paths with Rudolf Steiner: Memories], 147.

28      Andreas Fankhauser, ed., "'An Sant Maria Magtalena Tag geschach ein grose Schlacht.' Gedenkschrift 500 Jahre Schlacht bei Dornach 1499-1999" [On Saint Maria Magdalena Day a great battle took place. Commemorative publication: 500 years of the Battle of Dornach 1499–1999]. Special issue, *Jahrbuch für Solothurnische Geschichte* [Yearbook for Solothurn history] 72 (1999), 392.

Walther Lietha, ed. *Freiheit einst und heute: Gedenkschrift zum Calvengeschehen 1499–1999* [Freedom once and today: Commemorative publication on the Calven event 1499–1999] (Chur: Calven, 1999).

Peter Niederhäuser and Werner Fischer, eds. *Vom "Freiheitskrieg" zum Geschichtsmythos: 500 Jahre Schweizer- oder Schwabenkrieg* [From "War of Freedom" to historical myth: 500 years of the Swiss or Swabian War] (Zurich: Chronos, 2000).

Willibald Pirckheimer, *Der Schweizerkrieg. De bello Suitense sive Eluetico* [The Swiss war. On the Swiss or Helvetian War]. Translated from the Latin by Fritz Wille (Baden: Merker, 199).

29      Rudolf Steiner, *Anthroposophical Leading Thoughts*, letter from Nov. 30, 1924, p. 113.

30      Rudolf Steiner, *The Building at Dornach* (CW 287) lecture 4

31      Rudolf Steiner, *Ways to a New Style in Architecture*. CW 286

32      Letter [from Rudolf Steiner] to Walter Schwagenscheidt [1886–1968] from July 18, 1922, original in the Rudolf Steiner Archives, Dornach

33      In later years, this was how he [Pieter de Haan] formulated a very dear and cherished communication to the Architect Albert von Baravalle in my [Erika von Baravalle's] presence.

34      Ita Wegman, "The Old Goetheanum and the New Goetheanum "published anew by Peter Selg in *Ita Wegman: Memories of Rudolf Steiner* (Arlesheim, 2009).

35    From an oral communication by Christiaan Stuten.

36    Rudolf Steiner, *Ways to a New Style in Architecture*, CW 286

# 2.
# Eyewitness Reports

WILHELM SCHRACK

# Letter to Jürgen von Grone

When the Michaelmas issue of *Mitteilungen aus der Anthroposophischen Arbeit in Deutschland* [Communications from the anthroposophical work in Germany] containing the memoirs of Mrs. Grosheintz-Laval was first printed, Mr. von Grone had a conversation with one of the oldest members of the Anthroposophical Society in Germany, to which the following letter refers.

To the most honorable Mr. v. Grone!

Following our recent conversation about the laying of the foundation stone for the Dornach Building by Rudolf Steiner on September 20, 1913, in which I, along with many friends, was also allowed to participate, I may perhaps report on the following experience, which, similar to the participation in the laying of the foundation stone, has made the deepest impression on my life.

When I paid a visit to the Dornach hill one evening, I met the architect Schmid-Curtius from Stuttgart there. Soon, Rudolf Steiner came armed with Wellington boots, a coat, and a walking stick. About seventy meters away from us, Rudolf Steiner then walked in an arc forward, sideways, and backward again, often raising his gaze to the stars, and he also stretched out his stick to the stars several times. Thereupon, Rudolf Steiner lightly inscribed a small circle on the earth with the stick while, almost constantly looking up to the stars, stopped briefly, and suddenly thrust the stick into the soil and shouted, "This is the spot." Thereupon, he

asked Schmid-Curtius to hammer in a wooden stake at
this place.

With anthroposophical greetings,
Your Wilhelm Schrack

After such a long time, Mr. Schrack can no longer remember
whether this event took place one or several days before the
laying of the foundation stone. With regard to the time of day,
he remembers "that dusk had fallen when Dr. Steiner walked
around the site, feeling his way, and often held his stick up to
the faintly shimmering stars until he had found or determined
the sought-after place." Mr. Schrack assumes that it was likely
sometime between eight and nine o'clock in the evening.

MAX BENZINGER:

# An Eyewitness Report of the Laying of the Foundadtion Stone

*Documentation*

. . . We made a large wooden model for Dornach, where you could get inside and then see it from within. Herr Dr. Steiner calculated the thickness of the columns; it was interesting, this calculating. The first calculation was not right. I went back and looked at the columns because they did not seem right to me; and when Herr Doctor saw them, he immediately said that a calculation error had crept in. He calculated again and, truly, this took less than ten minutes for the seven columns. This time the strength and length ratios were correct. Then, he told me to prepare to manufacture the foundation stone for the Dornach building. It should consist of two dodecahedrons—specifically, the larger with a length of 63 cm, the smaller, 54 cm, and it should be made of copper. He left the rest to me, because I was his wizard (*Hexenmeister*), as he said. This was because one time, he was in Munich for three or four hours, and at six o'clock in the morning he gave Dr. P[eipers] the task, by eight o'clock, to make a model of the walkway that wouldn't be too steep. At eight o'clock, I was able to present P[eipers] with this model for Herr Doctor.

Now, I went to work calculating the surface areas of the foundation stone so that the diameter would come out right, and for that purpose I first made a small model. When it was far enough along, I visited a coppersmith in Munich, in whose workshop I manufactured the foundation stone. It was finished to the point where only the assembled surfaces needed to be soldered together. When the large dodecahedron was finished, I attached the small one to it, but then had to get ready, since I was to go to Switzerland to pack the furniture trucks and I also had to take equipment to a carpenter in Dornach; and so I arrived in Dornach on September 10, 1913. On September 17, Herr Dr. P[eipers] brought the foundation stone to Dornach.

On the same day that we were up on the Dornach hill determining the various points, the point where the foundation stone was to be laid was also determined. In the so-called Villa Hansi [House Hansi], right nearby the construction site, our construction office was set up, and that is also where the foundation stone was initially brought. We were still up at the construction site at 7:30 p.m. when Dr. Steiner stepped up and took a spade and made the first three groundbreaking strikes at the place where the foundation stone was to lie. Then Dr. Steiner gave the spade to the architects Sch[mid-Curtius], Ai[senpreis], von M[utach]; Dr. P[eipers], K[alckreuth], L[inde], Br[ummer], and last of all to me. Each of them dug three spadefuls, which were thrown into a sand cart. I was seized with a great shiver when I saw the action being performed and I myself being drawn into it; and I dug my spadefuls in deep reverence with the R-verse in thought.[37] By then, it was already quite dark, and I lit a lantern and led Herr Doctor down the hill, down to the Villa Brodbeck [House Brodbeck], where he lived. Herr Doctor had arrived in Dornach on September 15, and I brought him from the train station to Villa Brodbeck.

Then, I again went back to the building site. There, it was decided by the gentlemen that they should dig the pit themselves, and it was believed that this could be done in half a day and a night. Well yes, the gentlemen firmly believed this and drove the filled carts downhill, but already after a quarter of an hour one could see the result of their inexperienced work—after half an hour, one was already tired, and one learned to estimate the time for the work as more than imagined, because a pit of 6 m[eters] in circumference and 1.75 m[eters] depth certainly needs its time to be dug. The other day, roughly fifteen to twenty men worked; the same on September 18, 19, and 20; and it was finished right before the laying of the foundation stone.

While the excavation for the foundation was being worked on, I went with Br[ummer] to a carpenter in Arlesheim, and we made the wooden shell, in order that one could create an enclosure; so, it was a so-called shuttering for the outside and inside, because the foundation stone was to lie in a cement base. This foundation stone lies precisely in the axis from east to west, and Dr. Steiner himself determined this line at noon by means of a crystal sphere (*Kristallkugel*), which I brought from Basel. On September 19, 1913, Dr. Steiner came to me in the cellar of the house Villa Hansi, where I adjusted the sealing plate on the foundation stone and arranged everything so that the laying of the foundation stone could take place at any time.

Herr Doctor brought me two pyrites, a large one (length 30 mm, height 20 mm) and a small one (length 25 mm, height 15 mm), and told me to affix these two pyrites within the foundation stone in such a way that the small pyrite is suspended in the center of the large dodecahedron and the large pyrite in the small dodecahedron. Well yes, that was also quite a task, which could only be solved after long contemplation. Then, I had concerns about securing the closing cap and I said to Herr Doctor, "Yes, well, I can't get a welding apparatus to firmly solder this cap, so what am I supposed to do?" He said, "Well, why can't it be done another way?" I said, "Well, you can't solder it with tin."

He said, "Yes, well, why do you have a concern about that?" I said, "Well, if an object soldered with tin goes into the ground, then after years the tin becomes soft, and moisture would then get into the foundation stone." Dr. Steiner thought for a moment, then said, "Now, how long do you think it takes the tin to soften?" I said, "About eighty to a hundred years." Then a smile came over his face and he said, "Yes, well, in eighty to a hundred years it will look quite different up here." I perceived something of the greatness of this expression and thus I completely forgot to ask about the how.

When I had solved the problem of how to hang the two pyrites, I showed it to Herr Doctor; and only once he said "Yes, that will work" did I affix these two pyrites, each in the center of their dodecahedrons. On September 19, the foundation stone was finished, the soldering torches were filled with gasoline, and the tin was ready with the soldering fluid, so that nothing was forgotten. I carried tin and soldering fluid always in my bag, so that I would not forget it at the decisive moment.

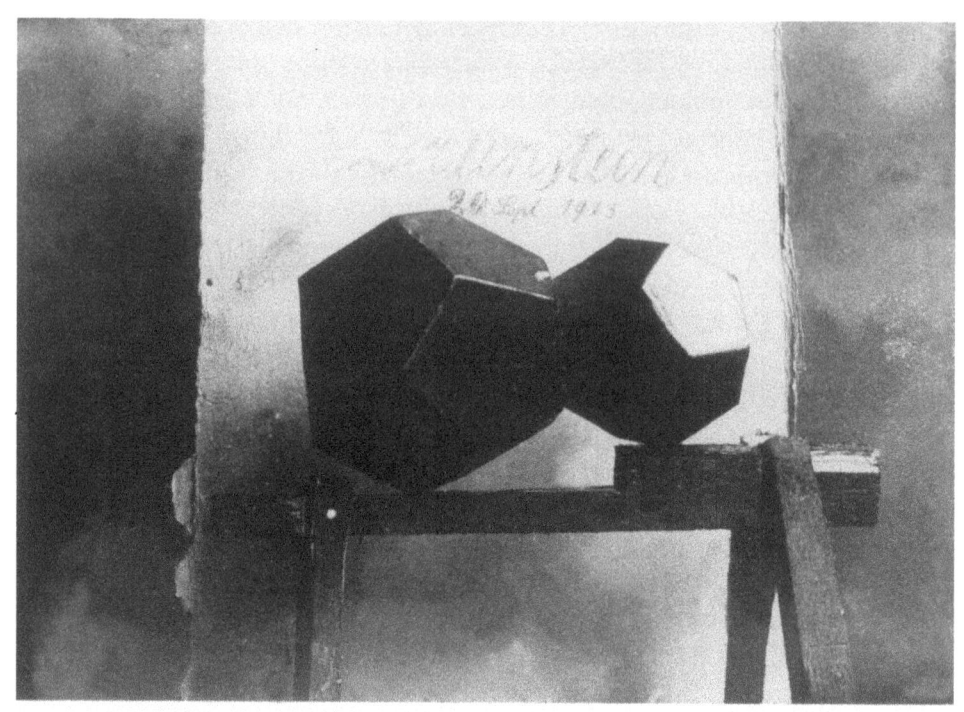

*Fig. 20: The foundation stone, 1913. [The "d" is missing from "Grundstein" (Foundation stone)].*

The pouring of the concrete for the foundation stone base (1 m high, 1.20 m long and 70 cm wide) was completed on September 20. At half-past eight, Dr. Steiner and Miss v[on] S[ivers] were in the construction office looking at the foundation stone. I had just finished my work, and there the conversation took place as written above. We were now only waiting for the bull skin to arrive so that Dr. Steiner could draw and write on it. It arrived at half past two in the afternoon, and Dr. Steiner immediately began to inscribe it [Fig. 3 & 4]. It was snow white, about 0.5 mm thick, 1.30 m long and 90 cm wide. Upon this certificate, he drew first a large egg-shape with lines going through, and he marked the end-points with the initial letters of the four cardinal points O W S N; then he drew the picture of the foundation stone and the R-letters on the faces.

The larger dodecahedron in the drawing was facing north. On the left and right were words which cannot be given here; underneath were drawn three moving lines; and below them were the signatures of the Board of the Building Association (*Bauverein*). The day and hour of the laying of the foundation stone were to be kept secret; and no one knew when the event was to occur, but all were eager for this moment. Then, after six o'clock, Dr. Steiner gave notice that at seven o'clock the ceremony was to proceed. As was always the case, so too here (something which actually should not have been done): the telephone sets were immediately put in motion and other members were notified, although actually only the members present would have been able to participate.

There was a peculiar mood outside. It had been raining all day, and the loamy soil was soaked so that one often stood in clay up to one's ankles and some ladies with low shoes lost their shoes. It was a real September day. Over the pit, a large canvas was stretched so that we had some protection from the rain—it was not just light raindrops, but already really almost pouring buckets. Though in the evening there were lighter drops. We had stacked up a woodpile next to the pit, about 1 m[eter] long and 1 m[eter] high. The evening was so dark, and it struck me as especially unusual that at this hour you could not see ten steps in front of you. It was good, for then the activity could proceed undisturbed and without prying eyes. At seven o'clock, Herr

Doctor arrived with the architect Schm[id-Curtius], both with blue aprons tied around themselves. I had already placed the foundation stone next to [the pit], and prepared two trowels, a carrying strap, and the soldering tools. About seventy members came together from the surrounding areas.

Now, torches and the woodpile were lit to illuminate the place a little. Then, Herr Doctor drew attention to the loftiness of the moment by reading the certificate out loud with all the names of the undersigned, saying also that this foundation stone is an image of the Human Soul. Then, he rolled up the certificate and inserted it into the container. Then I stepped into my role and soldered on the lid. It was still raining, but the fire of the wood-pile continued to burn merrily on. When I had closed the foundation stone, Dr. Steiner turned and spoke quiet words; then, the stone was harnessed and carried down into the concrete base in the pit by five people: Mr. L[inde], Br[ummer] on the left; the architect Sch[mid-Curtius] and Mr. Gr[osheintz] on the right; and Dr. P[eipers] grasping the large part at the back. It was placed in such a way that the large part lay to the east and the small part to the west, that is, converse to the dome structure. Then Dr. Steiner also went down. Thereafter he spoke for a half an hour. As I looked up—for I was so moved in my inmost being and so vividly bound up with all this, that I did not look up at all to the sky—but now I looked up, and there was the most beautiful and clearest starry sky; the stars seemed as if they were much closer. Venus and Jupiter stood very close together in the southwest and sparkled down, making it one of the most beautiful starry nights I've experienced (I was to experience this only once more, on New Year's Day 1923 in the morning, when the building had burned down). Then, earth was thrown in to completely fill the [concrete] enclosure, and it was covered for the time being with a wooden cover, and we proceeded from the depth [of the pit] back again upward. The fire still burned strong, and so did the pitch torches.

Then, Dr. Steiner again spoke and drew attention to the earnestness of this moment and discussed many things, including the fact that the four Gospels proceed from the east to the west and wait for a mirroring, which now occurs by the radiating back of what is most ancient from the Sun and Moon periods. He read it out loud two times, then the ceremony was over; it was 8:20 p.m.

I then accompanied Dr. Steiner with a lantern to the accommodations in Villa Brodbeck and returned again; most of the participants had gone off and only about twelve of us were still there. We removed the wooden cover and anchored iron rods into the enclosure, filled it with cement and sand, and concreted the whole thing shut, so with that everything was in order.

NELLY GROSHEINTZ-LAVAL

# Memories of the Commemoration of the Ceremony of the Laying of the Foundation Stone of the First Goetheanum

I would like to tell in simple words the course of events of the laying of the foundation stone on the physical plane. I would even like to go back a bit in order to describe essentially how this building, which was planned for Munich, was nevertheless at that time to be erected on this then untouched hill—for centuries called "Blood Hill" (*Bluthügel*).[38]

There we had two hectares of land and had our summer residence in the solitary House Brodbeck—today developed as Rudolf Steiner Halde. In the Fall of 1912, following the holding of the Basel cycle on the Gospel of Mark, Miss von Sivers was to rest there for a while with her sister Olga [von Sivers] and Miss [Mieta] Waller, while Dr. Steiner was to visit Édouard Schuré in Barr (Alsace), [France], and Christian Morgenstern in Graubünden, [Switzerland]. Then they were to travel further on to Italy.

In the *Nachrichten* [*für Mitglieder* (News for members)] of August 16, 1925, Mrs. Steiner—then Miss von Sivers—reported the following about this first stay:

> Green and rustic lay the hill, uneven and untouched, with the exception of House Brodbeck situated on the northwestern slope . . . . In a radiant autumn glow, the landscape lay at our feet; the cherry trees flamed red in the valley, like fire, like burning blood in the play of the sun's light. . . . And in all shades of yellow shone the mountains around the hill. For us city people, a blissful sight. I leaned out of the window filled with enthusiasm. But, on the following morning, Rudolf Steiner awoke as never before. Distraught, as if crushed, utterly grim; there was actually no reason for this; something

like this never happened to him—the one who, despite eternal hustle and bustle, lived in eternal harmony. It passed by. Nevertheless, I had the feeling—which has often returned in the course of time—that in this first night he foresaw many things which he had to forbid himself to consider in thought.

To the amazement of everyone, Dr. Steiner stayed in Dornach, wandering here and there, crisscrossing the whole area, and even climbed into all the Arlesheim caves.

Then he visited us in Basel, and the following conversation ensued:

Dr. Steiner: "What do you actually plan to do with this land?"

Dr. Grosheintz: "When I bought it, I told my wife that the future will show me why I had to buy so much land."

I: "I would like for us to build a rural community home there, where children can grow up in a proper way."

Dr. Steiner then spoke the words of destiny, "We have thought already of a Bayreuth."

We knew about the obstacles in Munich, and so my husband answered, "Dornach has no building laws."

"And Basel has a propitious theosophical karma," added Dr. Steiner.

Then, he told us about the steps in Munich whereby one only lost time, and said already at that time what he was to repeat so often: "Time, we don't have."

"Well," said my husband, "if you need the land, it is certainly there."

At the end of February 1913, there came the renewed refusal of the building project by the Munich Building Commission, and shortly thereafter the decision of the Johannes Building Association (*Johannesbau-Verein*) to erect the building on our hill. Since we only owned the front part—where the building now stands—we realized that the rear part must still be purchased.

Our Zurich and Bern friends, Prof. [Alfred] Gysi, Mrs. [Marie] Hirter-Weber, and Mrs. [Maria] Schieb, made it possible that the present site became a Swiss foundation.

It is important for me to mention that everything happened at Dr. Steiner's suggestion. For us to take the initiative for this change would have felt like a betrayal towards the dear, devoted Munich members. We felt how painful it must be for them to lose the building whose ground had already been purchased.

I was grateful to Dr. Wegman when she spoke the following words to me at that time:

> Should anyone say to you that it is unjust that it is built here, you may tell them the following: I (Dr. Wegman) was coming from Holland in 1905, on my way to Zurich to take up medical studies there. On the way, I stopped in Berlin, where I could then also hear Dr. Steiner, and I asked Miss von Sivers for advice about whether I should not rather study medicine in Berlin, where I would then be able to attend all of Dr. Steiner's lectures. And Miss von Sivers answered me, "Go to Zurich. Our whole movement is coming to Switzerland after all." (1905!)

Words of destiny!

Thanks to this advice from Miss von Sivers, Dr. Wegman was the only physician (among the members) with a Swiss diploma and was thereby able to offer Dr. Steiner the possibility of practical work in Switzerland in the field of medicine following the war.

Words of destiny also for anthroposophical work, since it surely shows that karma harbored within itself what was to protect the building, which was to become a home for many souls, against the impending storms of war.

Through this pronouncement by Miss von Sivers, one can also sense a danger, which for a time hovered over Rudolf Steiner's movement.

In 1911, from Geneva, the Swiss-German theosophical lodges were informed that the four lodges there—affiliated with Paris—had reorganized into seven lodges, thereby obtaining a national charter. This had been promptly granted by Mrs. Besant. And a national executive board (*Vorstand*) had been formed in Geneva, to which the administration of all the theosophical lodges in Switzerland was committed. This board was always to consist of the seven presidents of the seven founding lodges. According to the statutes of the Theosophical Society at that time, the general secretary of a section could not speak in the territory of another section without invitation. Thus, through the Geneva lodges, it was to be achieved that Dr. Steiner would no longer be allowed to hold lectures in Switzerland. It required an arduous struggle, led by Dr. Emil Grosheintz, until it was achieved that Mrs. Besant withdrew this Swiss charter and recognized the right of the Swiss-German lodges to consider themselves as belonging to Dr. Rudolf Steiner's stream.

It is not superfluous to remember this. The consciousness of the spiritual obstacles, resistance, and struggles had broadened and strengthened the souls of the people who had to bear the responsibility of collaboration.

And they were in an earnest mood when the moment came that the laying of the foundation stone could take place. I had almost said: earnest and worried, if it had not been the case that through Rudolf Steiner's being one was lifted up above the worries. One knew that one would receive the strength to bear the worries.

Now came the memorable day. Only three days prior, Dr. Steiner had indicated the date, and only a few people heard about it. On the day of the announcement—in the evening—Dr. Steiner broke ground first, and the members present then continued to shovel. For two days, work was done feverishly—during the day by workers, in the evening by members.

On September 20, the pit was ready. Nine steps led down into the depths. A small concrete enclosure awaited the foundation stone.

The ceremony was scheduled for 6:30 p.m., but could not begin until after 7:00. The day passed in an expectant mood. The foundation stone—two copper dodecahedrons soldered together, one larger and one smaller, not quite a meter long—had been brought. Rudolf Steiner himself had given the measurements. Later, engineer Englert told me that when he did the calculations for the building after the laying of the foundation stone, the calculation did not quite add up; there was always a remainder. And then he had noticed that the measurement of the foundation stone filled out this remainder.

The parchment for the certificate—made from the skin of a male calf—had been provided by Count Lerchenfeld. And Dr. Steiner was busy in the afternoon drafting the inscription on the certificate. He then read it to us. He also looked at the spot on which the fire that was to illuminate the event was to be built. From out of our old, dried-up, oak vine stakes, a mighty column was erected. Mr. Wilhelm Selling (from Berlin, Motzstr[asse] 17) piled it up and reassured us that as a former colonial official he knew how to do it so that the surroundings would not be endangered. The pitch torches had also been brought; carried high by members around the edge of the pit, they formed a fiery wreath.

During the day, the sky had clouded over, and as we gathered, a mighty wind arose. In the distance, thunder roared; lightning tore repeatedly through the darkness, and the landscape seemed ghostly.

When Dr. Steiner was reading the certificate out loud, a very fine rain began to sprinkle. But the real thunderstorm with pouring rain only unloaded itself when the ceremony was over. For the participants, the subsequent unleashing of the elements merged with the powerful, shattering impressions of the ceremony and formed a whole, which is reflected in some depictions of the ceremony. Still, all the participants were able to come home with dry clothes. But the pathless, loamy soil of the meadow, softened by the construction work, had seized some of the footwear and kept more than one overshoe; Miss von Sivers even had to forfeit a shoe.

Now at this point, the actual retelling of the first part of the activity will follow. However, with regard to its intimate occult character, it is more appropriate not to make the text available in this way to the members.

Essential communications were recorded on the certificate of the foundation stone. It was incorporated into the copper double-dodecahedron, which was then soldered closed. The foundation stone was brought down the nine steps—carried by Dr. Peipers on outstretched arms, held by two members on long straps—to the place where it was to rest. It was laid so that the larger dodecahedron lay to the east, the smaller to the west. That is, in a reverse-relationship to the building.

The architect Schmid[-Curtius] and Englert the engineer covered the stone with earth  upon which Miss von Sivers had laid a bouquet of roses—twelve red and one white rose.

Thereupon, Dr. Steiner reached out to those present around

the foundation stone—Miss von Sivers, Miss Stinde, Herr Dr. Grosheintz, Herr Dr. Peipers, the architect Schmid[-Curtius], the engineer Englert—with arms crosswise (*die Hände übers Kreuz*). Then all departed, lastly Dr. Steiner, from the depths of the pit.

Then, Dr. Steiner held that address which proclaims the answer that can be given to the audible cry for the spirit, where spiritual science can prevail with its gospel—the announcement of the spirit—that the Fifth Gospel can be proclaimed, if human souls will find their way to understanding. And, as the first words of this Fifth Gospel, there came the reading out of the Macrocosmic Prayer, "Thus prevail the evils . . . ," as a counter image of the microcosmic Lord's Prayer.

> So we now depart—taking with us in our souls the consciousness of the significance of the earnestness and dignity of the activity we have carried out—the consciousness of this evening that shall remain . . . igniting in us the striving for knowledge of a new revelation given to humanity, for which the human soul thirsts; from which it will drink, but only when it will fearlessly gain faith and trust in that which can proclaim the science of the spirit; which in turn shall unite what for a while must pass separated through the evolution of humankind: religion, art, and science. Let us take this, my sisters and brothers, with us, as something of a commemoration of this collaboratively celebrated hour that we no longer may forget.

Then followed the covering and concreting of the foundation stone in the presence of Dr. Steiner. Around 8:30 p.m. this momentous ceremony was at an end.

A few words of remembrance by Marie Steiner, written on August 16, 1925, should be added:

> The large torches that illuminated the pit into which the stone was sunk continually let pieces of flame from their bodies fall into it: a scene of terrific, somber seriousness and unforeseen greatness. For the words of Rudolf Steiner sounded over the uproar of the elements, rang out clear, great, fateful, and mighty.
>
> We were a little heap of poor human beings. Among

us a great one, such as history places only at very wide intervals at the turning points of time, who had subordinated his will to the will of the Spirit; who knew then that he was speaking at a time in which the evils were prevailing.

And ominously they gathered on the horizon of the Earth's events.

HEINZ MÜLLER

# Memories of the Goetheanum Fire on New Year's Eve 1922/23

*Spoken at the 30th anniversary commemoration in Stuttgart in 1952*

Dear and esteemed friends!
In an hour of remembrance such as this, it is certainly permissible to even say something personal:

As a ten-year-old boy, I entered the Gymnasium. Already weeks before, this event had cast its shadow. I went there full of expectation. On the first morning, after a Latin lesson, a history lesson was on the schedule for me for the first time. There, I heard—in breathless suspense—the story of the fire of Ephesus and the birth of Alexander the Great. Was it merely the fact that it was the first history lesson that caused it to make such a deep impression? The images of this event imposed themselves tremendously upon me. Everything rebelled inwardly against this abominable deed of the arsonist Herostratus.

When I was a young student living in Stuttgart for the first time, I was allowed to meet Rudolf Steiner. During one of the first conversations which he granted me, I confessed to him, after his question, that I would like to become a Waldorf teacher. But I immediately had to add that unfortunately this was not possible because during my first attempts to teach, it turned out that the student was so clumsy in speaking that he always became terribly hoarse after a short time. I spoke about this to Rudolf Steiner; he listened to everything in silence and encouraged me—when I was quiet—with a friendly "Hm" to continue speaking. At that time I knew nothing about speech formation (*Sprachgestaltung*), but I asked Herr Doctor if it was possible that he could give me some advice.

Again, he looked at me in a way that encouraged me to continue speaking. Already fairly embarrassed, I tried to stam-

99

mer out that I wished he could intervene helpfully here. "What are you thinking?" he asked finally. And again, I had to try to put into words what I could barely imagine. Very dissatisfied with myself, I suddenly heard Dr. Steiner's words: "Very good! I would like to try something in this direction and would be pleased if you would come to Dornach this summer, and, surely, as a guest of House Hansi." So . . . one day, I stood—shaken and ashamed—in front of the house, above whose door the words "Haus Hansi" (House Hansi) were written. And now, I was allowed to proceed in and out of the old Goetheanum every day for six weeks in the summer of 1922.

When I first stepped into the building—coming from the west, passing under the red window—the sun shone in wide, full rays through the colored windows. How often did I walk around the columns and marvel at the flood of colored light and its complementary colors in the shadows, and never rightly knew in what way to answer: How at all did this wondrous construction of light and color become humanly possible?

Looking upwards—from out of the twilight darkness came the flood of colors of the pictures in the large and small cupolas. We were allowed to spend one or two hours in the building at that time, and again and again we went from pillar to pillar and felt with our hands or with our eyes along the forms of the wood. Often, we heard Rudolf Steiner speaking during a guided tour through the building, and you can hardly imagine how it felt for young people who were granted this experience.

Half a year later, I came to the Goetheanum for the second time. The Christmas plays were performed in the carpentry workshop (*Schreinerei*). There were the great lectures during the Christmas days of 1922. Then came Sylvester Night [New Year's Eve]. And before our eyes and our ears the last afternoon and evening played out in the old building. While Rudolf Steiner was still speaking the introductory words before the eurythmy began, suddenly next to him came something very dark. By a technical error, the speaker's lectern, which had been transformed into Mephisto's castle, had been raised too early. Astonished, Dr. Steiner looked to the side, and the spook disappeared again. Then the curtain opened, and, arranging themselves one after the other, there stood the choirs of angels, in the foreground the three archangels—and the Prologue in Heaven began. Then the stage closed again and Rudolf Steiner held his lecture about the cosmic cultus.

After this experience, I sat on the edge of my bed on the second floor of House Friedwart. I let the day reverberate and tried to bring to mind what unheard-of things I had again been allowed to experience—then the telephone shrilled next-door. I heard the horrified call, "What, fire in the Goetheanum!" and I was already running up the hill. At the south portal, Rudolf Steiner comes toward me with big steps, saying, "You come with me right away, I need witnesses." Then, two more men join me. I think it was Dr. Kolisko and Dr. Stein. Dr. Steiner went with us immediately down to the boiler house. "Please, see how high the temperature of the returning water is!" 35 degrees I read off. "So, it is by all means normal," Dr. Steiner said, and we are already storming back up the hill. He opens the electrical cabinet, turns on all the lights in the building, and lets us check and see that no fuse has blown. And again his words, "So, again there is no fault; so it can only be arson."

We go in the south wing up to the White Hall; there it is unusually warm. "Smash the case out here and take out the ax, but pull your sleeve over your fist so you don't cut yourself," says Dr. Steiner to me, and then he points to a spot on the western side wall with the words, "Smash a hole here at once!" I had the ax in my hand and smashed into the wall of the Goetheanum. I don't know if you can empathize with what it means to smash with an ax like that into the beloved Goetheanum. "More! Hard!" And finally, a piece breaks through and falls inward into the wall. At the same moment, with howling suction, the air is drawn in by the flames shooting up inside. We step back horrified. At the same moment, we hear beside us Rudolf Steiner's voice, as if ashes had settled around it: "There's no more possibility to save it!" Outside on the terrace, lies snow. In the snow, we find a ladder, and as we set it up and climbed up, we came to a place at head height where three or four pieces of the outer wall had been pulled out. There was still some straw and tow lying there. And one could see, here was where the unfortunate work had been staged. I don't know whether Dr. Steiner said anything else.

We came back through the White Hall, went down the stairs,

and in the meantime the first people had also arrived. A fire chief also appeared, with whom Dr. Steiner once again went to the boiler house.

We said to ourselves: Just how is this possible? And: How logical were the individual steps thought out by Rudolf Steiner in this situation in order to prove right away just what had to be proven!

Now I would like to describe another scene. For a long time now, it burned, before anyone yet saw the flames from outside. When then the flames struck out—the lamps were still burning in the Great Hall—a few people dared to go once more up the stairs in the west and, under the protection of the organ loft, to take a last look into the Great Hall. On the chalkboard, in the front on the right, there were still the two verses that Rudolf Steiner had written down. I also wrote them down. And as I had written the last word, the light went out and the first flames struck in from above. We were called back since the danger of collapse was now increasing—and a little later the sparks were scattering about because both cupolas were breaking into each other. Soon, the columns were slowly bending apart at the top as a result of the heat. Like glowing, luminous lilies, they stood in the hot flames. Above the reddish glow, in the west, the portal still held. The entire west wing, built of the hardest wood, was still standing, and as I stepped up the hill in front of the carpentry shop, I saw Rudolf Steiner, who, pointing with his arm toward the west and to those standing near him, said "Impress this moment upon yourselves." Turning around, I saw the organ pipes just beginning to burn up and the flames colored a sort of green and blue. The eerie blaze of colors still stood like a memorial against the night sky as—from far away—the bells of New Year's Eve rang out.

These pictures, I wanted today to briefly place before your souls.

*Fig. 21: The Burning columns.*

Endnotes

37      This probably refers to the Rosicrucian verse

38      Memory of the Battle of Dornach in 1499; [see endnote 28.]

# 3.
# Various Aspects of the Laying of the Foundation Stone

FRITZ GÖTTE

# The Human Soul's "Cry of Longing for the Spirit"

*On the address of September 20, 1913*

The event of September 20, 1913, on the Dornach hill bears the seal of uniqueness. This "being unique" refers both to the history of the anthroposophical movement and to the history of humanity. Two thousand years ago, the Logos had betaken itself an earthly sheath: The Son of God had become human and had, through his sacrifice, laid the seed—that the creation born out of the Logos, humanity included, could escape the threatening death in materiality. The Mystery of Golgotha can be seen as a spiritual-physical laying of a foundation sone: It prompted the Resurrection of the End and of humanity, the building of the New Jerusalem of the Apocalypse. The laying of the Foundation Stone at Michaelmas 1913 is, on the contrary, the real echo of the foundation-stone-laying for the new becoming of the world and the new becoming of humanity at the Turning Point of Time; it is the echo thereof, from out of the Earth's humanity.

True awareness as to the significance of the laying of a foundation stone are sensible-supersensible acts. They thereby serve the world (which has sunk down from the divine world-origin and is thus consecrated to death), leading it upwards through the Being who, from the Son of God, has become the Son of Man—the Logos—back to the Father. Since the laying of the world-foundation itself, the greatest laying of a foundation stone was completed on the cross, upon which the World Soul was nailed; it was completed in one point, the intersection point of the world directions, the most painful contraction that is conceivable—in death on the cross. But this contraction in one point was only the necessary passageway for the Resurrection, through which the Logos would renew humanity and the world.

From the point of death emerged a new sphere, the sphere of the new life, which will lead to the spiritualization of all earthly beings clasped by death, to a true living in the spirit.

But that which must first be spiritualized is the human being. And every contact with the Logos, which becomes possible from the traditional Gospel and from a human thinking and cognizing that has become free to receive the Logos, is a continuation of what began with the Crucifixion and the Resurrection. Thus, human beings—in the sense of the Gospel of John—can, from their position as servants, become free friends of Christ, [and] who, sent out by Him, thereby become those who continue and fulfill His work. They then work on the formation of that substance, which is the substance of the foundation stone, for the new becoming of all creation. In this way, every human being can become the bearer and co-bearer of a foundation stone formed by the force of the Logos.

At the same time though, it is not only about the transformation and the new birth of the human being itself and the world substances given over to us as astral, etheric, and physical ["substances"] in our bodily nature. It is also about the transformation—one that corresponds to and is worthy of the Logos—of all substance alongside humanity, as it is to be found on Earth in the kingdoms of nature and their creatures. This substance, too, by way of the germinating and growing Logos-force in the human being, wants to be redeemed, i.e., it will be led back into that from out of which it came, but from which it fell away due to the path of human development—back into the Logos, from which, according to the Evangelist, everything that came into being in the primal beginning has come into being. The beings of nature have, in the course of their development, not yet been able to become what they should become according to the intentions of the Logos, in which the will of the Father lives. They could not become thus, because first the human being had to become what it should become. Now, however, their sacrifice must be repaid; the human being is called to be the redeemer or, as Novalis says, "the messiah of nature."

But this is the problem of a world aesthetics. Plotinus, the founder of the Neoplatonic School, grasped this in the third century after Christ when he said:

Everything formless is thus intended to take on form and archetype. As long as it has no part in the Logos and archetype, it is ugly and outside of the divine Logos . . . . That which is ugly, however, is also that which is still not completely permeated by form and Logos . . . . Thus, the beautiful body emerges through unification with the Logos, who comes from the Divine.[39]

Our world, however, is falling to pieces in our time, as far as both the social and the natural world are concerned. The human being who wants to "master" nature in the most external way— that is, with brutality—deprives it everywhere of its divinely ordained form; indeed, in their excessively egoistic craving, they drive it into extinction or destruction.

Into this world approaching its downfall, Rudolf Steiner placed the building of the Goetheanum. He who had struggled his whole life long for the Mysteries of the Logos in human cognition through to the knowledge of nature—he who had pursued the Logos Mystery in true religious feeling—now took hold of the spade and turned over the earth in preparation for the laying of the foundation stone on September 20, 1913. But this taking hold of the spade and turning over of the earth in service to the Logos is only a picture for the beginning of the taking hold and transformation of the Earth's substance on a grand scale. The redemption of the substance began at that time; it becomes converted from the force of truth into beauty. What Christian Morgenstern had written a year before (after the Helsinki cycle) began to be fulfilled:

To beauty leads your work:
for beauty streams in
at last through all revelation,
which it gives to us.

*Zur Schönheit führt Dein Werk:*
*denn Schönheit strömt*
*zuletzt durch alle Offenbarung ein,*
*die es uns gibt.*[40]

This revelation, however, was not a mere giving but one wrestled out of an individual human soul in self-transformation and self-sacrifice. It is a Logos-born revelation, which can show: "Matter is built up in the sense in which the Christ has gradually arranged it."[41] So also, in the original Dornach building, it is a matter of a beauty that emerged from truth. World Truth and World Beauty wanted to become Earthly Beauty in the building, which stepped into existence through the transformed and transforming Human Truth. *Divine* Sophia had become *Anthroposophia* (!) and this was to be visible to human eyes throughout long times in the building as matter-transfiguring Earthly Beauty; it was to bring humanity near to the Logos in the form of the beautiful. Through wisdom carried down and substance led upwards—in minerals, metals, and in woods, in the sense of Plotinus, through the "unification with the Logos, who comes from the Divine"—the "beautiful body" was to shimmer and shine into the world, which as realized world aesthetics was a summons, henceforth to raise the whole Earth into beauty through the work of human beings.

The great laying of the foundation stone for the new building of the world, for the New Jerusalem, which concerns Earth and humanity, was completed on the cross, in the sorrowful contraction of the World Soul into one point. Yet, from out this point proceeded the all-embracing sphere of the Risen One. And an image of this sphere was incorporated into our Earth in the form of the pentagonal dodecahedron on September 20, 1913. During the actual act of laying the foundation stone, Rudolf Steiner called this seed, which represents a twelvefold-enclosed sphere, a "symbol of the Human Soul." But just as the Christ, in going through the point of the cross as the Risen One, became the World Sphere, so can every human being—out of their encounter with death—seek and gain connection to this sphere if they make the dodecahedral foundation stone, as a symbol of the soul, into the expanding sphere within themselves. The human soul can become the twelve-sided enclosed sphere. And the "Human Dodecahedron" can shelter in the "World Dodecahedron" in the sense of the laying of the Foundation Stone at Christmas 1923. This path goes via Anthroposophia to the Logos of the Son and via this [Logos of the Son] to the Father; and [upon this path] to the Logos, by way of the Human Being, the elements and substances, which are still unredeemed today and which form the Earth, are taken up in selflessly devoted knowledge and in love-borne will.

These acts of the laying of the foundation stone in September 1913 and Christmas 1923 are fundamentally one. First, the physical foundation stone was laid into the Earth in 1913, and it was brought to completion at the end of 1923 by the second, formed in the sounding-together of human hearts. Rudolf Steiner, however, made it clear from the beginning [in 1913] that the "spiritual share" from the force of the human soul had still to be brought forth toward the physical foundation stone.

In their significance for the overall development of the anthroposophical movement, these two events are related to that which accompanied Rudolf Steiner from his youth in his study of Goethe's "Fairy Tale," and which found its first culmination in the fact that in Berlin, at the home of Countess and Count Brockdorff, on September 29, Michaelmas Day of the year 1900—for the first time in his life—he was able to reveal something of his actual mission: namely, to become "completely esoteric."[42] In the interpretation of the "Fairy Tale," in connection with the three kings, he spoke of the fundamental forces which fill up the three kingdoms or reservoirs, and which are also found as fundamental forces in the human soul—in thinking, feeling, and willing. And from there, the stream-of-becoming of the Heavenly Sophia reborn in the human being, the Anthroposophia of the Earth, goes outward—consistent with its inner nature—into the esoteric activities of the foundation-stone-layings of 1913 and 1923. The *Temple* had to rise up to the surface of the Earth out of spiritual necessity.

In view of the spiritual necessity of the physical building, the master builder pointed out at that time that "the interrelationship of the divine world-existence with the will, with the feeling, and with the divine-spiritual cognition, has yielded up the human soul." The detachment from the divine as a result of the birth of the 'I' in the human being, however, led to the splitting of the human soul. And out of this soul-situation of humanity, Rudolf Steiner sees himself prompted to appeal—with an unsurpassable insistence—to the "will to help" of the small group of people gathered with him around the pit of the Dornach foundation stone, as exponents for the whole of humankind. Try! Hear! Feel! . . . it sounds again and again to the ear of the participants in this cosmic and all-human act. And what should be tried? What should be heard? What should be felt? Sounding out from the souls of human beings should be heard and felt the "cry of longing for the spirit," and an attempt should be made at an answer thereupon.

Binding, in the depths of the spirit and the heart, is this call of a great one of humanity; binding not only for those who heard it directly at that time, but binding for all those who followed them in the generational stream of the movement—binding for the present, and for those who after them will come. And how far and how deep this obligation should reach is made clear by sentences such as these:

> Let us understand that this act [of laying the foundation stone in 1913] in a certain sense signifies a vow for our soul . . . . Let us understand that we, on today's date . . . wed ourselves to this spiritual evolutionary stream of humanity which we have recognized as right . . . . Let us try, my dear sisters and brothers, to take this soul vow: that we want to look away at this moment from all the pettiness of life . . . .

"It is the time," said the old man with the lamp in the "Fairy Tale." It was the time that Rudolf Steiner laid the foundation stone in that region of Arlesheim and Dornach, so historically significant for the Anthroposophical Society, in the Michaelmas time of the year 1913. It is today [1963]—after half a century—the time for us to bring before ourselves again the original impulses of the anthroposophical movement, which came to light at that time, in our seeing-thinking (*schauendem Denken*) and in the feeling of our hearts; and for us to renew in our will that vow which at the time of the laying of the foundation stone was reinforced not merely in words but through deed: in the love for the souls living in the circle of all humanity; in love for the Earth at our feet; in love for the higher worlds, which are able to incline graciously toward us—if we seek them.

And must we not will within the unity of the all-collaborative sensible-supersensible foundation stone? Do we not hear it—sounding out of the evils of the loosening 'I'-hood—the cry of the whole of humanity, the cry for the spirit?

It is truly the time!

Endnotes

39     Wilhelm Kelber, *Die Logoslehre*, (Stuttgart: Urachhaus, 1958).

40     In *We Have Found a Path.*

41     Rudolf Steiner, *The Spiritual Guidance of the Individual and Humanity*, lecture in Copenhagen on June 8, 1911, p. 56.

42     Rudolf Steiner, *Autobiography*, p. 201.

FRITZ GÖTTE

# The Macrocosmic World-Prayer, the Lord's Prayer, and the Foundation Stone

Three central, meaningful prayers have entered the consciousness of human beings in the course of human development:
the Cosmic Lord's Prayer, the Lord's Prayer of the Gospel, and
the Words of the Foundation Stone, the spiritual rock upon which
the General Anthroposophical Society was founded.

Concerning the temporal entrance into the consciousness of
humanity, the Lord's Prayer of the Gospels is the oldest. It was
given at the Turning Point of Time. The Macrocosmic Lord's
Prayer, which is not a human prayer, but rather a prayer of gods,
began to become the possession of humanity on September 20,
1913, when Rudolf Steiner, together with a few of the faithful,
laid the seed of the Goetheanum foundation stone into the Earth.
Subsequently, not the Earth, which contained the seed, but the
humanity living upon the Earth rejected and destroyed the building that had grown out of it. The great master builder continued
to build in spirit by uniting his own human heart with other human hearts in the building of the community. And the substance
in which this unification took place was a "prayer," the praying
of which he taught during the Christmas Conference, day after
day, standing among his disciples.

Concerning the temporal *coming-into-being* of these three
archetypal prayers, the Macrocosmic Lord's Prayer is the oldest. When it was proclaimed, at the earthen pit on the Dornach
hill, it was designated the "most ancient Macrocosmic World-
Prayer." It is a prayer of gods, a component of that religion of
divine beings whose "object" is humankind, which, as Genesis
says, despite its deep fall, is predisposed to be of divine essence.
By allowing human consciousnesses to take up this prayer of

gods, the seed was thereby laid for the divine-heavenly and hu-man-earthly religion to unite. The "Macrocosmic World-Prayer," within the sublime triad of the archetypal prayers, moves again and again through human spirits and human thinking-feeling souls (*Menschengemüter*). It is a first member of the foundation stone, out of which can grow the tenth hierarchy—the hierarchy of humanity—which, in free human deeds, inserts itself into the World Building of the threefold (themselves further threefold-ed), third, second, and first divine hierarchy.

The second spiritual member in these hierarchy-founding "stones" is the Lord's Prayer, which Jesus taught following the Jordan Baptism through which he had accepted into himself the Logos—the Son of the heavenly Father—and had become Jesus Christ. This prayer is the answer to the gods' lament and the gods' question of the Macrocosmic Lord's Prayer.[43] The young Jesus, born as an earthly human being out of a long chain of lineage, had received it (as the Fifth Gospel teaches) in the voice of the Bath-Kol, when he collapsed in the midst of the miserable people crying for help at the pagan altar and his soul was rap-tured into the spiritual worlds. In Jesus, who received baptism in the Jordan, there lived this Cosmic Lord's Prayer; in him it was ensouled. In him were present the world sorrows of the gods for humanity's plight of sinking into the evils; but also, in him was present the immeasurable need of the "labored and burdened," who, entangled in the earthly, lacked the upward-looking view into the actual primal and essential foundations of their own be-ing. By entering Jesus, who was ensouled with the suffering of gods and human beings, the Logos—God and human being to-gether [now]—was able to become the Mediator and the Savior of gods and human beings.

And as such, the Logos taught human beings to pray. It taught them to evade the workings of evil, saying, "Take heed that you do not make your spiritual striving a spectacle for humanity" [Matt. 6:1].[44] For praying in the synagogues and on the street-corners would draw them into the stream of the outwardly earth-ly, making them hypocrites. That is why the Gospel of Matthew goes on to say, "When you pray, go into your innermost chamber and shut the door. In this way, send your prayer upwards to the Fatherly Ground of the World in the kingdom hidden from the senses. And the Fatherly Ground of the World, before whose gaze the invisible lies open, will satisfy you" [Matt. 6:6]. And what it taught was and is, up to the present day, the prayer which line-by-line is the answer to the gods' woe, such as was given voice in the Macrocosmic World-Prayer for the sake of humanity. In such a way, the religion of humanity and the religion of the gods weave together in the space—which is free from evil—of the Lord's Prayer. The soul enters into the Fatherly Ground of the World and into the human soul enters the Father, in whom also the three-times-threefold hierarchies are sheltered. The creator of this "space" is the Son, in whom the human soul itself finds its own way home on the way to the Father.

Thus, the Lord's Prayer of Jesus Christ can only be fully understood, and it can only be prayed in its full depth, when we inwardly join it together with the first archetypal prayer, the gods' Lord's Prayer of the Fifth Gospel, which is the "Gospel of Knowledge" (*Erkenntnis*).

When the Macrocosmic World-Prayer is transformed, interwoven into the Lord's Prayer, which the Savior taught us how to pray, then the third archetypal prayer—the Foundation Stone— lives in this as the Lord's Prayer come alive in a new way.

On January 28, 1907, when Rudolf Steiner spoke in Berlin about the Lord's Prayer, he had already begun to build on that substance in society which, streaming out from anthroposophy, will become *building*. Yes, this lecture is already building and foundation stone substance. And plunging into the deed further still, in the same year, May 1907, in Munich—at the Fourth Annual Congress of the Federation of European Sections of the Theosophical Society—the first building elements appeared, which were now no longer of a supersensible but of a sensible, visible nature: a uniform red color for the whole room; a table, also clad in red, with the signs of the zodiac; the columns J and B (Jachin and Boaz); as well as, on the side walls, the seven columns, which, painted on boards, showed the motifs of the later Goetheanum columns. In 1907, the master builder began to form and build anthroposophy itself, and, indeed, in a double sense: on the one hand, into visible forms; on the other hand, in the preparation of the substance of the spiritual foundation stone. Then, on September 20, 1913, the physical foundation stone was sunk into the Earth and another contribution was given to the "*other* foundation stone," the spiritual part of it, by placing the cosmic Lord's Prayer of the "Gospel of Knowledge" alongside the Lord's Prayer of the Gospel of Matthew [Matt. 9–13].[45] Thus does the Lord's Prayer run through the history of the building.

But what happened in Berlin on January 28, 1907? The occult structure of one of the archetypal prayers, the only one hitherto known to Christendom—the Lord's Prayer—was unveiled. The fundaments of human nature are represented in the square: physical body, ether body, astral body, and I. Over above them rises the triangle with Manas, Buddhi, and Atma. The square, however, is the human being, who became a "lower" human being as the "I-hood" loosened itself from the sheltering of the divine primal foundation. Thus prevail (as the cosmic Lord's Prayer points out) those "evils" whose wellspring is the I become free. They generate sickness and lack of brotherhood in the daily bread and thus also in the physical human bodies; debt and counter-debt in the etheric body and in the intercourse of human beings with each other; temptation in the astral body, the place of cravings; and egoism in individual and communal life.

The triangle hovering over the square of the lower human being is the "higher" human being who recognizes the evil and the good in the I, and—by loosening astral body, ether body, and physical body from entanglement in the evils—leads them upwards again to a higher level of being, transforming the astral body into Manas, the etheric body into Buddhi, and the physical body into Atma. The "upper trinity," however, represents "not merely the three highest principles of *human* nature," as it is said in the 1907 lecture on the Lord's Prayer, but also the "three principles of the Godhead itself." In *Manas* dwells the Holy Spirit; this is *Name* in the Christian archetypal prayer, in which "name, concepts, or ideas of things" are represented.[46] In *Buddhi* lives the Son as in the *Kingdom*, which is the "bearer" of the divine will. In *Atma* lives the Father, who in his "archetypal essence" is *Will*. "His will be done . . . ."

If we look back from the closing words of the third archetypal prayer of humanity, from the Foundation Stone, to the Macrocosmic Prayer and the Lord's Prayer, then we can recognize that something is working in the "lower" quaternity of the latter, in so far as this quaternity is given over to the "prevailing of the evils"; this something was described at Christmas 1923 as the prevailing of the "darkness of night" in the earthly stream of being. In it, everything that is entangled in earthly temporality streams toward the abyss. The four members—the I, the astral body, the etheric body, and the physical body, originally of divine substance—are drawn into the streaming transitoriness, the wresting away from which Christ himself wanted to teach through the petitions of the Lord's Prayer. With this prayer, he opened for all human beings that wellspring of active and effective life which is connected with the innermost essence of his mission on Earth, in that he wants to lead us onward to the Father, to the divine primal ground of everything, also of human beingness. For he is the Savior, the World Healer, in that he does nothing but the will of the Father, in whom the wholeness—and that is the healing and the salvation—of the world is resolved. No one comes to the Father except through the Christ, who is one with him. That is why, for the whole of humankind, he gave the answer to the lamentation of the gods in the Macrocosmic Prayer, and he gave it for all those who have fallen into the prevailing of the evils in the earthly stream. And the Lord's Prayer is the way out of the lower quaternity into the redeeming sphere of the divine trinity.

The answer of Christ Jesus, which was given from the sphere of the Earth as the Lord's Prayer to the Macrocosmic Archetypal Prayer, is, however, also present in the Foundation Stone of 1923.

The *Will* of the Father lives in the first third of the great Foundation Stone Trinity in the words: "For the Father-Spirit of the heights prevails in the world depths generating beingness." And to the human soul, which in the ever-repeated practice of "spirit remembering" (*Geist-Erinnern*) penetrates into the primal ground of the divine and the prime original divinity of its own beingness, and learns on Earth more and more to do such will as has its origin in the heavens, it is said: "And you will truly live in Human World Being." Will of God and will of human being become united in Atma, the physical body redeemed from the evils. Here the physical body becomes selfless, and the divine will in it does not let the human being upon the Earth ask for more than the daily bread. In the portioning out of bread, the way is prepared for brotherhood.[47]

The *Kingdom* as the "bearer" of God's will—which pours out into the world creating and shaping—comes to us in the deeds of the Son, when "spirit contemplating" (*Geist-Besinnen*) is practiced. The kingdom appears when we prepare ourselves for it: "For the Christ Will in the surroundings . . . . Where the surging World Becoming Deeds unite one's own I with the World I": there, debt disappears, that "which is at fault against the community," the debt in and between human beings.[48] And more and more "from the outset, the encounter of every person with every other person [will be] a religious activity, a sacrament."[49] Buddhi force then prevails in the social life. Equality reigns in the kingdom, which is the kingdom of the Son, streaming from the will of the Father.

The *Name* with which the Lord's Prayer begins, calling on the divine and the human "upper trinity," points to the ideas of creation in the purity which prevails in their eternal, divine names. To rise to them, the Foundation Stone summons the human soul: "Practice spirit beholding" (*Geist-Erschauen*) that is, produce the thinking tranquility, the deepening of thinking into devotion, by directing it to things and beings. In such a way, Manas forces are unfolded. They allow the entrance into the spheres of the Holy Healing Spirit, in whom the thoughts, in the light and in the illumination of their universal worldliness, implore for the encounter and unification with the hidden light, that which glimmers in the thought-force of the human being. In this the human individuality—in a first step—wrests its freedom to reach the spirit through thinking means: To begin to free the astral body from the prevailing of evils, so that it no longer opens itself to the temptations from the realm of the lower, but instead awakens to that which pours itself into it in the force of the Holy Spirit's divinely pure name "to freely will" and thus enables an individual contribution to a free spiritual life upon the Earth.[50]

In the lament of the Cosmic Lord's Prayer, we also hear, "And forgot Your names, You Fathers in the heavens." In the Lord's Prayer of Matthew's Gospel, the Christ-Jesus calls upon *the* Father. In the Foundation Stone, however, not only the names of the divine persons of the Trinity are sounded, but also the names of all those who belong to the three-times-threefold hierarchies, who since ancient times have been experienced as "the Fathers."

Will, Kingdom, and Name—or we can also say: Father, Son, and Spirit—come to life again in the Foundation Stone in a way that gives a testimony to humanity of a forward-working and forward-striving of the Christ impulse upon the Earth, proving true Rudolf Steiner's words: "The destiny of Anthroposophy wants to be that of Christianity at the same time," and:

> It was not so that we might hold fast to the few words of the Gospels spoken in the first decade of the foundation of Christianity that the Holy Spirit has been poured down; but rather, he has been poured down so that ever new and renewed can the message of the Christ be told.

We may add: To tell new things also through the unveiling of the Fifth Gospel in its immeasurable breadth and depth, as it began on September 20, 1913, at the first laying of the foundation stone in our movement.

The actual empowerment for Rudolf Steiner to speak in the sense of a fulfilling "continuation" of the Gospel, however, does not come only from the fact that he was able to again name the "names" of the Fathers. His deed is the naming of the true, i.e., eternal names of beings and things, which comes from *seeing-cognition* (*schauenden Erkennen*). The ability of seeing-cognition is based on taking up the inner continuity, which through human cognition in its self-altering and self-transforming, goes through the millennia. Rudolf Steiner has described this inner stream in his book *The Riddles of Philosophy*. And what he accomplished emerged not out of some kind of atavism, which could have made him into a "clairvoyant," but rather it is a result and consequent continuation of humanity's cognitive efforts. What he achieved is the ability, from the rocky ground of mere natural-scientific sensory experience and the thinking bound to it, to strike—in a scholarly manner—the waters of life. This deed of his is Christian because it has taken hold of the continuously progressing earthly stream of being, in so far as it also concerns human cognition, and did not abandon this cognition to its own devices, so that it would go entirely into the wasteland, but rather led it upwards in the given historical moment. With his Pauline philosophy, Rudolf Steiner himself, the servant of Christ, had an effect on the evil-prevailing earthly stream of being, so that good becomes of that which only from heads is to be aimfully guided.

But that is not all: One sign, which shows that this way is a continuation of the Christian work, and which develops further what is described as the work of salvation in the four tradition-al Gospels, is the fact that Rudolf Steiner did not establish an exclusively religious, pseudo-Christian realm of effective ac-tivity *above* the earthly, but rather grasped that which is "be-low us." The turning towards this "below," however—since Goethe's luminous depictions of the three "reverences" in his *Wilhelm Meister Journeyman Years*—we can call the Christian element. Christ himself, out of divine mercy, has descended into an earthly body—to the "lower" sphere, which, from out of the true world coherence, has sunk to the Earth along with its human beings. In the Foundation Stone, Rudolf Steiner by no means merely connects the human soul to the upper world of the Trinity and the hierarchies, but rather, *at the same time*, he shows the soul as anchored and rooted in the human *body*: the soul mem-ber of the will in the metabolic-limb system; the soul member of feeling in the rhythmic beating of heart and lungs; the soul mem-ber of thinking in the nerves and senses of the head enthroned in kingly tranquility. Earthly bodiliness and heavenly bodiliness of the human being appear in the Foundation Stone from the spiri-tual point of view—the heavenly as bodiliness, the bodily in its heavenly beingness. And the practice in spirit-remembering, in spirit-contemplating, and in spirit-beholding points to the forces which, in the spirit of the Lord's Prayer, transform the four-fold formed, evil-prevailing human beingness by way of the divine principles of the upper triangle into the true Human Soul, which begins to live in the sanctification of the Name, in the entrance into his Kingdom, and in the fulfillment of the Will out of the Father Ground of the World.

The regular rhythmic inner working with the Foundation Stone, properly cultivated, means the direct continuation of the work of salvation in which Christ-Jesus has instructed us by teaching us to pray the Lord's Prayer. The First Goetheanum building and its foundation stone are bound together with this work. And the General Anthroposophical Society is rooted in the Goetheanum building that was physically taken away; together with its foundation stone, the one laid in bodily form in September 1913; and the "other" Foundation Stone, the "spiritual part," which was added on at Christmas 1923. Both foundation stones, however, are consubstantial and cannot be separated from one another.

In 1913, when Rudolf Steiner completed the laying of the foundation stone with the double pentagonal dodecahedron, he described the stone in his address as the "*symbol (Sinnbild)* of the Human Soul." Already at that time, it was about the "Human Soul," which was called upon three times in 1923. Rudolf Steiner, turning to the north, south, east, west, called all the high names of the hierarchies—petitioning them as "protectors" and "steerers"—all the names that are also mentioned again in 1923. One has the impression: this address, even then, already belonged to the "other," the spiritual foundation stone.

The stone with its twelve pentagons is the "symbol (*Sinnbild*) of the Human Soul." But, around it and with it an action is performed, and it changes in its course. By designating it as the true embodiment of spiritual truth (*Wahrzeichen*, lit. "true sign") of the striving towards knowledge, towards love, towards strong action," the three-membered human soul comes to life in these words, and by sounding the three lines of the Rosicrucian verse, it is consecrated under hammer blows into the "*sign (Zeichen)* of the Human Soul. . . . The stone has thereby become a *sign* from the *symbol*," said Rudolf Steiner.

The activity strives on. From the "sign" of the Human Soul, into which its "symbol" becomes, in that the soul reads in it "the eternal World Word," will the stone become "the *sheathed one*" (*zum Verhüllten*). A riddling word! But Rudolf Steiner explains the reason for this third change of the human soul, for he says: The stone, from the sign, now becomes sheathed, "by our entrusting it to the Earth." But another hint is given to those gathered around the pit, which permits us to consciously live through the "sheathing": "The deepest depths of the World Mysteries—they become livingly bonded with the soul when this soul is able to give itself the sheath from the kingdom of the hierarchies." Even then, the "other" foundation stone within the friends [gathered] was addressed to such an extent that their "human souls" were included in that threefold transformation of the physical foundation stone, the "symbol" of the Human Soul.

Was this different when the spiritual foundation stone was laid on Christmas Day 1923? Only cautiously can one try to answer this question. The physical foundation stone lay in the Earth since 1913, transformed by that act. From this seed has grown the visibly built Human Soul—for that is the Goetheanum building. Anthroposophia, the innocent soul of humanity from primordial times, had become physically incarnated in a building. The fire of Sylvester Night [New Year's Eve] 1922 to 1923 took it away again from thence, back into the worlds of the spirit, from which the human soul had come to speak out of stone, wood, and color—that is, through the raised up and transformed substances of the Earth. But it only went thence to come back again through the master builder, proclaimed as word, and to become building again: *Building of the community of living human souls*. A new seed was planted, of the same essentiality and the same germinating and growing force as the first, so that the human soul might be built up as a *spiritual* Goetheanum from the soul substance of a growing number of human beings. The bodily—albeit spiritually consecrated and transformed in the spirit—foundation stone was entrusted to the Earth, the body of Christ. The "other" foundation stone was formed and sunk into the heart, the dwelling place of human souls, so that they might find themselves in the community of the soul of humanity. It is as if, there with Rudolf Steiner, when he led the act of laying the Foundation Stone in the Christmas Conference, the words of consecration and transformation of September 1913 had also resounded: "May it be sheathed!" as he said in the Christmas Conference:

> And from these three forces—from the Spirit of the heights, from the Christ-force of the surroundings, from the Father-effectivity (*Vaterwirksamkeit*), the creative Father-activity, which streams out of the depths— we want, in this moment, in our souls, to form the dodecahedral foundation stone, which we will sink into the soil of our souls, so that it will be there as a strong sign (*Zeichen*) in the force-filled foundations of our soul-beingness, and, in the future of the work of the

Anthroposophical Society, we can stand upon this firm foundation stone.

This "other," the spiritual foundation stone, just as the first one, is laid for *effective activity* (*Wirksamkeit*). The building of humane human-community is to grow out of it and the will "to collaboratively carry the anthroposophical willing through the world." It is to be a "sheathed one" in our hearts. But this means—if we take the sheathing words of 1913 seriously— nothing other than that we ourselves must learn to give the sheath to our souls from the kingdom of the hierarchies. For we—each unique one—since December 25, 1923, have been foundation stone bearers and foundation stone ensheathers, just as the whole Earth has been since September 20, 1913.

But we can only learn this giving-of-a-sheath to ourselves, if we daily employ that "thinking tranquility" in ourselves, through the Foundation Stone rhythms given for each day of the week, of which Rudolf Steiner spoke on December 27, 1923.[51] Then the limb human being will wrest itself from the evils prevailing in the earthly stream of beings and will find its "sheath" in the first hierarchy and the Father; the rhythmic human being in the beat of heart and lungs in the beings of the second hierarchy and in the Son; the nerve-sense human being of the head in the Archai, Archangeloi, and Angeloi, in the sheathing force of the Holy Spirit.

We have called the Cosmic Lord's Prayer, the Lord's Prayer, and the 1923 Foundation Stone Words prayers, archetypal prayers. The first sounded from the spiritual worlds through the Bath-Kol (which means "voice of heaven"). It came, as the Fifth Gospel says, from the Sun region, which we may picture as the place in which the Christ still dwelt at that time. The second sounded from the mouth of the Christ, who in the meantime, from the Sun region had come to Earth and had become human being. Through the Bath-Kol, God spoke; but through the Lord's Prayer spoke the *God-Human*, the Son of God and Son of Man; and through the third archetypal prayer of humanity spoke the *human being*, who, as exponent of the Earth-humanity, had purified his soul to such an extent that he could unsheathe the occult content of the Lord's Prayer and convey the Macrocosmic Lord's Prayer of the Fifth Gospel, through which we may participate in the gods' thinking and feeling, in the gods' religion. And ultimately, through this human soul the Foundation Stone entered into our center, within which the other two archetypal prayers resonate and sound together below the surface.

Since primordial times, the Macrocosmic World-Prayer sounds from the heavenly heights and its call is the ancient, holy *Aum*. Since the Turning Point of Time, the Lord's Prayer lives among us, the praying of which the God-Human—as the earthly answer to the lamentation of the gods—laid upon the heart of all human beings, and its call is the powerful "Our *Father*, you who are in the heavens." Through the force of Rudolf Steiner, who, in the pain of the fire-risen Goetheanum, transformed the building of the human soul into the Word, there has been resounding upon the Earth since December 25, 1923—that is, for 33 years—the third human archetypal prayer, the Foundation Stone, and its call is no longer "Father" but rather "*Human Soul.*"

The one calling in the World Prayer is the divine world. The one who calls in the Lord's Prayer is the Christ-Jesus. But who is it that calls, "Human Soul," searching heart and sense of those called upon? The accompanying words to the Wednesday rhythm of December 26 speak of the "human soul called upon from it itself." This is from one's own higher I, which is on the way to unite with its Angelos. On Friday, December 28, indication is made of the "World Rhythm" from which the words calling for us "to practice" resound. This is the sphere of the Christ, who is effective in the world rhythms, and the sphere of Michael, who, as the Leading Thoughts say, "chooses the rhythmic world as his dwelling place." However—the higher I, Michael, the Christ . . . are not those calling on the human soul fundamentally one? Does not the angel speak in the higher I; through [the angel speaks Michael] the leader of the times; and through him again the one whose countenance Michael is? The spiritual world calls always; and in addition, we may full well say for ourselves in silence: And also, its most faithful servant, that human soul who bore the name Rudolf Steiner.

And why should we not call the Words of the Foundation Stone a prayer? Because our time has devalued the word "prayer" by imbuing it with egoistic pleading? Rudolf Steiner, in his Berlin lecture on "The Lord's Prayer," gave back to prayer its archetypal character by moving it back to the immediate vicinity of meditation: If the egoistic wishing is switched off, so he says there, and the "Not my, but Thy will be done" lives in the praying, then, if one

> reaches this foundational mood (*Grundstimmung*) as the real prayer mood, then Christian prayer is exactly the same—only with more of a coloring of feeling—as what meditation is, and originally this Christian prayer was nothing else than what meditation is.[52]

The call "Human Soul" and the threefold "Practice . . ." is prayed by the gods alongside us. Their petition to us is prayer. In the "Enwarm our hearts, Enlighten our heads . . . ," we petition the Divine Light, the Christ Sun, in the essence of its being for its existential help. We pray. In the Foundation Stone, what Rudolf Steiner said in relation to the Lord's Prayer wants to become reality: prayer in the Ur-Christian sense is meditation. We can add: And meditation again becomes prayer.

There are many paths that the human souls who gathered around Rudolf Steiner at Christmas 1923 may traverse towards the Foundation Stone; and many paths which, when they have united themselves with [the Foundation Stone], lead to work in the community, in the anthroposophical, as well as in the human community of the world. [The paths] will be different according to the destiny of the one traversing them. No one will dispute the other's path. Fundamentally, they are all valid, and what error is in them will—for the pure seeker—be corrected by a spiritual might. But I think there is one thing in which all inner experiences accord in the spirit of the Foundation Stone: The richness sheltered in it is immeasurable. And if one wanted to grasp these riches, one would have to say with John the Evangelist: "So I believe, the World-All itself would not have enough space for the books in which they would be written" [John 21:25].

Endnotes

43     The wording is quoted here again:

> AUM, Amen!
> The evils are working
> Witness to a loosening egoity
> Selfhood's debt from others incurred
> Experienced in the daily bread
> As heaven's will no longer prevails
> For human beings have been separated
> fromYour kingdom
> And forgotten Your names
> You Fathers in the heavens.

*AUM, Amen!*
*Es walten die Übel,*
*Zeugen sich lösender Ichheit,*
*Von andern erschuldete Selbstheitsschuld,*
*Erlebet im täglichen Brote,*
*In dem nicht waltet der Himmel Wille,*
*Da der Mensch sich schied von Eurem Reich*
*Und vergaß Euren Namen,*
*Ihr Väter in den Himmeln*

44     We bring this and the following quotation from the Gospel of Matthew in the translation by Lic. Emil Bock.

45     The expressions "other foundation stone" (*anderer Grundstein*) and "spiritual part" (*geistigen Teil*) are taken from the address given on September 21, 1923, for the tenth commemoration of September 20, 1913. See Rudolf Steiner, *Das Schicksalsjahr 1923 in der Geschichte der Anthroposophischen Gesellschaft* [The destiny-year 1923 in the history of the Anthroposophical Society], 642. First published privately under the title *Eine Erinnerung an die Grundsteinfeier zur Befestigung des anthroposophischen Wesen* [A remembrance of the foundation stone celebration for the fortification of the being of anthroposophy), edited by Marie Steiner (Dornach: Philosophisch-Anthroposophischer Verlag, 1923].

46     The quotations are taken from Rudolf Steiner, "The Lord's Prayer, Considered Esoterically", lecture in Berlin on Jan.

28, 1907.

47      See Rudolf Steiner, "What Does the Angel Do in Our Astral Body?", lecture in Zurich on Oct. 9, 1918. Herewith, and with the following illustrations, the three basic motives of the spiritual-soul age as described in this lecture shall be indicated, as well as their connection with the three members of the foundation stone.

48      See note 46.

49      See note 47.

50      See note 47.

51      See Rudolf Steiner, *The Christmas Conference*, address in Dornach on Thursday, Dec. 27, 1923, p. 113.

52      Cf. e.g., the writing of the church father Origen "On Prayer," from which it can be seen how close prayer and meditation once were.

FRITZ GÖTTE

# From the Laying of the Foundation Stone in 1913 to the Laying of the Foundation Stone in 1923

*Part I*

It is part of the destiny of the foundation stone—in which we are all united in the depths of our being—that we cannot communally commemorate the fortieth anniversary of its incorporation into the Earth. We cannot, out of a communal resolution, rise on this day into that region of spiritual motifs from which Rudolf Steiner drew this earthly-spiritual central motif of an anthroposophical movement of the Earth and, on September 20, 1913, shaped the sacred act of laying the foundation stone in the excavation pit at Dornach. Instead, the foundation stone can only be written about by including in spirit all those who in some way participate in it and feel committed to it.

Whoever occupies themselves with the foundation stone will soon realize that they have reached the central or primal motif of the whole anthroposophical being upon the Earth. The laying of the foundation stone is the first and most significant act in building, and building presupposes a community of those who are willing to build. Before all building, a development takes place in what is spiritual, which at the given moment leaps over into what is earthly, seizing it, and willing to transform it. Thus, if we want to understand the foundation stone and the building erected over it, we must first turn to the prehistory of the laying of the foundation stone. This prehistory leads us to the 15th of May, 1905, in Berlin, where Rudolf Steiner began to speak "Über den verlorenen und wiedergefundenen Tempel" (On the lost and re-found temple). Already the first sentences spoken at that time leave no doubt concerning what it is about.

> In the pictures of the teaching in the Mysteries, the idea of today's lecture is usually called the picture of the

> lost and re-found temple . . . . I will have to speak about theosophy and about the whole practice of life, because with this theme we have to speak about everyday work.

Rudolf Steiner then speaks of that kind of construction which leads into the depths of the Earth, of tunnel building, and remarks that such would not be possible without higher mathematics, without good knowledge in geology, practical engineering, etc. To continue:

> Just as one cannot build a tunnel, for example through the Simplon, without this knowledge, so likewise one cannot approach the building (*Bau*) of human society with a few general concepts. But—he adds—today, everyone feels called to be able to help in the building (*Bau*) of the human social body . . . . And the ignorance of the fact that for the organism of state and society there are equally great laws (just as they must be observed, for example, in the tunnel-constructions)—that is the real misfortune of our time.

The thought of building comes to light here in its whole comprehensiveness. For temple building does not mean merely to build a sanctuary somewhere isolated from the social life. Temple building is only an expression of that higher building art which creates the building of the community, yes, the building of humanity. And only the one who knows the great laws of the community building,

> only they who proceed from *these* laws could help to build. Statesmen, social reformers, etc., are nothing without theosophical foundations. Therefore, all the work that is being done in this field today is extremely piecemeal.

The laws, the inner blueprint, of the community are given in such theosophy, which was later called anthroposophy; and anthroposophy is in no way mere doctrine for the satisfaction of the intellect and the soul, but rather through and through a blueprint which, when it has been studied thoroughly enough by a person and spiritually brought to realization within themselves, becomes—by the inherent force of *knowledge* through the *feeling-perceiving* (*Empfindende*) experience—the *will to build*. It becomes the will to build, in a double sense: It becomes the establishment, from the materials of the Earth, of a built temple; and, on the other hand, it becomes the work on the forms and organization of social life. When it is seen in the real sense of the regaining of the temple lost during the development of humankind, then both of these elements are inseparably one.

But a third thing is added. In this context, Rudolf Steiner also speaks of the true essence of Freemasonry:

> In the original brotherhoods lived the thought that the human being has a task, and that task is to build up the lifeless world. Wisdom has thereby become action by flowing into the lifeless world . . . . The task of Freemasonry is to shape the world so that it is a garment of the spiritual. The human being should work on their spiritual I, so that their outer edifice (*Bauwerk*) becomes an image of the spiritual.

But along with this "outer" edifice (as the explanations in the following lectures on the subject "On the Lost and Re-Found Temple" show) one must also consider the shaping of the "outer" bodiliness, which as physical body, etheric body, and astral body should at some time ensheathe a "holy of holies" through the human being's work of building.

> The human being has passed through the kingdoms of nature,

it says in the second lecture on May 22, 1905,

> The I-consciousness finally merged into it. Astral body, etheric body, and physical body and the I together form the Pythagorean □ [square].

This Pythagorean □ [square] is God-created and God-given. Judaism

> added to this the divine Self, which comes to us from above downwards in contrast to the I coming from below. Thus, the square had been made into a pentagon
>
> ⌂ .

But this means nothing other than that to the area of the four "lower" members of the human temple of the body, a fifth is added in which, from the force of the Holy Spirit, works the higher I of the human being, the Spirit Self or Manas. While all the building art of the past was an expression of the sentient soul and the intellectual soul, the building art of the future must be of a Manas character.[53] And if an anthroposophical movement wanted to build in the age of the spiritual soul, this could only be achieved in the unfolding of that which has been predisposed in the spiritual soul as seeds of Manas. This applies to the work on that temple building which must be formed out of the human "lower" sheaths; this applies also to the building of the human community; and it applies thirdly to the actual building formed out of the substances of the Earth, which was begun as the Johannes building (*Johannesbau*) and then completed as the Goetheanum.

The threefold building impulse of anthroposophy is, through and through, *Manasic being*.

## *The unfolding of the blueprints*

Two years after Rudolf Steiner had spoken "On the Lost and Re-Found Temple," a first step of the building impulse inherent in anthroposophy became visible. During the *Theosophical Congress* in Munich, during Whitsuntide 1907, the entire hall was clothed with bright red material. Left and right of the busts of Fichte, Schelling, and Hegel appeared the columns J(achin) and B(oaz), inscribed with verses, and "both side walls and the back wall" were, as E. A. K. Stockmeyer has reported, "decorated by the seven columns of about 2.5 meters in height, painted quite simply on large boards." They already showed in the capitals the motifs of the later Goetheanum columns.

The lost temple, re-found as anthroposophy, began to step forward into appearance. And it worked in souls. For example, *E. A. K. Stockmeyer* says: "That Dr. Steiner could give new columns with these unique capitals without placing them in an appropriate room and having a ceiling supported by them" seemed unthinkable to him, and he began with intensive questioning, which then turned into attempts at his own planning. We learn details of Rudolf Steiner's indications at that time concerning the whole design: that the room should have no windows; that light should be received only from a single opening, which, as in certain buildings of the past, would let the sunlight fall on a "certain point" inside at the spring equinox at nine o'clock in the morning; that there was to be a zodiac on the main vault. And, not without shock, we hear from the one who two years earlier began his remarks about the temple by referring to the necessities of tunnel construction, that the room should be hewn in rock, preferably in granite. (Summer 1905)

As it did in E. A. K. Stockmeyer, anthroposophy also worked as a building impulse in other friends, for example, in *Sophie Stinde*, of whom Rudolf Steiner said after her death that the spirit of her soul further prevails "as the soul of our building." At the end of 1908, E. A. K. Stockmeyer made a model, which prompted his father to erect a building in the forest solitude of *Malsch near Karlsruhe* [Germany]. In the night of April 5 to 6, 1909, the laying of the foundation stone took place, the words of which have been handed down to us—words to which we will return in Part II.

Thereafter, in mid-October 1911, came the opening of the *Stuttgart building* at Landhausstrasse 70. It was the first time that the work of the anthroposophists was given a permanent sheath. Rudolf Steiner gave for this building the verse:

> Who enters, bring love to this home.
> Who stays inside, seek knowledge in this place.
> Who goes out, take with them peace from this house.

> *Wer eintritt, bringe Liebe diesem Heim.*
> *Wer drinnen weilet, suche Erkenntnis an diesem Ort.*
> *Wer austritt, nehme Frieden mit aus diesem Haus.*

This verse has consecrated the evenings of the Free Anthroposophical Society [*Freien Anthroposophischen Gesellschaft*] every week for years.

Rudolf Steiner said significant things in the lectures of October 15 and 16, 1911, about the color and sculptural design of such anthroposophical work spaces, which will remain valid for a long time. Everything culminated in the words about the necessity of building and designing in this way because anthroposophy needs sheaths [*Hüllen*]. Since it needs sheaths, however, it must, out of pure spirituality, reach into the materials of the Earth in order to constructively transfigure them. For it is something terrible to engage with theosophical reflections in philistine rooms, as we are obliged to do.

Certainly, a greater perfectibility is already achieved if, through individual concentration,

> purely in thought, we can erect such a temple place around us.

But

> In order not to form the wrong mental picture about the necessity of such a building, we must tell ourselves that when we, in the branch work, devote ourselves to our contemplations, it is necessary not only that we establish the conditions of our concentration as individuals, but also that we are disturbed as little as possible by our environment.

Since we have not only a physical but also a supersensible organism, we must support our thinking and willing.

> We can do that if we establish for our unconscious, that is, for the etheric and astral bodies, such conditions as can best be established when we are in an occult environment. Therefore, such a building is a great benefit and becomes a necessity for us.[54]

The laws whose application could be considered here were, said Rudolf Steiner, the laws of "so-called white magic."

On December 12, 1911, a few months after the opening of the building at Landhausstrasse 70, the *First General Assembly of the Johannes Building Association (Johannesbau-Vereins)* took place in Berlin. Rudolf Steiner held a sweeping lecture showing the transformations of the temple-building impulse throughout the different epochs.[55] He dwells with particular emphasis on the *Temple of Solomon*. He says about this:

> What does the Temple of Solomon want? It wants the same thing that the temple of the future should want and can alone want.

And there is no question that Rudolf Steiner wanted thereby to give an indication of a promise that lived hidden in the Temple of Solomon, as well as of [that promise's] fulfillment—only present in spirit and not yet become physical reality—which would be given in the Goetheanum building. The fulfillment would come from the growing-in of the fifth principle (the higher I, the Manas), coming into the earthly world, and which should find an adequate ensheathing for itself in a materiality raised-up via the Manas force of the builders themselves. Another intimately connected line goes from the working-in-each-other of the Cain impulses of Hiram with the Abel-Solomon impulses on the Temple of Solomon across to the new building which wants to arise in the age of the spiritual soul. The mighty Occidental impulse of the *Order of the Knights Templar*, which in spirit was tied to the ancient temple idea and physically to the site where the Temple of Solomon had stood, also plays a significant role in the whole, as is shown in the above-mentioned lectures of 1905.[56]

Prepared by anthroposophical activity, humanity must work towards the forces of *selflessness* by developing the seeds lying in the spiritual soul, and thereby making these selfless forces visible in an edifice of humanity (*Menschheitsbauwerke*).[57] The motif of the selflessness of the room had already appeared in the lectures at Landhausstrasse—the walls were to disappear, as it were, through the designs of color and allow those who dwell within them to enter into relationship with supersensible beings. Now, however, in the First General Assembly of the Johannes Building Association, the Manas quality of the anthroposophical "will to build" appears before our eyes with all clarity. *"What shall we build?"* asked Rudolf Steiner at that time in Berlin; and he answered:

> Out of what spiritual science can give to us, we must find the possibility of creating an interior space which, by virtue of its effects of color and form and of other things, by virtue of what it contains in itself of artistic presentations, is at once enclosed—and, in every detail, is such that the enclosure is not enclosed, that everywhere we look, it summons us to penetrate through the walls . . . .

And he succinctly concludes:

> *To have walls—and to have no walls*, that is it, that is what will answer to the temple art of the future; interior space that renounces itself, that no more develops *egoism* of space, that is *selfless* in all. What it presents in

> colors, in forms, are only to be there in order to let the
> World-All itself enter in.

The Manas forces of the world had come close enough to the Earth and to humanity, initially revealing themselves in the teaching structure of anthroposophy, but then moving with world necessity into the phase of the will to build. At the close of his lecture, Rudolf Steiner said:

> For the response to the question of whether, in a certain broader sense, anthroposophy is understood today depends first of all extraordinarily much on an answer that we cannot give with *words*, that we cannot express with thoughts, but much depends on our going over *to the deed* . . . .

In other words (do not be offended by this expression): Anthroposophy had to take the hammer in hand. And soon thereafter, we see the first of all anthroposophists as a master builder among those he called his friends, himself creating with the hammer on the Dornach hill.

## A tragic interlude

One cannot report on the prehistory of the building and the laying of the foundation stone without remembering that event which took place two days after the Berlin General Assembly of the Johannes Building Association [began], and the destiny which this "attempt" had. Rudolf Steiner spoke in concrete form of an endowment (*Stiftung*) that was to be made from out of the spiritual world, and he emphasized that this should not be confused in its essence with what is called a "foundation" ("*Gründung*") in the earthly sense. The "*Society for Theosophical Way and Art*" (*Gesellschaft für theosophische Art und Kunst*) was such an "endowment" or bestowal. He called what was to be founded a "*way of working*" (*Arbeitsweise*), which went back to that individuality who in another context was called the "great leader of the Occident." That which was to come to life with the "Society for Theosophical Way and Art" was only a part of a great whole.

In these considerations, we are interested in this "endowment" first of all because it was connected, among others, with the Stuttgart building and the Johannes building. But further, we are interested in it because here, as in a first seed, a work of human beings was to come about in which the force of self-lessness had to be appealed to in an absolute sense, a way of working which was—in the spiritual-soul age—to pre-form a part of the coming Manas culture (of the sixth post-Atlantean epoch). He, Rudolf Steiner himself, came into consideration in this "endowment" only "as the interpreter, [initially,] of the fundamental principles that are present as such only in the spiritual world alone . . . ." Nothing was connected with the offices to be established—which were precisely designated—other than "duties; no honors, no privileges." And there could be nothing other "than the absolutely free willing to belong to such a way of working," i.e., nothing other than the fulfillment of the lower I by the forces of the higher I. The membership can only rest

> upon the representative of spiritual interests and on the recognition of spiritual interests—at the exclusion of everything, *everything personal.*

As it was, the "endowment" was not able to function as such. In 1915, Rudolf Steiner had to say "that the 'Society for Theosophical Way and Art' does not exist at all."

One personality in the appointed circle had drastically violated that provision which said: "to the exclusion of everything, everything personal." It was not the quality of the Spirit-Self [Manas] that arose, but instead egoism, and this brought about the failure of the attempt of the spiritual world for this time.

We reference this tragic interlude because it carries something of a prelude to those later tragedies which, out of the membership, accompany the path of the great master builder far beyond his death. For the building to which Rudolf Steiner called us to be as builders cannot be built with attitudes and from stones in which selfishness is sheltered. But where the temple of humanity is being built, jealousy, the need for recognition, and personal grievances are all the same evils at work in ourselves as was the case with the three journeymen at the casting of the brazen sea of which the *Temple Legend* speaks.

# The laying of the foundation stone
## on September 20, 1913

Completely penetrated as Rudolf Steiner was by the necessity—since anthroposophy, having taken up the questions of the time, had reached contemporaries as *thought* and *word*—to now give an answer in deed, we see him on the evening of September 20, 1913, standing in the earthen pit and, with 3, 5, 7 strikes on the small, 12 strikes on the large part of the double pentagon dodecahedron, which represents the foundation stone, carrying out the historic work of consecration. The herald of world wisdom in the thought and in the word has seized the hammer. The Solomonic being of wisdom and the Cainite being of deed stream together in a humanity-encompassing cultic act in full harmony.

"What does the Temple of Solomon want?"—for which Solomon called Hiram—this is a question that Rudolf Steiner asked on December 12, 1912, in Berlin, in order to answer: "It wants the same thing that the *temple of the future* should want and can alone want." Nine months and one week later, he, a builder, stood in the Earth itself to lay the seed for the temple of the future with his own hand. Not at an arbitrary position on the planet, but at a place that he—as Nelly Grosheintz-Laval reports, as is likewise proven in his letter to Baron Alexander von Bernus—had previously investigated physically and spiritually down to its foundations.[58] The whole surrounding landscape and the history of humankind in the stream of time spoke in unison with this act on the Dornach hill.

We only understand this act correctly if we recognize the deep spiritual obligation that lay in it for those participating at that time and that arises for all those who, afterwards—as of now [1953], four decades—come into contact with its substance as descendants. For it is not a matter of mere doctrinal content, but rather of forces which were initially the *will to knowledge* and which henceforth have turned knowledge into the *will to deed*. They are aimfully directed forces, not non-binding, capricious ones. The anthroposophical movement had arrived at the decisive act at this historic moment. It connected itself with the "condensed kingdom of the elements." From this moment and from this place began the immediate work of redemption by anthroposophy on the Earth. This required the strong and complete commitment to the recognized task by the participating individualities, and so it is consistent that the builders *obligated* themselves to the building thought. That came to be expressed in the word "*[to] vow*" (*angeloben*) used by Rudolf Steiner in the act of laying the foundation stone and, thereby, the content of the certificate, the spiritual foundation stone itself, which contains the Rosicrucian verses, is designated the "*formulation of our vow*" (*Angelobeformel*).

This evening act of the 20th of September is a renewed appeal to the Manas forces which are hovering over the anthroposophical movement, an act of calling them into the sphere of the earthly world, so that the re-found temple may arise in threefold ways through work of human beings: *in the design of the Goetheanum building; in the form of the building of our own human essence; and in the form of the building of the human community.*

But human beings who will to build are obliged to hold constantly before their eyes throughout their whole life, from the moment they have awakened to this realization, the words spoken by Rudolf Steiner on the occasion of that attempted "spiritual endowment" of the "Society for Theosophical Way and Art," which say that membership "will always only rest upon the representative of spiritual interests and on the recognition of spiritual interests—*at the exclusion of everything, everything personal!*"

For that is the foundation stone!

We do not need foundation stone mysticism, which asserts itself here and there. We need the clear insight into the master builder's will to build. The history of the foundation stone can be a master teacher for us. It teaches that we need those who can build, who—out of themselves, from out of the spiritual soul, upon the clearly indicated *schooling paths*—unfold the seeds of the Spirit-Self [Manas] for themselves and *in the community.*

And we may know that we thereby fulfill a historic task: The preparation of the sixth post-Atlantean culture, the content of which depends not only on what we alone think today, but on what we collaboratively *do*. For we have now become—through the laying of the foundation stone on September 20, 1913—a *society of building*, and can no longer divest ourselves of the duties bound with it.

Endnotes

53      Cf. Rudolf Steiner's fundamental remarks on architecture in connection with human development at the Second General Assembly of the Johannes Building Association (*Johannesbau-Vereins*) in Berlin on February 5, 1913.

54      Here a question may be raised: Where in Germany, after the destruction of Landhausstrasse 70 by bombs, is there an anthroposophical workroom that can be said to represent an "occult environment" and which is a great benefit and necessity for the flourishing of our work?

55      Rudolf Steiner, "An Art and Architecture that Reveal the Underlying Wholeness of Creation: Complementing the Modern Tendency to Analyse and Dissect," in *Architecture as a Synthesis of the Arts*, lecture in Berlin on Dec. 12, 1911, p. 3f. Original German title, "Und der Bau wird Mensch: Die Ziele des Johannesbau-vereines" [And the building becomes the human being: The goals of the Johannes Building Association].

56      Rudolf Steiner, *The Temple Legend*, lecture in Berlin on May 22, 1905, p. 136f.

57      See note 47.

58      Reprinted in the 1950 Easter issue of *M.A.DE.*

FRITZ GÖTTE

# From the Laying of the Foundation Stone in 1913 to the Laying of the Foundation Stone in 1923

*Part II*

With the laying of the foundation stone in 1913 as the first step in the construction of the Goetheanum, Rudolf Steiner began to make the Mystery of the Temple, which has been carried through the millennia, into an "open secret" entirely in the sense of Goethe—a secret that was to stand before the world in all clarity. The secrets of the world and of the human being were brought by him, according to the new stage of humanity, into strict thought form, and what was previously hidden in the wisdom cultivated in the Mystery sites henceforth emerged openly before the people, accessible to elaboration and acquisition in free thought. That is why the emerging building was not called a temple, but rather the "Freie Hochschule für Geisteswissenschaft" (Free School for Spiritual Science) and it received the name of the one who had spoken of the open secret for the first time, and who in his "Fairy Tale," through the mouth of the old man with the lamp, let it be said: "It is the time"—the name of Goethe.

But Rudolf Steiner knew that what happened was only a seed in an environment that bore everything but nurturing forces for what was emerging. The seed needed protection, and this could only come from human souls who, in free inner activity (*Freiheit*), commissioned themselves as guardians. Thus, it is to be understood that Rudolf Steiner, at the moment of the laying of the foundation stone, strongly emphasized this thought of guardianship and obligation by saying:

> Let us understand that we, on today's date, feeling our souls bonded with what we have symbolically sunk into the Earth—that we wed ourselves to this spiritual

evolutionary stream of humanity which we have recognized as right,

and spoke of a "vow of the soul."

This avowing of the self, as it occurred at that time in the excavated pit of the Dornach hill, indicates a living condition of spiritual life in general. The spirit does not appear on Earth without commitment. Only the adversarial demonic powers take effect without commitment, but human beings fall prey to them. They reach out unrestrainedly and seek to make into their servants all those souls who are living unconsciously or striving egoistically. The progressive spirit who has as its goal the redemption of humanity and of the dying Earth and who, from out of the decline, will deliver new, higher life, needs that soul cultivation which alone can spring from the free individuality that is conscious of itself. Free spiritual life is not formlessness and non-bindingness, but rather has to do with formative force, which proceeds from those who, in finding free I-activity, consciously place themselves into the service of the leading spiritual powers in the kingdom of the divine hierarchies.

Only from such ways, in which the life in personal impulses (from the satisfaction of a lower egoism to those subtle forms of egoism which even a scientist or artist may pursue) is upwardly cleansed to ever purer, unselfish service, can there flow in from the spiritual worlds into the earthly world that which bears the progressive development of humanity.

One can have the impression: What was completed among human beings down in the earthen pit that received the foundation stone on September 20, 1913, has to do with a kind of formation of a vessel for the free, creative spirit. And the spiritual worlds have filled up this vessel. The whole scene is illuminated by the beginning revelation of the Fifth Gospel. Human souls were made worthy to participate in that knowledge of the gods, in that religion of the gods, which expresses itself in the ancient primordial "Macrocosmic World-Prayer." This intensification of the instreaming of the spirit is the answer to the fact that human Is, out of their relation to the reality of a world above, joined the world under their feet, the kingdom of the "condensed elements," as Rudolf Steiner said, in fidelity to the spirit—a process that was repeated significantly after the second laying of the Foundation Stone in 1923.

## II.

It was of deep inner concern to Rudolf Steiner that the events of September 20, 1913, should not fade from the consciousness of the members. After this laying of the foundation stone, he began to cultivate something that would henceforth gain an ever-greater significance in the emerging society: memory.

On the eve of the first anniversary, September 19, 1914, he gathered the members around him in the carpentry workshop and said:

> But today, my dear friends, I would like to remind you first and foremost of those ideas, perceptions, and feelings that ran through our souls when, one year ago, here on this hill, we laid the foundation stone for this building.

He speaks of these feelings, which "at that time fully glowing—glowing in the most beautiful sense of the word; namely, glowing with divine fire—have passed through our souls." And just as he had already in 1913 begun to raise that World Cross into consciousness by requesting that those around him "feel . . . what in the lands in the east, west, south, north, those human souls out there feel . . . ," so he called up this motif again in 1914 with the words:

> We tried to bring before ourselves how we can look out from this hill to the north, south, east, and west, and how we want to be of service to that spiritual life which we are convinced is needed by that humanity in the north, south, east, and west, if the Earth's evolution should proceed in a way corresponding to what is intended by the spiritual hierarchies.

Once already, there was mention made of this World Cross. That was when Rudolf Steiner, on the night of April 5/6, 1909, completed the laying of the foundation stone for the Malsch building mentioned in the previous article. At that time, as E. A. K. Stockmeyer reported from records of his sister, [Rudolf Steiner] said:

> May the light of the spirits of the East light upon this building. May the spirits of the West stream it back.

> May the spirits of the North consolidate it and the spirits of the South warm it through, so that the spirits of the East, West, North, and South stream through the building.

Thus, the words of the laying of the foundation stone were already always bonded with this, which—in the Christmas Conference of 1923, when the Foundation Stone for the General Anthroposophical Society was formed—concludes each of the three great invocations to the human soul: "The elemental spirits hear this in the east, west, north, south. may Human beings hear it!"

With impressive continuity, such motifs run through Rudolf Steiner's life and activity. They appear—always the same—at new stages of development. The world directions of east, west, north, south, are immersed in the Christmas Conference, and even further so in the establishment of the three classes of the Free School for Spiritual Science, of which it was said in the opening lecture: "The three classes were originally already there in the Anthroposophical Society, only in a different form, up until the year 1914."

## III.

When one reviews the years from 1913 to 1923, it can become a certainty that during this time the threefold building impulse of anthroposophy has been steadfastly effective. The building of the temple of body and soul for the higher I is always being spoken of. All spiritual-scientific proclamations up to 1913, everything that is described in particular in the books *The Philosophy of Freedom, Knowledge of the Higher Worlds?, Occult Science: an Outline*, and in *Theosophy*, served the self-knowledge of the human being and the transformation of their sheaths into the temple of the spiritual light from out of the force of the I. The three soul forces of the human being—the thinking, the willing, and the feeling—were to be built into the housing or vessels of the spirit, so that in the rising apocalyptic age in which humanity comes into contact with the threshold of the spiritual world, through the force of one's own being, that which comes forth out of the divine guidance can be brought together and held in a new way. Already from the address of September 20, 1913, the call resounds to us:

> Let us try to make clear how the interrelationship of the divine world-existence with the will, with the feeling, and with the divine-spiritual cognition, has yielded up the human soul.

The building (*Bauen*) of the physical building in the design of the Goetheanum and the building (*Bauen*) of the human temple of the body—in the working-through of the soul body and the other sheaths by the I—were, for Rudolf Steiner, always interwoven with each other. Both building impulses of anthroposophy were and are the effects of one and the same primordial being. On the eve of the first anniversary of the laying of the foundation stone, on September 19, 1914, as World War I was unfolding on the battlefields outside, Rudolf Steiner said to the members gathered in the carpentry workshop:

> What the members of our souls show us is that they can come into inner conflict, inner soul warfare with each other.

This is the loosening of the soul forces from those higher bonds spoken of a year prior [1913]; these are the "evils," the "witnesses to a loosening egoity" which are spoken of in the sublime language of the "ancient eternal" Macrocosmic Prayer. And with innermost conviction and confidence the view is directed from there to the growing building, which is built from the substance of Manas, the purified and harmonized soul forces. Thus, it is said on September 19, 1914, after having spoken of the "fighting against one other":

> And the type and manner by which we are tuned, how our state of soul is—whether we are more inclined to live into a thing with the feeling element or more in an intellectual-spiritual state—this is again found in the membering of forms in our building . . . .

and

> These soul members will only conduct themselves rightly when each one finds its corresponding weight with which it, so to speak, draws the human being to

the only true earthly task called for by the spiritual hierarchies, whensoever the soul members join together harmoniously.

It is pointed out here that the three-membered human soul—which itself lives in thinking, feeling, and willing—by penetrating these soul members from out of the I and, in this way, harmonizing them, forms itself into a vessel. And only that soul which acts in accord with the hierarchical beings—becomes a vessel for them—is able to fulfill its earthly task in the real sense.

The connection between the building and the human soul forces becomes even more significant and more concrete in the lectures held a few weeks later for the co-workers at the Goetheanum building and which were published under the title *Der Dornacher Bau als Wahrzeichen geschichtlichen Werdens und künstlerischer Umwandlungsimpulse* (Dornach, 1937). Rudolf Steiner said there on October 24, 1914:

> We have built willing, feeling, and thinking with our building, and as it thus is, so are willing, feeling, and thinking in human nature mysteriously connected with one another.

They are connected in a new, higher, so to speak ideal form, which stems from the I-force of the great master builder himself. He continued:

> If I walk from west to east in this building, I move myself in the same way as the sphere of will of the human being moves.

It is the walkway through the western main portal toward the Representative of Humanity who—in such a manner as from a higher will—strides towards us from the east out of the small cupola.

> If I direct my gaze from below upwards and observe the forms of the columns and architraves, then I delve into the secrets of the sphere of feeling of human nature.

Out from the round of the columns speaks the being of the European folk souls, so that the observer lifts up their own feeling into the region of the archangels, expanding it to an unegoistic feeling of the widths.

> If we study that which arches in the painting of the cupola over the building, that which we experience within the building, then we study the secrets of the human sphere of thought.

It is the gaze that looks through the cupola and its motifs that, flying over the sense-perceptible firmament, raises itself to the eternal aims of the gods. Thinking becomes seeing, to which the World Thoughts open.

Whoever enters deeply into these words of Rudolf Steiner, which he spoke on October 24, 1914, begins to suspect out of what tremendous, unified soul- and spirit-force Rudolf Steiner created: Building (*Bau*) and human soul, purified in the fifth principle of Manas, clasped together in one, and the meaning of the words which Rudolf Steiner spoke at the First General Assembly of the Johannes Building Association in Berlin on December 12, 1911, opens up:

> In loud tones, there speaks to us across the times: *The Temple is the Human Being!*


## IV.


But the third member of the unified, threefold building impulse of anthroposophy, the building of the human community, also came forward from the beginning in connection with the foundation stone. The laying of the foundation stone in 1913 was not an internal act that touched only the [Anthroposophical] Society as such. The master builder's gaze, completing the activity in the pit, went directly hence into the whole of humanity, whose social life is a testimony to the self-loosening of I-hood, in that in it "prevail the evils." "Let us feel ourselves surrounded by human souls in which there resounds the cry of longing for the spirit!" he said. And only

> if we can hear the longing call of humankind for the spirit and want to erect the building of truth (*Wahrbau*) from which is to be proclaimed more and more the message of the spirit—if we feel this in the life of the everyday world, then we rightly understand ourselves

on this evening.

The building should be erected for the sake of humanity and for the sake of the Earth as a building for the instreaming of truth, as a center for the whole of social life, which longs for new principles of design and creation from the spirit.

When the first anniversary of the laying of the foundation stone was celebrated, Rudolf Steiner spoke in all concreteness of the task of the building, "which, in the most eminent sense, is to serve to harmoniously unite human souls across the Earth." Yes, he indicated how deeply the fate of humanity and the fate of the Anthroposophical Society hang together. Even the point in time of final completion for the building—which in fact did not take place as intended, but was delayed—seemed to be full of significant destiny; for Rudolf Steiner said at that time:

> Had the thought of completion in July (1914) been realized, then we would now be able to perceive how—during the entire construction of this house dedicated to our holy cause—we could have looked down, as we did look down at the time of the laying of the foundation stone, to the north, south, east, and west, upon peace that prevailed among human beings.

But: "Now it has turned out differently!" When these words were spoken, one had to look upon a world that could call up "truly deep sorrowful feelings." These sorrowful feelings, however, streamed into the physical building of the Goetheanum and into the willing-to-become building (*Bau*) of the anthroposophical community. In both, Rudolf Steiner's will to help was actively effective.

When he spoke to the members for the first time after the outbreak of the First World War, he pointed out the first of the principles of the Society, namely, "to cultivate within ourselves a seed of human beings with an attitude of fellowship beyond all nations."[59] And under the weight of the events "out there" in the world, Rudolf Steiner came in order to remind us, with tremendous earnestness, of the responsibility to humanity's history which we bear and yet so easily pass over, saying:

> And if we could, for example, in our own ranks gathered here around our building—which is to be an ex-

pression of our spiritual striving—if we could now strongly place into our hearts, into our conduct with one another, an exemplary image, a model, a model of the attitude of fellowship, then it would have to be this thought [to cultivate within ourselves a seed of human beings with an attitude of fellowship beyond all nations.]

Certainly, one can say that these words resonate with the fact that the co-workers in the Goetheanum at that time were assembled from people of different folk, some of whom, in part, were at war with each other. Nevertheless, this word of the exemplary image and model, which trusted in a peace-testifying force in the whole of humanity, applies to all living and working together of those who have begun to take up anthroposophy in their hearts. And never may the force of peace disappear from the heart, which comes from the building, itself consumed by fire—that force of peace of which it was said at that time, on August 13, 1914, and of which it will still be said for a long time to come:

In these times, when everything seems to be shaken, let us strive to be a group that cherishes peace and harmony in every heart, so that everyone has the best thoughts about everyone, without envy, without discord.

Rudolf Steiner added to these words those which no one should erase: "Without this, the world outside cannot move forward either."

Thus, the necessity to overcome envy and discord in living together with others, and the effort to thereby cultivate a "model of the attitude of fellowship" (which Rudolf Steiner said [to] "strongly place into our hearts, into our conduct with one another") stands as a grand motif before all those who regard anthroposophy not only as a construction of doctrine, but as the inner substance out of which the building (*Bau*) of human community must be erected.

# V.

Fundamentally, the Goetheanum building was the foundation stone for the work of the art of building social forms towards which Rudolf Steiner was striving, with the Anthroposophical Society as a model for humanity, towards the stage of Manas. In this building, the forms spoke as a whole—not only an inscription above the gate—the Mystery words "Know thyself." And through the beholding of these forms, the most diverse people were lifted up into their higher selves, into a communion with their own Manas, in which they could unite in peace with their fellow human beings. But the building was at the same time the spiritual archetype of the emerging Europe: The archetype of the folk souls of our continent, which revealed themselves in the round of columns and architraves and were arched over by the unifying cupola, the archetype of a humane community. Rudolf Steiner, in creating the Goetheanum building, was at the same time the master builder of social forms.

One may say: Whoever took the entirety of the building into their senses and their heart, founded community in themselves. But one must add: It was only with this foundation stone in the heart that the real work of building began. The laying of the foundation stone in us was a deed of the great master builder. The building itself could only be erected by us ourselves, keeping ourselves vital and in a process of growth.

This is the reason why Rudolf Steiner, already at the third commemoration of the laying of the foundation stone in 1913, spoke of the "other foundation stone" which was to complete the physical foundation stone that had been given over to the Earth. On September 20, 1916, at the close of the commemorative lecture, he says:

> But in many of our souls there lives an honest, genuine will; and this honest, genuine will—if it is true to itself—will add understanding to the honesty of the will; and then—in all our souls—*the other foundation stone* will be able to form. This other foundation stone would like to carry spiritually into the world, in various and manifold ways, that which we ourselves wanted to establish, for the sake of our ideal, upon the *physical*

foundation stone which, three years ago, we sacredly entrusted to the Earth, here on this hill (emphasis
Götte's).[60]

On the tenth anniversary of the laying of the foundation stone,
on September 21, 1923—thus already in view of the Christmas
Conference—Rudolf Steiner took up this theme of the other
foundation stone again.[61] He emphasized that the foundation
stone "should not be only what it immediately presented itself
as" and pointed to the "spiritual part." This happened after the
Goetheanum building had fallen as a sacrifice to the flames on
Sylvester Night [New Year's Eve] of that year [1922/23]. Rudolf
Steiner said, standing as he was between the fire and the Christmas Conference:

> Today we may perhaps express this, that even if ini-
> tially the building, which grew out of this foundation
> stone ceremony (1913) has passed away, the spiritual
> part may nevertheless preserve its fastness . . . .

This commemorative lecture of the year 1923 is basically a
unique appeal to the wakefulness of the members, an urgent
warning against "sleepiness." To speak in this way was a burning necessity, for the fire that had consumed the building of humanity a few months prior was still not enough of an admonition
to make of the Society what was called for to fulfill its duties in
the world. With the view thereon, that what had burned down
was "what had grown out of that laying of the foundation stone
ten years ago," Rudolf Steiner said:

> It comes to mind [the warning against sleepiness; the
> admonition to wakefulness] because today one really
> must have the most enthusiastic longing in the truest
> sense of the word, that only what was spiritually direct-
> ly connected with that laying of the foundation stone,
> what spiritually permeated that laying of the founda-
> tion stone—that only this can signify a laying of the
> foundation stone for a building which perhaps only
> under tremendous difficulties and efforts can be built
> up, of which today perhaps extraordinarily little still
> stands: *I mean the spiritual part!*

And he added:

> Despite the heavy misfortune that has affected us, this laying of the foundation stone [of 1913] should remind us less of that misfortune than of what our task is in building.

But it was precisely this "building" that Rudolf Steiner had to do without, that disciplined effective activity in the construction of a community body from the strict building plan of anthroposophy itself. In the course of the years, he had to point to the necessity to live and let live, and, on this 21st of September 1923, to the "sloppiness" with which people handled the membership cards, thus allowing adversaries to continually creep into the meetings; to the inner-societal enemies of naiveté, illusion, and a lack of capacity for discernment. Regarding these qualities, he characterized naiveté as a maidenly being, chubby, and coquettish; illusion as an elderly dame with horn-rimmed glasses and pointed nose; while the third inner adversary was introduced as "Leberecht Freiherr von Unterscheidungsvermö- gen" (Baron Live-Rightly von Capacity for Discernment).

That was three months before the Christmas Conference. The elaboration of the "other foundation stone," the "spiritu- al part" of what Rudolf Steiner had laid within the Earth as a physical foundation stone on September 20, 1913, had not come about. The hope of the master builder for those builders who should have enacted the social edifice was unfulfilled, and the visible archetype of the community in the narrower sense, and of an evolving Europe in the wider, was annihilated by fire a few months before.

The loneliness of Rudolf Steiner in these weeks, the burden of the historical mission that, without us, could not be fulfilled, is—to our shrunken possibilities of experience—un- imaginable.

## VI.

But Rudolf Steiner did not retreat. His will to build, fed out of the world forces of the threefold building impulse, remained unbro- ken. The path to the construction of the Human-Body-Temple was given and inserted into the culture of humanity. The Temple on the Earth, with which the transfiguration of the whole planet—with all that is on it—had been initiated, had stood visibly on Earth; it was physically annihilated, but it would shed light from the spiritual worlds through the centuries and the millennia as a spiritual-earthly fact, irremovably inserted into the evolution of the Earth. But what about the third: the edifice of the social forms of the community?

We can only look again and again with deep trembling, in devotion, and in humility at what the great teacher, who increasingly also became a master builder, accomplished with the laying of the Foundation Stone of the General Anthroposophical Society in the Christmas Conference of 1923, beginning on December 25. For this Christmas Conference has nothing to do with what is related to our personal gain, no connection with what we could somehow "invoke" "for ourselves."

What degree of loneliness was connected with this second great laying of a foundation stone for Rudolf Steiner, we know directly from him. On July 18, 1924, in Arnhem (the Netherlands), he pointed out that what was undertaken at Christmas 1923 was a "venture," since the spiritual powers guiding the anthroposophical movement could also have "withdrawn their hands."[62] Not understood and abandoned by the members, taking that tremendous "venture" towards the spiritual world, Rudolf Steiner has completed his third great building deed, which relates to the human community.

The "other" foundation stone, which Rudolf Steiner entrusted to our hearts at the Christmas Conference, summarizes his entire effective activity up to now. And we understand it correctly only if we take into consideration a great deed which happened on the way from the foundation stone in 1913 to the Foundation Stone in 1923. At that time [1913], Rudolf Steiner joined together foundation stone and Earth body, i.e., spiritual world and earthly material. In 1923, he founded the stone not only in our souls, but rather in an organ of our body: in the human heart. And the Foundation Stone itself is not spirit per se, but rather spirit effectively working in the three members of our human beingness. The Foundation Stone of 1923 is not conceivable without the deed of 1917, at which time Rudolf Steiner published in the book *Riddles of the Soul* his research results on the threefold structure of the human organism, by which was proved the connections: of thinking with the bodily basis of the nervous-sensory system; of willing with the bodily basis of the metabolic-limb system; and of feeling with the bodily basis of the rhythmic system in breathing and circulation.

Therewith, a decisive building deed in the evolutionary history of humanity has taken place. From now on, the human soul could not be looked upon in any other way than as three-membered, and its three-membered revelation in the soul as thinking, feeling, and willing could not be thought of in any other way than in connection with the bodily-material foundations. The higher world of the human soul was seen as bound with the "lower," the earthly part of the microcosmic human being.

But in the Christmas meditation, in the Foundation Stone of the General Anthroposophical Society, this deed experienced its coronation; and Rudolf Steiner, when he placed the Foundation Stone into the hearts of the assembled anthroposophists at ten o'clock in the morning on December 25, 1923, referred expressly to the events of 1917 by saying:

> My dear friends! When I look back today at what could be taken from the spiritual worlds while the frightful storms of war were surging through the world, this must be paradigmatically summarized in this trinity of verses which have just sounded upon your ears.[63]

In these verses of 1923, the human limbs and the will living in them were connected with the first hierarchy of the Seraphim, Cherubim, Thrones, through which speaks the World Father Being, whom Goethe once called the "Master Builder of All Worlds." The heart-lung beat of the rhythmic system and the feeling living in it were connected with the second hierarchy of the Kyriotetes, Dynamis, Exusiai, through which speaks the Christ Will in the surroundings. The head of the human being, the seat of the nervous-sensory system and the thinking living in it were connected with the third hierarchy of the Archai, Archangeloi, Angeloi, through which speaks the World Thoughts of the Holy Spirit.

In unfathomable spiritual depths, the laying of the foundation stones of 1913 and 1923 are connected with each other. One can only intimate at their inner connection. At that time,

Rudolf Steiner said "the interrelationship of the divine world-existence with the will, with the feeling, and with the divine-spiritual cognition, has yielded up the human soul" and in the "ancient primordial Macrocosmic World-Prayer" we were allowed to hear the god's lamentation of the prevailing of the evils as the witnesses to a loosening egoity. In the Christmas meditation, when we rightly live through it, the new self-binding of the soul forces will be found out of the force of that I that called itself the Son of Man and is spoken of in the closing stanza of the "second foundation stone" as the World Spirit Light, and is that which, at the beginning of our calendar, entered the earthly stream of being, in order to enwarm human hearts and to enlighten human heads in the wasteland that engendered the state of separateness from the spiritual world origin.

In the laying of the Foundation Stone on December 25, 1923, Rudolf Steiner joined the three-membered human essence with the hierarchies and world origin of the Trinity—calling all their names high—and thus responded, as the representative of Earth humanity, to the lamentation of the gods and the question of the gods, which lies in the words he proclaimed in the laying of the foundation stone on September 20, 1913: "And forgot Your names, You Fathers in the heavens."

Endnotes

59     Rudolf Steiner, "Das Hereinbrechen der schicksals-schweren Ereignisse als Konsequenz des Materialismus" [The onset of fateful events as a consequence of materialism] August 13,1914. In: *Schicksalszeichen auf dem Enwicklunswege der Anthroposophischen Gesellschaft*, (Dornach, 1943).

60     Rudolf Steiner, *Architecture, Sculpture, and Painting of the First Goetheanum*, (Dornach, 1934).

61     Rudolf Steiner, *Das Schicksalsjahr 1923 in der Geschichte der Anthroposophischen Gesellschaft* [1923 Year of Destiny in the history of the Anthroposophical Society], July 18, 1924, Arnheim, (Dornach,1940).

62     Rudolf Steiner, *Karmic Relationships*, vol. 6, lecture in Arnhem on July 18, 1924, p. 122.

63     Rudolf Steiner, *The Christmas Conference*, address in Dornach on Dec. 25, 1923.

ELISABETH VREEDE

# "When Mercurius Stood in the Scales"

## *The Stellar Script*

The forthcoming opening of the Goetheanum on Michaelmas [1928] brings before our souls that September evening when, as night was breaking in, the foundation stone for
the house devoted to spiritual science was laid by Dr. Steiner
in a ceremonial act. Under the invocation of the hierarchies,
the foundation stone, the double dodecahedron, "symbol in its
double twelve-memberedness of the striving human soul, sunk
as a microcosm into the macrocosm," was laid down into the
"condensed kingdom of the elements." To it was added the certificate which contains the formulation of the vow of the human
being towards the spiritual world. This document closes with the
words:

> laid by the Johannes Building Association in Dornach
> on the 20th day of September 1880 after the Mystery of
> Golgotha, that is, 1913 after the birth of Christ, when
> Mercurius as the evening star stood in the Scales.

With these words, the foundation stone was wedded also to the
starry heavens. A certain constellation is pointed out with a few
words, a constellation which is considered so significant that it
appears next to the mighty names of the hierarchies on the document of the foundation stone. We can ask: What does this expression wish to say to us, that which occurred in that moment,
at that place, as that stone was sunk into the Earth, upon which
also the new Goetheanum rises on its foundation stone?

Let's proceed from the purely external constellation that is
mentioned there: Mercury in the Scales. If we open a so-called
ephemeris for the 20th of September 1913, then we find that
on the same day about eleven o'clock in the morning the plan-

et Mercury had crossed over the celestial equator downward, so that in the evening it still stood in the 1° of the sign of the Scales.[64] Not far from it stood the Sun, with which, shortly before, it had been in conjunction. Through this conjunction, Mercury had passed over from the west side of the Sun as morning star to the east side, thus becoming the evening star, and had moved away from it only 3½°, for the outer eye still quite imperceptible. Now since the Sun sets on September 20 in Dornach at 6:30 CET, Mercury was at that moment, when the actual laying of the foundation stone took place, directly on the horizon in the setting Sun. But, since it had just crossed over the equator, Mercury stood in the "autumnal point," the autumnal equinox, which the Sun first reaches on September 23. The equator, however, intersects the horizon of every place directly due east and due west. The east-west line always designates the intersection points of the celestial equator with the horizon. Consequently, Mercury was standing precisely in the west-point in relation to the building, that is, it was lying directly on the longitudinal axis of our strictly "oriented" Goetheanum, crossing the equator downward, due to the simultaneous rotation of the Earth and due to its own movement (Fig. 22).

Just like the foundation stone itself at the act of consecration, that which we can explore purely astronomically should come to be for us a *symbol* and then a *sign*. Let us ask first: Is the fact that "Mercury as the evening star was standing in the Scales" in itself something so special?

In answering this question, we must thoroughly renounce all that we may have taken in from an external "astrology." After all, the statement "Mercury in the Scales" is not referring to a unique or only exceptionally existing constellation, where one can—trivially said—lick one's fingers, because it is so "interesting," or even to special "aspects," from which one wants to discern very special future perspectives or destiny connections. The position is in itself a quite ordinary one, always returning in the respective season. Since the Sun itself always crosses the equator on September 23 or 24, and Mercury can never move very far away from it, so as evening star on September 20 it is actually almost always in the sign of the Scales (as morning star it would be in the Virgin).[65] The designation "Mercury as eve-

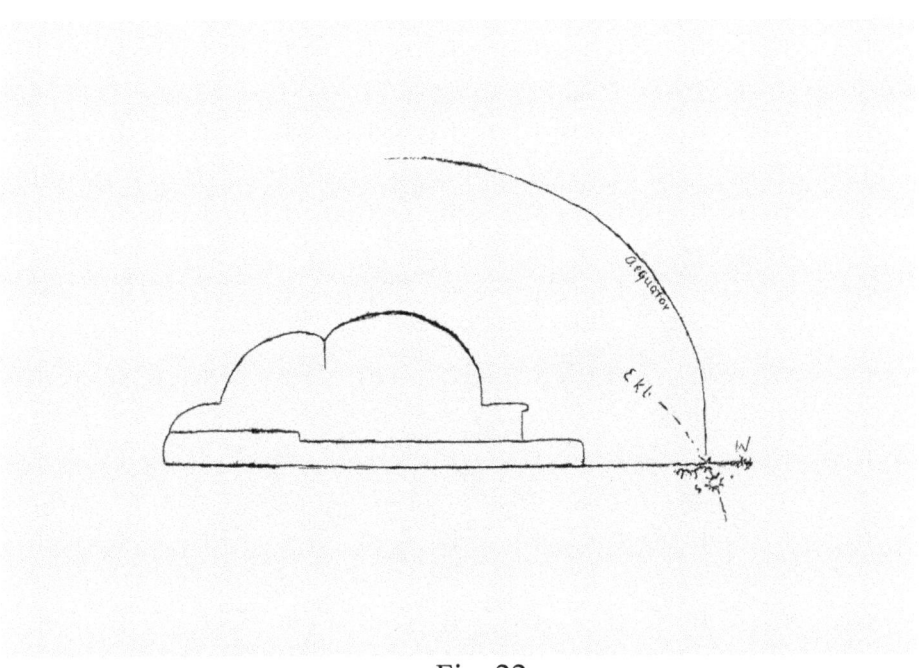

Fig. 22

ning star in the Scales" would apply to almost half of all years on September 20. We must soar upwards to other mental pictures to discern the significance of the constellation, and in doing so, we will depart more and more from a popular astrology in order to ascend to spiritual-scientific Imaginations.

Already the first drawing, which is reproduced here again as a sort of ground plan (Fig. 23), speaks an Imaginative language. We see the longitudinal axis of the building—the only axis of symmetry, which goes from west to east, and which is also the axis of symmetry of the foundation stone—(these relationships also apply to the Second Goetheanum) leading directly to Mercury diving below the horizon, which has exactly its position of equilibrium between heaven and earth—equator and ecliptic—and between the world above ground and the world below. This symmetry axis is at the same time the will-axis of the building. In this direction, the words and will impulses, flowing down from the stage and the speaker's lectern, flow into space. For their part they meet the sign inscribed in the world ether standing upon the horizon and equator at the moment of the building's

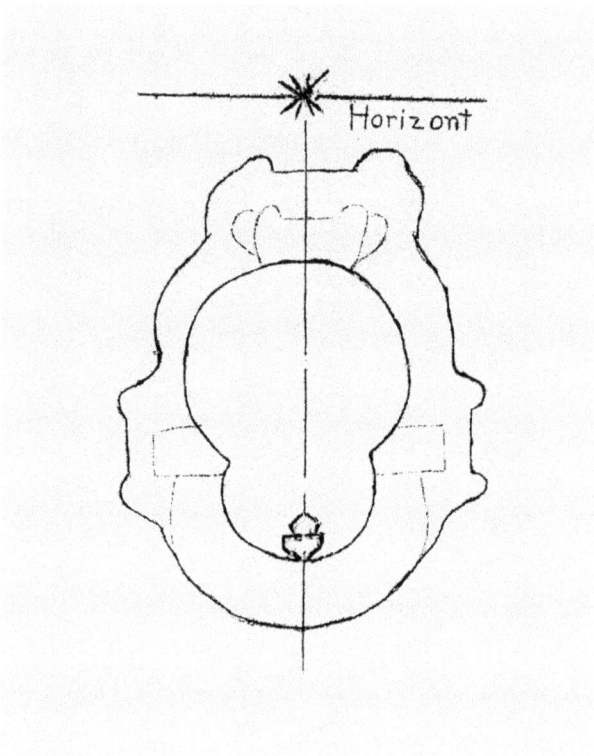

*Fig. 23.*

birth—Mercury. A Scales-position, an equilibrium-pose, which could not be more grand.

But what does this Mercury in the Scales between heaven and earth say to us? It should be a sign for us, which we learn to read like a letter from the stellar script.

We find in the cycle held in Torquay in August 1924—*True and False Paths of Spiritual Research,* lecture 10—the depiction of how those who awaken spiritual consciousness in themselves at first feel an inner Moon rising within. It is not the external Moon that is to have an effect here—otherwise the human being would become a somnambulist and ultimately a medium—but rather the night effects of the Moon are conjured into the consciousness of the day. The spiritual begins to become illuminated. There the forces of the lunar sphere live in the human being and build thereins a second human being. The outer Moon is only like a sign for these spiritual Moon-effects, its light becomes the general elixir of life, which one feels oneself within.

> Then, gradually, the spirit star Mercury rises in this night conjured into the day. Out of this twinkling dawn and dawning twinkle, in which Mercury encounters one, that being emerges which is then designated as the divine being Mercury. One needs him. One needs him absolutely, otherwise confusion ensues. . . . And thereby, insofar as one gets to know him, one can now govern, willfully govern, the second human being, which is enlivened within oneself.

The Moon alone would transmit to us merely visions, indeed imaginations, but of such a kind that one cannot know whether they present a reality.

> But, by stepping into Mercury's activity, these imaginations proceed to the essence of their being. And so, you become conscious of the Mercury effects while your visionary world flows into a true perceptual world of the spiritual.

Thus, we see, like an Imagination of the cosmos itself, Mercury standing in the Scales on the evening of the laying of the foundation stone: the messenger of the gods for true Imaginations, glimmering on the horizon, in the Scales between heaven and earth! We have to do here with a spiritual being who is symbolized for us in the planet Mercury, and who has this planet as a divine body, in a sense, outside or beside itself. The planet Mercury goes its prescribed course; it is like the sign for the effective spiritual forces ruling in the whole Mercury sphere. The planet Mercury shows the progression of these effective forces. In the present Earth era—the "World of Accomplished Work"—here the star-world reveals its "effectiveness" (cf. Dr. Steiner's letter "To the Members" in the *Nachrichten* [*für Mitglieder* (News for members)] no. 43, Nov. 2, 1924, and also the first and second *Rundschreiben* (Circular letters) [of the Mathematical-Astronomical Section at the Goetheanum], Sept./Oct. 1927).

Mercury is considered in occult tradition to be the god of the combining intellect. That he is, but only for the brain-bound intellect. For the spiritual researcher, he is the guide into the world of true Imaginations. As such did the old initiates likewise know him, in their own way. Mercury was Hermes for the Greeks and the same being was called Thoth by the Egyptians. He was the inventor of the arts and sciences, which were spread among the people in time immemorial by Osiris, the spouse and brother of Isis. The Egyptians depicted the being, the destinies of these gods with the help of the stellar script, "the script that the heavenly bodies write in the world-space" (cf. [Rudolf Steiner's] lecture "Hermes," printed in *Die Drei* [The three] 5, no. 11). This stellar script portrayed entirely real experiences for the ancient Egyptians. They knew: In the most distant past there was a living clairvoyance among human beings. That was the time when Hermes or Thoth taught human beings, when Osiris formed the script, which was modeled after the stellar script. One felt in one's soul the forces of Isis and Osiris, of Hermes; they were present from the very beginning. Sun, Moon, and Mercury were symbols for these forces. But they were symbols that at the same time had something to do with what they portrayed, like the letters of a script—only not such a script as we have today, but rather exactly like the celestial script that was taught to human beings by Thoth. "As above, so below." When the Sun and the Moon circle in the heavens and place themselves in relationship with the constellations, it is like a revelation of spiritual-supersensible forces. These forces have called forth this positioning and have provided themselves with a means of expression in the celestial writing for supersensible powers and forces.

In this celestial script, Osiris was the Sun; at the same time, the Egyptians felt within themselves the active solar force of Osiris. In these olden times, it lived in them as the power of the clairvoyants. At that time, the people were immersed in a clairvoyant culture; there worked Osiris, there also Hermes. They lived in atavistic Imaginations. Hence, Osiris understood how to shape the picture-writing from the celestial script, the hieroglyphics, which the uninitiated looked upon in shy reverence. But now took place that which would later be told in the Osiris-Isis legend.

Osiris had a brother, the evil Typhon (= breath of air). Typhon killed the benevolent Osiris by tricking him into lying down in a coffin and then closing and locking it. The coffin was then doused with lead and cast into the sea. It came to Byblos in Phoenicia. After a long search, Isis finds the coffin and brings it back to Egypt; again, Typhon seizes Osiris and tears him into fourteen pieces. Only after great hardship does the grieving Isis succeed in finding the parts and then buries them. She gives the land to the priests and has a rite for Osiris established. Now, various events play out between Typhon and Isis and between her son Horus and Hermes, but we need not enumerate them here.

With this legend there will also begin important experiences for the human soul in the transition from the holy hieroglyphic, borrowed from the celestial script, to the abstract writing notation of a later time. "Osiris" does not represent a unique being, but rather the time of clairvoyance in general. Typhon is that being (he corresponds to Ahriman), who kills the old clairvoyance and wants to replace it with the intellect, initially in the form of cunning, craftiness. "The breath of air kills the light being"— in this picture lived reminiscences of the old Lemurian time, when the breathing of light was superseded by the breathing of air! For, after all, Egyptian culture was a recapitulation of the ancient Lemurian epoch. But now, Osiris can no longer be the Sun. He can only reflect the sunlight in a dimmed form. He has become the Moon; the fourteen pieces into which he was torn are the fourteen days around the full Moon. But Isis, the faithful spouse, is the new Moon; always the dark, passive half, opposite and facing Osiris.

Hermes in this celestial script is also twofold. As Thoth he is the morning star, the god of wisdom, who descends to Earth with winged feet. As evening star, he is Hermes Psychopompos (Anubis or Hermanubis, among the Egyptians), the guide of the souls into the underworld, who brings them to Osiris. For Osiris, after his violent death, is no longer to be found among the living in the upper world, but must be sought among the dead, in the underworld. Therefore, only death—or initiation— leads to Osiris. In the Egyptian so-called "Book of the Dead" one finds the scene presented where Thoth-Hermes—or also the jackal-headed Anubis—as the scribe of the underworld, leads the souls to judgment by Osiris.

In our fifth post-Atlantean cultural period, the old Imaginations must arise anew. Therefore, we need Mercury as the evening star in the Scales; we absolutely need him.

As Sun, Osiris has set; the time of the old clairvoyance is irreversibly past. As Moon, he is again present. This event is also expressed by the stellar script. It is said that the death of Osiris took place when the Sun stood in the 17° of Scorpio and the full Moon rose on the opposite side. We have there a pronouncement (it is found, among other places, in Plutarch, "On Isis and Osiris"), which is stated completely in the sense of the later astrological way of thinking. It already contains speculations and no longer has the pure pictoriality of the actual legend. Indeed, Dr. Steiner also said something about this indication: "So also, those who connected their thoughts to the Osiris myth have referred back to quite specific star constellations" (Lecture, Jan. 5, 1918). At another place, Plutarch relates the number 17 to the age of the Moon, which is two days beyond the full Moon, and thus, clearly shows that it is understood to be in the process of waning.

Let us take the picture of the setting Sun in the sign of the Scorpion, which was the sign of the underworld and of death. It stands not far from red Antares. Osiris disappears into the underworld, but soon after, he rises again as the full Moon in the eastern sky. Hermes accompanies him. Indeed, Mercury is like a kind of Moon to the Sun, as he was also for the Egyptians, who already had Mercury and Venus orbiting around the Sun. Mercury behaves, in some respects, in relation to the Sun as our Moon does in relation to the Earth.

The constellation depicted here—the Sun in the 17° of the Scorpion, the full Moon in the Bull by the Pleiades—is again not something unique that could lead, for example, to a specific historical date. These relations between Sun and Moon return again and again in regular time intervals. We have here an example of "rhythmical astronomy." Every 19 years, both the Sun and the Moon will be in nearly the same place in the sky where they were before this period, so that the phase of the Moon is also the same. This is the so-called Metonic cycle, which is added to the other Sun-Moon rhythms, like the Saros period, etc. Considered in this way, the killing of Osiris by Typhon is also a recurring, continuously effective event. Every 19 years, one could say, whenever in the November days the Sun stands in the 17° of Scorpion and at the same time there is a full Moon, an impulse will again be given for the clairvoyance to fade away a little more. At least, that's how it was during long spans of time. But at some point, the end is reached. Far beyond the Egyptian time, almost into our time, there has been atavistic clairvoyance. Then, however, the effects change and the same constellation must now be read in a completely other sense.

For the ancient Egyptians, Osiris had disappeared from the side of Isis. A lead coffin remained on the Earth at Byblos in Phoenicia, the country where the letter script was invented. Upon papyrus barques, Isis sails over marshes and rivers seeking Osiris. The old legend seems to us like a typhonic presentiment of the art of printing, which ushered in the fifth post-Atlantean age. Today, those who seek Osiris, without becoming torn apart by Typhon, must go to the dead themselves. The dead, said Dr. Steiner, are today the only human beings who read the celestial script. From the dead we can learn it, if we can find common forms of experience with them.

Let us return to our constellation for the laying of the foundation stone! It is outwardly something like a reminiscence of the Osiris-Typhon constellation. The setting Sun; the Moon, not yet completely risen, standing in the Bull, between full Moon and last quarter; Hermes-Mercury, accompanying the Sun into the underworld; the descending lunar node not far from the Sun, for it is a few days after a lunar eclipse. We must not interpret the picture in the old sense, because the experiences and the way of experiencing of the Egyptian age are irreversibly past. Yet, the fifth post-Atlantean age is the recapitulation and should be the Christened resurrection of the third epoch. We have, as it were, the task to create the counter-image of the Osiris-Isis legend. We move from the lead coffin and the typhonic schemes of the earthly intellect away towards a newly risen Osiris force; through a new celestial script to a truly cosmic experience. We should not look up to the heavens in mourning, like the Egyptian. The new stellar script is not only written by gods, but also experienced by human beings in freedom (*Freiheit*). For between the tragic experience of destiny in pre-Christian times and today's experience of the stellar script, there lies precisely the event of Golgotha. Indeed, the indication for the constellation at the laying of the foundation stone is not an indication of an inescapable fate, but much more that of a vow!

Again, Hermes-Mercurius can teach us arts and sciences if we are willing as scientists to follow Hermes-Psychopompos into the world of true Imaginations, which initially for us may appear degraded as an underworld. If not, we will become Typhon or Seth—so also was the evening star Mercury called by the Egyptians when, not recognizing its relationship with the morning star Mercury, they considered him as a being unto himself. The artist will be accompanied by the Sun messenger Mercury as morning star, the god of wisdom. The Greeks called him Apollo in this form also; for the Egyptians he was Horus, the son of Isis and Osiris, who remained in constant battle with Seth. Both, however, were going towards unification with the Sun, towards the inferior or the superior conjunction. We can address both together in this sense as the Archangel Raphael, who stands in the west.

And this can be our vow when looking upon the constellation of the laying of the foundation stone: May the divine being Raphael-Mercurius lead us to the true Imaginations of a new science, a new art. Gabriel alone, the lunar emissary, shall not be enough for us. Mercury shall also lead us past the crags of the Venus entity. Lucifer shall not confront us when the Imaginations go on to their being, but the empty consciousness shall stand in place of the picture-filled world of Mercury's consciousness. Then, we penetrate to the experience of the Sun.

We have spiritually traversed the path that is also recorded for us in a celestial script through the planetary world from the Moon to the Sun. And when we arrive in spirit at the Sun, there is no glowing ball of gas, but rather a world of Inspiration. There Michael meets us in his radiating garment of spiritual beings who have sprung from the powers of the Sun; his luminous word will one day stream to eagerly awaiting, thirsting souls.

Endnotes

64      This is the astronomical Mercury, the small reddish planet which is always near the Sun—and not the planet commonly called the "evening star," Venus. Also here the *sign* of Scales is spoken of, not the constellation of Scales. This difference was indicated in the 11th and 12th circular letter of vol. 1, The *Rundschreiben der Mathematisch-Astronomischen Sektion* (Circular letters of the Mathematical-Astronomical Section).

65      Speaking astronomically, "evening star" refers to the planet that follows the Sun, that is, both after it rises and sets. It can be "morning star" at the time of the sunset if it has a position to the west of the Sun. It would then set before the Sun and therefore be invisible altogether in the evening sky.

WALTHER BÜHLER

# "When Mercurius Stood in the Scales"

## *The Cosmological Aspect of the Laying of the Foundation Stone*

It is the innermost concern of anthroposophy to connect the spiritual in the human being with the spiritual in the universe in a way that is appropriate to the modern consciousness of humanity. Only this expansion of consciousness will at the same time be able to create the moral atmosphere out of which humanity can meet the dangers that threaten the development of the fifth cultural epoch. For in this epoch, technology will take a turn, as yet hardly imagined in its extent, towards the seizure of cosmic forces, which will show itself to be the polar opposite of the mastery of the forces of the atom.

Rudolf Steiner said:

> While science has, over the course of centuries, looked only at those things which have effects alongside each other on Earth, and has renounced all looking up to what is most important in the happenings of the extra-earthly, the extra-telluric, as it approaches the Earth, precisely in the fifth post-Atlantean time the utilization of the forces coming in from the cosmos will come into consideration.

This highest concern of spiritual science finds its expression in the forming of the foundation stone of the Goetheanum; it is assembled from a small and large dodecahedron as a "symbol in its double twelve-memberedness of the striving Human Soul, sunk as microcosm into the macrocosm." It is therefore essential that this foundation stone—and with it the whole building—appears in a corresponding and significant way within space and time. On the one hand, the symmetry axis of the foundation stone points to this mystery, which together with the longitudinal axis of the building is strictly aligned from east to west; on the other hand, the foundation stone document closes with the words:

> laid by the Johannes Building Association on the 20th day of September 1880 after the Mystery of Golgotha, that is, 1913 after the birth of Christ, when Mercurius as the evening star stood in the Scales.

Thus, the laying of the foundation stone appears to be tied-in with the central event of the history of humanity and the planetary rhythms in the fixed-star periphery.

Dr. E. Vreede has dealt in detail with the indicated constellation in the *Rundschreiben der Mathematisch-Astronomischen Sektion am Goetheanum* (Circular letters of the Mathematical-Astronomical Section at the Goetheanum) 2, no. 1. The date chosen for the laying of the foundation stone was the day shortly before the beginning of autumn, on which the planet Mercury—in the sense of today's astronomy—crossed the celestial equator or passed through the autumnal point of the ecliptic, that is, just entered the sign of Scales. In the relationship of the starry sky to the Earth, each time the Sun or a planet passes through the spring or autumn point there is a unique situation of equilibrium, which contributed to the choice of name for the sign of Scales. At this point in time, the respective heavenly body rises, in every location on the globe, exactly in the east—at six o'clock local time—and sets exactly in the west and stands everywhere equally distant above and below the horizon. The enactment of the laying of the foundation stone at the evening hour emphasizes this equilibrium situation, in that Mercury, standing precisely in the middle between "upper and lower world," between zenith and nadir, between north and south, reaches the horizon exactly in the west-point, following the Sun, which had just set. Thus, it is a truly mercurial—that is, mediating and harmonizing—constellation between many polarities. But also, the idea for the construction of the Goetheanum connects with it spatially. For Mercury now streams directly into the opening of the main portal in the west and along the symmetrical axis of the building.

The planet Mercury, among all the luminaries of the heavens, connects most strongly with the morning and evening forces. While the planets beyond the Sun, after the time of their invisibility, reappear as morning stars in the east, culminate at midnight in the most glowing brilliance of the loop formation and shine the whole night to emerge as evening stars in the west, Mercury appears to us, when at all, only in the morning or the evening twilight. It is the only star of the sky which can never be seen at midnight—but also not at noon.[66] In accordance with this, the best visibility of Mercury falls in the course of the year in the time of the spring or autumnal equinox, while [in contrast] the full Moon and the planets beyond the Sun reach their optimum visibility at the beginning of winter—standing in the constellation of the Bull or the Twins. Mercury remains, as it were, stuck "in the childhood" of its particular development of phases. From the special connection of the laying of the foundation stone to the true star of the morning and evening forces, the question arises as to whether the objective of the Goetheanum building is particularly joined together with this weaving of forces—perhaps in contrast to the noon and midnight time—or whether it has a special significance at all.

Dr. Vreede already referred to Rudolf Steiner's explanations in the cycle *True and False Paths of Spiritual Research*: In the consciousness-night of the beginning body-free experience, "the spirit star Mercury" meets the spirit student "out of this twinkling dawn and dawning twinkle" as a soul guide. "One needs him absolutely, otherwise confusion ensues." In the abundance of pictures activated in the Moon sphere, whose content of truth initially cannot be controlled, "the divine being Mercury" points the way to the real Imaginations. "And so, you become conscious of the Mercury effects while your visionary world flows into a true perceptual world of the spiritual." One of the most central tasks of the fifth cultural epoch will be the complementing of outer sense perception by supersensible seeing, the transformation of the dead shadow pictures of the sense-bound intellect into living, free Imaginations. In this overcoming of "the intellectual fall into sin," the Central European people will have an essential contribution to make; indeed, they must lead the way forward. Rudolf Steiner remarked, in connection with the planetary impulses reflected in the seven columns of the large dome of the Goetheanum, that the *Mercury column* is assigned to the European folk. In this task, a developmental step of the third cultural epoch assigned to the constellation of the Bull is repeated. Now, in our time, as the vernal equinox passes through the Fishes, this task should resurrect in a concrete, albeit polar way, with the corresponding metamorphosis—permeated with the consequences of the Christ event.

In the Egyptian Osiris myth, this foundational step of the evolution of humanity's consciousness is reflected in an archetypal way. The death of Osiris, his incarceration in a lead coffin achieved through cunning—a deed of the ahrimanic opponent Typhon—was at the same time a personal experience for the Egyptians. They experienced in the ever-stronger binding of the soul-being to the physical corporeality the extinction of the old, Sun-filled Imaginations sounded through by Inspirations. In their place, there had to gradually come the imaginative mental pictures, mirrored, Moon-like, by the brain, the content of which was to flow more and more solely from the sense world. The division of the corpse of the Sun god into fourteen pieces found by Isis also points to this transition; their number indicates the fourteen phases of the waxing or waning Moon, in which the unified Sun-round of the day appears split up into fourteen pale, nocturnal counter-images.

According to Plutarch, the death of Osiris took place when the Sun stood in 17° of the Scorpion and the full Moon rose on the opposite side—thus, on an *autumn evening*. Rudolf Steiner has again called attention to this tradition (lecture, Jan. 5, 1918). In a significant way, the death of the Sun-god coincides with the Sun descending in the course of the year. After the passage through the autumn point, the day-star has to cede the rulership to the night, which has now become longer. In the mighty bull sculptures, in which the Sun shines between the horns, the Egyptians brought to expression the source of inspiration of their cultural period: the spring point located in the Bull. At that time, the autumnal point thus lay in the Scorpion, the opposing constellation. In this constellation, the sight of the Sun was exchanged for the cold, not self-luminous Moon, and the Sun, just set, wandered through the autumnal point in this constellation of the underworld and death. In this constellation, the Egyptians experienced a weaving of forces which paralyzed the rising forces of their culture and opposed their own being. Thus, at the same time, they were probably also not able to wrest free an inner spiritual resurrection from the experience of nature's decline in the autumn. According to the known Metonic cycle,[67] such a constellation repeats itself in exact form every 19 years. Dr. Vreede already pointed out: We must assume that at that time, the old clairvoyance suffered in this way, every 19 years, a renewed impulse for a further fading away. However, this opposition repeated itself in an approximate form each year, manifesting as the first full Moon of autumn, which today appears in the Fishes, but at that time had to appear always in the Bull. Connected with the described experience was the melancholy of the Egyptians, which may have permeated the life of that time especially in the later part of the epoch like a general pessimism of culture.

However, into this twilight of the gods, this mood of the Kali Yuga, there promisingly shines the birth of the Horus child, the later-born Son of the Sun. The sight of him in the arms of the World-Mother Isis bestowed consolation to the "sons of the mourning widow" as a luminous star pointing to the future of the new World-Morning. Nevertheless, just as they experienced the robe of Osiris in the Sun's rays, the Egyptians identified Horus, the son of Isis welcomed from the divine realm, with the planet Mercury as the morning star. The growing offspring was called to avenge his father in a new battle with Typhon, to herald a new, brighter age. While *Mercury* shines out as a guiding star at the laying of the foundation stone, at the same time a mysterious thread is tied to the sources of the Egyptian Mysteries, from which the contents of the Osiris-Isis myth descend. This becomes even more significant when we look at the fixed-star background of the foundation stone constellation.

The auspicious age has dawned with the modern age, which receives its impulses above all from that which the Sun radiates to us from the constellation of the Fishes. The position of the vernal point in the respective zodiacal constellation determines, so to speak, the ascendant, the rising constellation of an age. This fact finds a unique, pictorial expression in the northern Arctic, the land of the midnight Sun. In our [Central European] latitudes, each zodiacal constellation rises—taking approximately two hours—over the eastern horizon every twenty-four hours.

This is not the case in the Arctic or at the North Pole itself, where all stars circle horizontally above the horizon that coincides with the celestial equator. There we now find the constellation of the Fishes on the horizon, which, considered in the framework of the Platonic world year, is in a *unique*, majestically slow, rising which lasts 2160 years. As the *enduring ascendant* on the north polar horizon, the respective constellation marks the progress of its age on the rest of the Earth. The opposing constellation sets at the position lying opposite during the same period of time— namely, (in our cultural epoch) at the constellation of the Virgin. At the North Pole, the Sun rises and sets only once each year. This *unique* sunrise (and sunset) of the year takes place there in these constellations and is accompanied by weeks of dawn (or dusk) reddish-twilight. It coincides with the passage of the Sun through the vernal (or autumnal) equinox. Fishes and Virgin, as bearers of the vernal and autumnal points, thus become the con- stellations of morning and evening. Their connection could be designated: the fixed-star World-Axis of the age.

During the duration of the laying of the foundation stone, the star-*picture* [constellation] Fishes rose in the east, the star- *picture* [constellation] Virgin set in the west![68] The fixed star axis of the fifth cultural period therefore coincided with the axis of the rising building. At the head of the Virgin constellation, the Sun and Mercury, the only two planets which embody a 33-year rhythm (see Easter issue of this year "Vom 33-jährigen Rhyth- mus" [On the 33-year rhythm]), find themselves together and momentously weave their streams of forces in the same direc- tion. It is the direction to which the spirit-born *word* of the artists and speakers should sound [from the Goetheanum].

In lectures of November 1917, which have now been pub- lished under the title *Individuelle Geistwesen und allgemeiner Weltengrund* (Individual spirit-beings and general world-foun- dations), Rudolf Steiner has described the problem of the whole future humanity of the Earth from a certain cosmological point of view. Thereby, a new light falls on the meaning of the foun- dation stone constellation.

Rudolf Steiner shows how the West, in America, in an indi- rect way via the magnetic field of the Earth and the duality of the north and south magnetism, will succeed more and more in placing cosmic forces into the service of humankind, forces connected with the mid-day forces, with the constellation of the Twins. In contrast, the East will try, in an indirect way via the lower animal nature of the human being, the Centaur in us, to use the forces of the celestial Centaur, of the constellation Archer—the midnight forces—in order, among other things, to "seduce the European East as well" in a group-egoistic way.

"It will just be a matter of mustering the uncertain courage to do these things. In certain circles, this will already be summoned. . . . A great struggle will arise in the future. Human science will extend to the cosmic; but human science will try to extend to the cosmic in diverse ways. It will be the task of the good, the salutary science to find certain cosmic forces which can arise through the interaction of two cosmic directional streams on the Earth. These two cosmic directional streams will be: *Fishes -Virgin*. Above all, the secret will be to discover how that which functions from the cosmos in the direction of the Fishes as a solar force connects with that which functions in the direction of the Virgin. This will be good, my dear friends, that one will discover how from two sides of the cosmos morning and evening forces can be placed into the service of humankind—on the one side from the side of the Fishes, on the other side from the side of the Virgin. One will not concern oneself with these forces in instances where one will try to achieve everything through the dualism of polarity, through positive and negative forces. . . ."

The central task of the middle, especially of humanity in Central Europe, is *hygienic occultism*, which will develop between the mechanical occultism of the West and the eugenic occultism of the East (see cycle *In geänderter Zeitlage* [The Challenge of the Times]). Rudolf Steiner's indication about the zodiacal cross of the two opposing pairs of constellations Fishes-Virgin and Twins-Archer reveals the cosmological aspect of the different forms of occultism mentioned above. At the same time, however, it becomes apparent how the constellation at the laying of the foundation stone from the very beginning places the idea for the construction of the Goetheanum building within the whole of humanity, i.e., wants to connect it responsibly with the healing forces of progress of the future. We may imaginatively picture how the figure of the Representative of Humanity—which

179

would stand in the small cupola in the east, as if coming from the direction of the constellation of the Fishes—varies in the world-axis Fishes-Virgin, which has been connected with the symmetrical axis of the building since the hour of the laying of the foundation stone. The left arm pointing to the heights, before which Lucifer falls, points at the same time to the south, where the constellation Archer culminates. The right arm pointing into the depths, under which Ahriman is entangled in the Earth gold, points at the same time northward, where, under the Earth, the constellation of the Twins is found. In the latter, at the time of the laying of the foundation stone, the planet *Mars* is found, which has passed the St. John's point of the Sun a few days prior. Thus, it radiates into the counter-axis of Twins-Archer and astrologically affronts Mercury in the west in a sharp square aspect. We are reminded that the *descending* half of the Earth's evolution is designated as the Mars period. It must be superseded, through the impulse of the Mystery of Golgotha, in the second half of Earth evolution, so as to become an *ascending Mercury period*.

If we try to investigate, to pursue "how that which functions from the cosmos in the direction of the Fishes as a solar force connects with that which functions in the direction of the Virgin," then we come up against, among other things, the interplay of forces between Sun and Moon which play out during the Easter period. In our time, the *Easter Sun* stands in the constellation *Fishes*, while the first *spring full Moon*, decisive for the dating of Easter, is always a full Moon that brings its effects from the constellation *Virgin*. However, we celebrate Easter only on the Sunday following the Easter full Moon, i.e., always only with the waning Moon. We may sense the Moon element in the way it is explained in the Helsinki cycle, "as a corpse in the cosmos," and perceive its overcoming through the opposing Easter Sun's death-conquering might of resurrection forces. The stream of forces between Fishes and Virgin, which becomes effective in the counterplay of Sun and Moon, is revealed in this way again as a revelatory mystery of the efficacy of the Christ impulse. At the same time, the meaning of the *movability of the Easter festival* becomes clear, in which, among other things, the above-mentioned Metonic rhythm continuously plays a part. It is the sustainment of a living, rhythmic processuality in the force-streams of the Fishes-Virgin axis to which our attention should be drawn anew every year. The fixing of the Easter festival would not only extinguish this annual call to look up to the cosmos, but at the same time would undoubtedly mean a victory of those powers which strive to eliminate by all means the morning and evening forces for the development of humankind.

With regard to the respective Easter constellation, a Sun-Moon opposition, in the constellation axis decisive for our cultural period, we are reminded of the above-mentioned ominous Sun-Moon constellation to which the Egyptians looked with trepidation. The former seems like the contemporary polar counter-picture of the latter. The victory of the Moon over the Sun in autumn, which resulted in the death of Osiris, is contrasted with the victory of the Sun over the Moon element in spring, which evokes the celebration of the resurrection of the Sun-being. In the right view of the Easter constellation, we today take hold of a mood of consciousness which sees the working of the Christ-being in the 33-year life of Jesus of Nazareth as a sunrise radiating upon Earth-humanity; experiencing him [the Christ], we wrest from the powers of darkness the light of a new age.

In the strangulation of the intellect, struck by the Scorpion sting of the past, the human being experiences the lingering darkness of Kali Yuga in the spiritual battles and turmoil of our time. It is possible for us to waste away in an attitude of resigned agnosticism, cynical cultural pessimism, and paralyzing catastrophic anxiety and thus conjure up the unredeemed ghosts of the past, with which Typhon seeks to continue his work of destruction.

But anywhere we succeed in seeing an earthly fact of nature and the human kingdom in the cosmic light with the help of spiritual science, a new, individualized solar force becomes effective in our soul, the approach of which the Egyptians saw in the Imagination of the Horus child. Maturing as "spirit-star Mercury," he wrests us continuously from the forces of decay, in order to lead our being into the spiritual of the Universal-All, toward resurrection. United with him—in face of not only the dying-away nature in autumn but also of the descending forces of our age—we can hold the Scales.

Endnotes

66      Venus—also called Phosphorus or Lucifer by the an-
cients—can shine at the time of its most radiant brilliance next
to the noontime Sun, thus breaking the implied regularity of the
two planets below the Sun.

67      Every 19th year, the same lunar phase falls on the same
date.

68      The [*constellation* of] stars of the Virgin shine at present in the zodiacal *sign* of Scales.

ERNST BINDEL

# The Symbolic Significance of the Pentagonal Dodecahedron as the Foundation Stone of Spiritually Significant Buildings

If one wants to get a reasonably adequate idea of the symbolic use of the pentagonal dodecahedron as a foundation stone for spiritually significant buildings, one must first arrive at a clear view about the shape of this body. Therefore, the reader cannot be spared the necessity of first following some elementary mathematical-geometrical considerations.

There are two solids in the world of forms that are bounded by twelve congruent plane surfaces: the rhombic dodecahedron and the pentagonal dodecahedron. The former features rhombuses (diamonds) of preferred shape: the length ratio of its two corner lines ("diagonals") is the same as that of the side of a square to the diagonal of the square (1: $\sqrt{2}$). This body can be thought of as being formed from a cube if each of the six faces of the cube has a four-sided pyramid placed on top of it, the faces of which are inclined less than 45° towards the base. Different minerals crystallize as rhombic dodecahedrons—for instance, the garnet—which is why this crystal form is also called garnetohedron.

The pentagonal dodecahedron is, as its name suggests, bounded by congruent pentagons. However, it must be distinguished whether these pentagons are regular—that is, have sides of the same length and angles of the same size (108° each!)—or not. There is also the possibility of pentagonal dodecahedrons whose bounding pentagons are not completely irregular, but rather deviate from the shape of a regular pentagon insofar as only four of the five sides are of the same length—the fifth being longer or shorter. The five angles are therefore also of different sizes, but in such a way that the pentagon has an axis of symmetry which

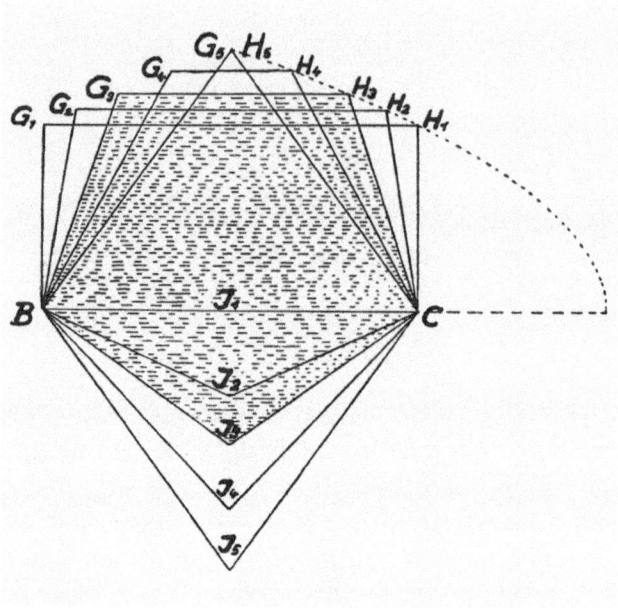

*Fig. 24.*

forms the central perpendicular on the deviating fifth side. In the figure provided, a number of such "symmetrical pentagons" are grouped around a shared diagonal (BC) (Fig. 24).

Consider the pentagon whose corners are successively the points $G_2$, B, $J_2$, C, and $H_2$. The four sides $G_2B$, $BJ_2$, $J_2C$, and $CH_2$ are of the same length, whereas the fifth side $G_2H_2$ is longer than the four mentioned above. If, on the other hand, we take the symmetrical pentagon with the corners $G_4$, B, $J_4$, C, and $H_4$, the side $G_4H_4$ is shorter than the four others of equal length. Between the two symmetrical pentagons mentioned lies the one whose face is highlighted by dashes, and which has all sides of equal length and correspondingly all angles of equal size, that is, a pentagon which is not only symmetrical but also regular. Let us consider, in the figure, the case where the deviating fifth side has shrunk down to zero, so that the corners $G_5$ and $H_5$ coincide; then the symmetrical pentagon has become the rhombus of the rhombic dodecahedron.

184

Seen in this way, the rhombic dodecahedron and the many possible pentagonal dodecahedrons are related. They form a chain of shapes, the last member of which is the rhombic dodecahedron. What is the first member of this chain? The cube, not as a hexahedron, but rather as a dodecahedron, comprised of a division of each of the square faces into two rectangular halves! Indeed, let's look back at the series of symmetrical pentagons! The first to present itself is the one with the five corners $G_1$, B, $J_1$, C, and $H_1$ in the shape of a bisected square ($J_1$ is the center of BC!). On the way from the cube to the rhombic dodecahedron, there are many possible dodecahedra with symmetrical pentagons, one of which is distinguished by the fact that its bounding pentagons are actually regular.

In the described figure, five stations of this series of forms are noted whose corresponding dodecahedra shall now be placed before us. First, the cube (as a dodecahedron!); second, a dodecahedron with all symmetrical pentagons, whose one side is longer than the other four of the same length; third, the dodecahedron with all regular pentagons, i.e. the regular pentagonal dodecahedron; fourth, a dodecahedron with all symmetrical pentagons, whose one side is shorter than the other four of the same length; and fifth, the rhombic dodecahedron (Fig. 25).

In the world of crystals, only the pentagonal dodecahedrons with merely symmetrical pentagons occur; never does the special form of the regular pentagonal dodecahedron appear. What this is connected with cannot be discussed here. Suffice it to say that it would contradict the laws of crystals if there were regular pentagonal dodecahedrons. These statements are not meant to imply that the length of the edges of the dodecahedral crystals would follow the given considerations. With crystals, it depends solely on the angles. A crystal can grow with different speed in different directions, but under all circumstances it keeps to the angles prescribed by the laws of crystals. Our assertion that there can be no crystal with the form of a regular pentagonal dodecahedron must therefore be restricted to the fact that the edge angles of the bounding pentagons can never have the value of 180°. Thus it is, as it were, denied to the mineral world to produce a regular pentagonal dodecahedron angularly, that is, to bring fivefoldness into appearance in a pure way. This succeeds only in the plant world situated one level higher, whose blossoms can form completely regular pentagons or pentagrams in the rose family of the flowering plants. In the mineral world, dodecahedra with merely symmetrical pentagons are found on the crystals of cobaltite and pyrite, which is why *these* dodecahedra are also called pyritohedra. They usually prefer the second of the five forms presented. In the photograph provided, one sees in the upper row on the left a garnetohedron (rhombic dodecahedron), in the middle a pyritohedron, whose dark surface turned to the front clearly shows the deviation from the regular pentagon, and on the right a cobaltite crystal; the lower row shows again two pyritohedra, the left fully formed, the right one as a cube with a hipped roof only on the front cube-surface as the beginning of a pyritohedron formation (Fig. 26).

The pentagonal dodecahedrons, especially the regular one, have fascinated the spirit and heart of the seeking human being since ancient times. The oldest reports about them that have come down to us date back to the time of Greek culture and the name Pythagoras as the one who devised the construction of the five "cosmic bodies" (*kosmischen Körper*). Four of them, the tetrahedron, the octahedron, the icosahedron, and the hexahedron (cube), according to the Pythagorean view, as reproduced by Plato in his dialogue *Timaeus*, configured the four earthly elements fire, air, water, and earth, and the fifth, the pentagonal dodecahedron, was used by God to serve as the contour of the entire world. In his book *Les Grands Initiés* [The great initiates], Édouard Schuré has tried to give a broad description of the course of instruction to which those were subjected who entered as novitiates into the school of Pythagoras in the southern Italian colony of Kroton. They had been presented with questions in a kind of aptitude test, among which was, for example, this one: "Why is the dodecahedron enclosed within the sphere, the figure of the universe?" If they were found worthy to proceed through the school, then they took over with their schooling the obligation to keep silent about the insights into the mysteries of the universe which became known to them. If they broke this silence, they committed the most severely punished betrayal of the Mysteries. Thus, it is said that the Pythagorean Hippasus, who first inscribed the pentagonal dodecahedron in the sphere

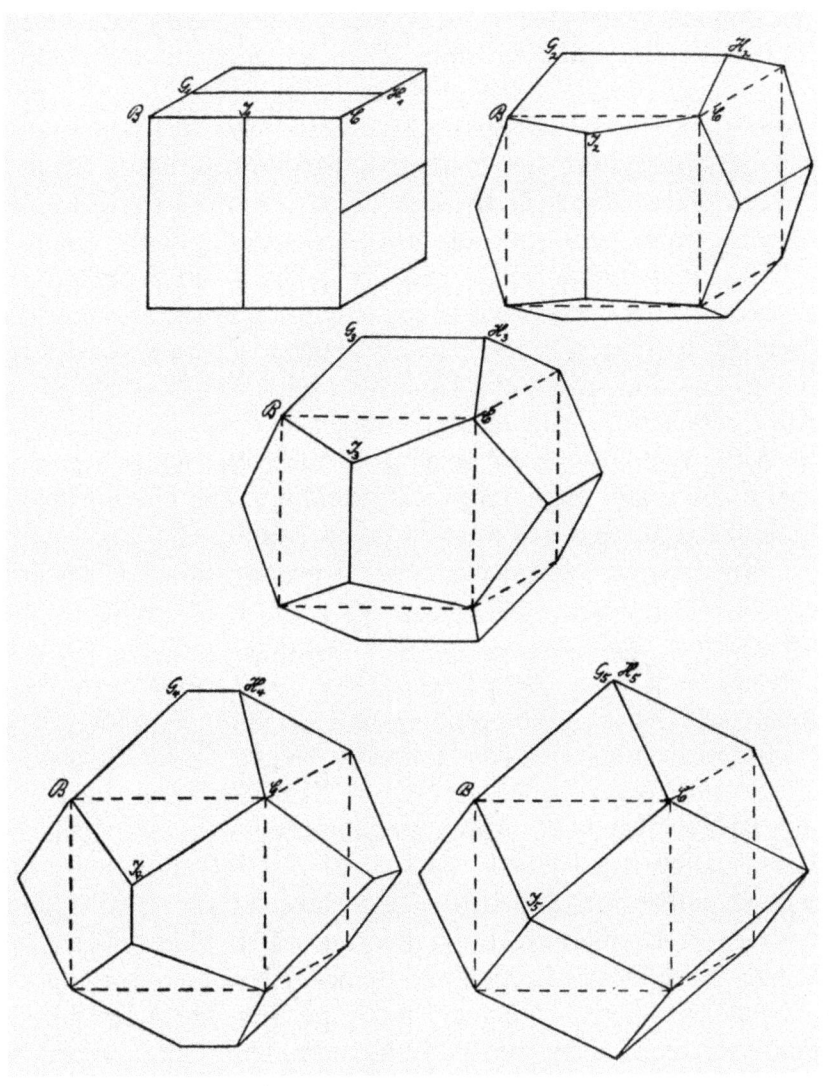

*Fig. 25: The cube on which the four dodecahedrons are based is indicated by dashes.*

and published this discovery, perished in the sea as punishment for this impiety. The projection of the pentagonal dodecahedron from its center onto a sphere of the same center, however, provides a division of the sphere's surface into twelve congruent spherical pentagons. It is hardly compatible with the division of the celestial sphere from the ecliptic into twelve spherical lunes reaching from the north pole to the south pole of the ecliptic, which is still common in astronomy today. It would perhaps be a worthwhile initiative to pursue the legitimacy of that other dodecahedral division of the celestial vault.

Bronze dodecahedrons have also been found north of the Alps, which, hollow inside, have round openings of various sizes in the middle of each pentagonal face, and whose age and meaning are still a mystery to archaeology. The circumstances of their finding make Roman origin probable.

Knowledge of the occurrence of pentagonal dodecahedral crystal forms is also very old. On Elba and in the southern valleys of the Alps running out to Piedmonte—though, remarkably, nowhere else—those pyrites close to the regular form were found, which may have been venerated as natural wonders.

Later, in modern times, Johannes Kepler, in his first work *Mysterium Cosmographicum* (World Mystery, [literally, the cosmographic mystery])—which made him famous and which the mere twenty-five-year-old published in 1597—employed the regular pentagonal dodecahedron to take up a kind of middle position in the universe of the then-known six planets Mercury, Venus, Earth, Mars, Jupiter, and Saturn. He wanted to bring the distances of these six planets from the Sun into a lawfulness that was intended by the World Creator. The written aspect of his work was preceded by a kind of inspiration which he formulated in the following sentences: "The Earth is the measure for all other orbits. Let it circumscribe a dodecahedron (meaning the regular pentagonal dodecahedron); the sphere encompassing it will be Mars. To the Mars orbit circumscribe a tetrahedron (meaning the regular tetrahedron); the sphere encompassing it will be Jupiter. For the orbit of Jupiter circumscribe a cube; the sphere encompassing it will be Saturn. Now, place within the Earth's orbit an icosahedron (meaning the regular icosahedron); the sphere inscribed in it will be Venus. Within the orbit of Ve-

*Fig. 26: Pyritohedra [with cobaltite (top-right) and garnetohedron (top-left).]*

nus, place an octahedron (meaning the regular octahedron); the sphere inscribed in it will be Mercury. There you have the foundation for the number of planets."

With this idea realized in his *World Mystery*, Kepler made the dodecahedron into a foundation stone of the solar system by placing the dodecahedron in the middle between the sphere of the Earth and the sphere of Mars, and thus, in the middle between the six planetary spheres, as a measure for all six planetary distances from the Sun with a supporting collaboration from the tetrahedron and cube, on the one hand, and the icosahedron and octahedron, on the other hand. He raised it to the rank of a World Dodecahedron. On its inner sphere, the Sun located in the center is orbited by that planet [Earth] whose mission it is, at the end of its development, in addition to the already-existing wisdom, to implant love from all that lives and weaves on it.

It is well known that Rudolf Steiner used the pentagonal dodecahedron as a foundation stone for the First Goetheanum, and later for the new building of the first Waldorf School in Stuttgart. Less well known may be the concrete details of how the First

Goetheanum came to have its foundation stone manufactured and installed.

It was at the beginning of September 1913 that Rudolf Steiner ordered the production of a double pentagonal dodecahedron for the foundation stone from a copper sheet one millimeter thick. It was to consist of two differently sized regular pentagonal dodecahedrons, joined together by one of their pentagonal faces, in such a way that these two faces had a collaborative center and that their bounding edges were parallel. This double form was chosen because the First Goetheanum consisted of two domes of different sizes oriented in the east-west direction. The following dimensions were given: 68 cm for the diameter of the sphere enclosing the large dodecahedron, 54 cm for the diameter of the sphere enclosing the smaller dodecahedron. Thus, all corresponding lengths of both dodecahedra were in the ratio. With these dimensions, a good approximation was reached where the enclosing sphere of the smaller dodecahedron fit exactly into the large dodecahedron. (The exact length ratio of two such dodecahedra is $\sqrt{15-6\cdot\sqrt{5}}=1{,}258\ldots$, whereas: $34{:}27=1{,}259\ldots$) So, according to Kepler's *World Mystery*, the radii of the Mars sphere and the Earth sphere had this ratio, too; however, today's astronomical measurements do not give the ratio 1.258... for the ratio of the mean distances from the Sun of Mars and Earth, but instead 1.523..., a large deviation.

Around the middle of September, the excavation of a pit for the foundation stone was begun and at the bottom a concrete container was built to hold it. It was only on the day before the laying of the foundation stone, on September 19, that Rudolf Steiner handed over to the manufacturer of the foundation stone two pyrite minerals—a larger pyritohedra, 30 mm long and 20 mm high, and a smaller one, 25 mm long and 15 mm high—with the request that the larger one be suspended in the center of the smaller copper body, the smaller one in the center of the larger. During the laying of the foundation stone on the evening of September 20, he slid in a rolled-up parchment certificate through an outer surface of the foundation stone that had been left open. This was then soldered shut by a sealing plate that had been kept ready. The double dodecahedron, which by the given dimensions had the stately lengthwise extension of about 96 cm, was placed in the container intended for its reception in the same way as the whole double-dome construction was then oriented afterwards—namely, the larger dodecahedron in the direction of the east-oriented smaller dome. The sketch provided, which is drawn at a scale of 1:12, illustrates the size and bearing of the double dodecahedron (Fig. 27).

Rudolf Steiner then went to the foundation stone and tapped with a hammer first three times, then five times, then seven times on the smaller dodecahedron and then twelve times on the larger one. Then, he threw earth three times on the foundation stone with a small triangular trowel, the shape of which was the determining triangle of a regular decagon; the others of the Executive Board of the Johannes Building Association did the same. In his address he called the foundation stone "a symbol of the Human Soul, which consecrates itself to our great work . . . . [A] symbol in its double twelve-memberedness of the striving Human Soul, sunk as microcosm into the macrocosm." At the same time, the importance of the place where the foundation stone was laid was indicated by him in the words:

> We stand, led by karma, at this moment, in the place
> through which important spiritual streams have passed:
> Let us feel within ourselves on this evening the serious-
> ness of the situation!

Thereby, he alluded to Arlesheim, to the flight of St. Odilia from her threatening father, and also, as will be shown, to localities of the Grail stream.

When the First Goetheanum went up in flames on St. Sylvester's Night [New Year's Eve] from 1922 to 1923, its foundation stone remained unharmed. The Second Goetheanum building now also rises above it. Even before it was erected, the new founding of the General Anthroposophical Society took place with the Christmas Conference of 1923, in which Rudolf Steiner took up the motif inherent in the foundation stone form in the sense of the Christmas meditation in the words:

> . . . and when we unite these three forces—the forces of
> the heights, the forces of the surroundings, the forces of
> the depths—in this moment, into an organized, formed
> substance: then, in our soul-comprehension, we place

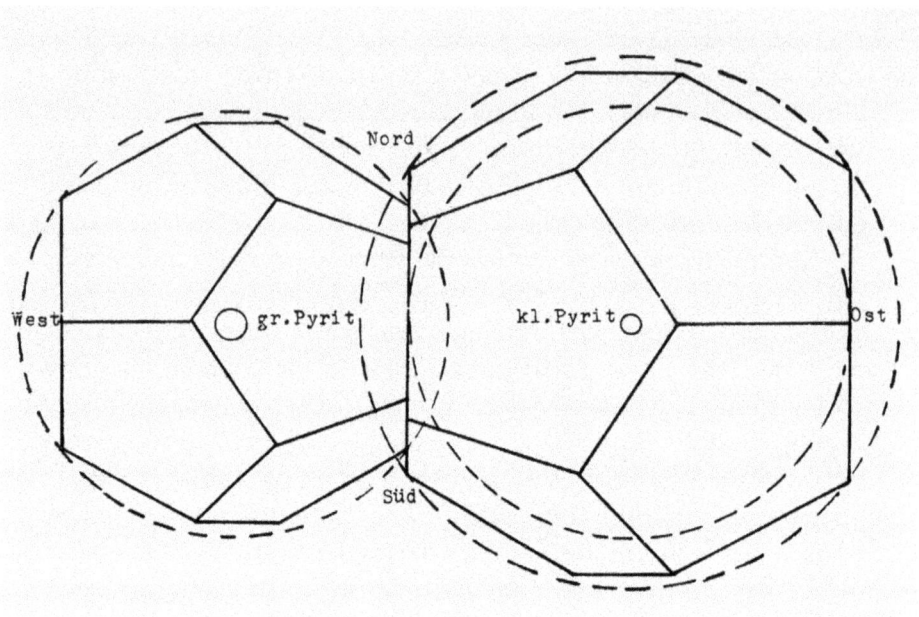

*Fig. 27. [Nord = North; Ost = East; Süd = South; gr.[oße] Pyrit =*
*lg. Pyrite; kl.[eine] Pyrit = sm. Pyrite]*

the World Dodecahedron into an encounter with the
Human Dodecahedron.

Then come the astonishing words of the "dodecahedral imaginative Formation of Love" (*dodekaedrischen imaginativen Li-
ebesgebilde*), and at the conclusion of this spiritual Foundation
Stone of 1923 emerges the term "dodecahedral Stone of Love"
(*dodekaedrischer Liebesstein*).

Two years earlier, on December 16, 1921, the foundation
stone for the new building of the Stuttgart Free Waldorf School
in the form of a simple pentagonal dodecahedron had been laid
in the presence of Rudolf Steiner. It, too, survived the destruction of this building during the Second World War and still rests
under the entrance hall of the school building, which was restored in 1953. To celebrate the laying of the foundation stone,
Rudolf Steiner gave an address in which he spoke an aphorism

that would be inscribed on a certificate and was destined to be sunk into the ground along with the cornerstone. The actual laying of the foundation stone was done by him with the words:

> This certificate is sunk here into the pentagonal do-decahedron, and with this pentagonal dodecahedron, which is the symbol of the active force of the human heart and human spirit which we want to exert with all our strength upon everything that takes effect in this school—with this pentagonal dodecahedron, we want to sink this certificate into the Earth.

Clearly, these words appeal to the will, working with its force into the spirit and heart of the human being, that true magician of the human being's essence who, if only one wills rightly, is able to accomplish everything, even the seemingly impossible: "Him I love who desires the impossible." The certificate entrusted to the foundation stone contains a vow which emphasizes again and again the importance of the dodecahedral form:

> Let prevail—what the spirit strength in love—
> Let be effective—what the spirit light in goodness—
> From certainty of heart,
> From steadfastness of soul,
> To the young human being,
> For the working-force of the body,
> For the intimate-warmth of the soul,
> For the brightness of the spirit
> —Let prevail and be effective—what these can provide.
> May this place be consecrated to those who
> Find meaning in their youth from their
> Human caretakers,
> Gifted with strength, devoted to light.
> Those who here lower down
> The stone as symbol,
> Remember in their hearts the spirit,
> Which here shall rule, so that
> This stone solidifies the foundation
> Upon which should live, rule, and work:
> Liberating wisdom,
> Strengthening spirit might,
> Self-revealing spirit life.
> This they want to profess:

In Christ's name
From pure intentions
With good will.

(42 signatures)

*Es walte, was Geisteskraft in Liebe*
*Es wirke, was Geisteslicht in Güte*
*Aus Herzenssicherheit*
*Aus Seelenfestigkeit*
*Dem jungen Menschenwesen*
*Für des Leibes Arbeitskraft*
*Für der Seele Innigkeit*
*Für des Geistes Helligkeit*
*Erbringen kann.*
*Dem sei geweiht diese Stätte:*
*Jugendsinn finde in ihr*
*Kraftbegabte, Lichtergebene*
*Menschenpfleger.*
*In ihrem Herzen gedenken des Geistes,*
*der hier walten soll, die, welche*
*den Stein zum Sinnbild*
*hier versenken, auf dass*
*er festige die Grundlage,*
*über der leben, walten, wirken soll:*
*Befreiende Weisheit*
*Erstarkende Geistesmacht*
*sich offenbarendes Geistesleben.*
*Dies möchten sie bekennen:*
*In Christi Namen*
*In reinen Absichten*
*Mit gutem Willen. —*

*(42 Unterschriften)*

Afterwards, in the address that followed, it is said again towards the end that for our thoughts, sensations, feeling, and will impulses, *this foundation stone alone is the symbol.*

How can one understand that precisely the pentagonal dodecahedron is able to be the symbol for what the human spirit and the human heart, by virtue of a good will acting in pure intentions, are able to enact in Christ's name? What makes this spatial form in particular a Formation of Love, a Stone of Love?

This symbolism is by no means so obvious, and it might be difficult, even with all striving toward an answer, to give a tangible, rationally understood interpretation. What does our spatial form achieve purely mathematically? It encloses the three-dimensional space with the figure of fivefoldness, the regular or, as far as I'm concerned, only symmetrical pentagon, and needs exactly twelve of such fivefoldnesses for it. One can also say that we proceed from the number five as a surface and, through such surfaces enclosing a body, we arrive at the number twelve in space. What this discloses in the deeper sense can be fathomed when one immerses oneself in the essence of the two numbers five and twelve. The former [5] presents itself from the regular pentagon and, connected with it, the pentagram as the carrier of the so-called divine division, also called the continued fraction or the golden section; the latter [12] as the number of fullness, due to its being the first to contain such a multiplicity of divisors. But with these two characteristics, one touches, so to speak, only the hem of her garment and has also not yet grasped how the one number is connected with the other. Just as the form of a pentagonal dodecahedron pushes forth the twelvefoldness from fivefoldness, so likewise does a regular dodecagon from a purely mathematical point of view (Fig. 28).

In it, each interior angle with its 150° = 5 x 30° is complemented by its exterior angle with its 210° = 7 x 30°, leading to the full angle with its 360° = 12 x 30°, which appears in the center of the dodecagon.

Where the human spirit succeeds in rising to the height of the purest knowledge of truth, it may be an advance from a fivefoldness to a twelvefoldness, where the whole is first enclosed. Let us remember above all Rudolf Steiner's epochal spiritual deed, which he accomplished by bestowing upon the usual doctrine of the senses the necessary completion with seven further senses. Proceeding from the consideration of the "five senses," which are familiar to superficial thinking, he arrived by means of the "active force of the human spirit" at the twelvefold organization of the essence of the senses, which first fully encompasses the sensory human being.

Yet, first and foremost, the "effective force of the human heart" could make it plausible for us that our spatial form also

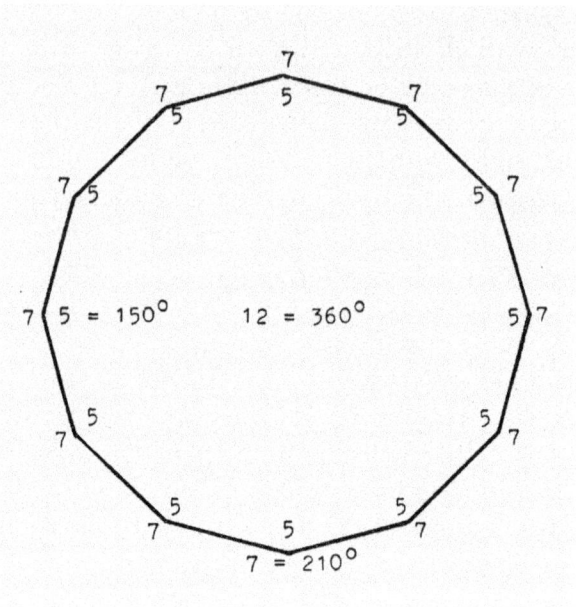

*Fig. 28.*

deserves to be called a Formation of Love, a Stone of Love. Is there an event in which, by the force of love, a twelvefoldness springs forth out of a fivefoldness in such a way that the effective agent would be precisely a will of love increased to the highest degree? Only the human being in their deepest, most sublime form would be capable of such a deed of love. All four Gospels describe such a process as the "Feeding of the Five Thousand," which is carried out on the directions of Christ by the twelve disciples. Here, the pair of numbers is already present in the number of those who were providing food, the twelve, and those who were being fed, the five thousand. But this pair of numbers appears even more memorably in the symbol of the food served. Five loaves are available, of which twelve baskets full of fragments remain after the food had been eaten. The fact that we are here concerned not with a sensory-physical process, but rather with an imagination of real spiritual significance, comes through to one who reads this story of the giving of nourisment not merely in a simple way but somewhat more closely. In the picture of the five loaves and the twelve baskets full of fragments, heavenly forces are experienced, a stellar food is offered. This becomes particularly clear by the addition brought in all four Gospels that with the five loaves there were "two fish" (Greek, *dúo ichthúas* [Matt. 14:17, *δύο ἰχθύας*]) because with these are to be understood those heavenly forces which are connected with the stellar region of the Fishes. A twelvefold celestial nourishment surrounds the Earth and upon it the living creatures in the form of the twelve-part zodiac. The Sun, on its annual trek through the ecliptic, carries this nourishment, by and by, down to the Earth, in the lighter part of the year, that of the seven heavenly loaves from the Ram to the Scales, in the darker part of the year, that of the five heavenly loaves from the Scorpion to the Fishes. In the deed of love of the Feeding of the Five Thousand, the Sun-force of Christ, the "Lord of the heavenly powers on Earth," disposes of them with full power in such a way that it can offer the five heavenly loaves with the two fish; and the miracle of the feeding consists in the fact that out of the five loaves come twelve baskets full of fragments. Whoever in inner activity, filling themselves entirely with Christ's will of love, is nourished by the heavenly forces that physically reach us through the Sun in the darker part of the year—to such a person is given the fullness of the whole heavenly world, the twelvefoldness of the starry round. This experience, in a supersensible way, forms the content of the miracle of the giving of nourishment. It will be granted as an act of white magic to the "five thousand," the many who live in the Age of Fivefoldness—and that is we ourselves, the members of the fifth post-Atlantean cultural period, in which the vernal point in the heavens is to be sought in the zodiacal constellation of the Fishes. The present significance of the miracle of the feeding has creatively inspired the poetic heart of Conrad Ferdinand Meyer in his poem glorifying it, *Alle* (All) (printed at the end of these considerations). With the Feeding of the Five Thousand, a deed of love of the most extensive kind is granted to our humanity standing in the sign of fivefoldness, that number which has been marked by Rudolf Steiner partly as the number of evil, partly as the number of crisis, partly as the number of freedom (*Freiheit*). It could also be comprehended as the number of the will; for only in its becoming free does the real good as well as the real evil become possible.

A still clairvoyantly inclined humankind of early times saw a cosmic human being in the twelve-membered zodiac circle, which, like the seed in the womb, was bowed together into a circle. The head was found in the region of the Ram, the pair of feet, touching the head, in the two Fishes. The hip region of this cosmic human being, revered by the ancient Indian wisdom as Purusha, lay in the constellation of the Scales. This, together with the six light constellations up to the Ram, thus corresponded to the sevenfoldness of the upper human being, whereas the five dark constellations from the Scorpion to the Fishes were related to the lower human being, with his will striving toward deed.

From each of the twelve zodiacal domains, one intuitively sensed certain forces operating down onto Earth and humankind. Again, according to the ancient Indian view, from the domain of the Fishes rained down everything that is capable of muddying human existence—age, illness, and death—everything that once so shook the prince Siddhartha that he left his homeland, wife, and child to live solely for the striving for inner enlightenment, until this was granted to him while sitting under the Bodhi tree and allowed him to rise to the rank of a Buddha, an enlightened one. Still going far beyond this, the ancient Egyptians considered the region of the Fishes to be the house of Seth, the adversary of Osiris. Our age, standing in the sign of the Fishes, is also particularly connected with and would have fallen to the forces of suffering and demonic possession, if precisely the Feeding of the Five Thousand had not taken place and, as a presently continuing effect, takes place again and again. Through it, the "Christ in us" has been implanted in the human will, empowering it to a mighty creative force for the Good. The Gospel of Matthew looks at this present and future situation in the words:

> From the days of John the Baptist, and now more than ever, the kingdom of heaven will be found through the will: Those who harness their wills can freely take hold of it (chapter 11, verse 12 in the translation by Emil Bock).

What is intended with the Feeding of the Five Thousand is distinguished only by the contrast with the Feeding of the Four Thousand. These are the ones living in the fourth post-Atlantean cultural period, in the Age of the Ram with its head, its forces of cognition. They are fed with the seven heavenly loaves, the lighter part of the zodiac, corresponding to the upper human being. The Feeding of the Four Thousand is only found in Matthew and Mark and is therefore missing in Luke and John. It was primarily a feeding of the cognitional human being with heart-evoking wisdom and did not yet, or did but little, encroach upon the sphere of will. In the picture of the feeding, this is expressed by the addition of only "a few small fish" (Greek, *olíga ichthúdia* [Matt. 15:34, ὀλίγα ἰχθύδια]) to the seven loaves—and in as much as, after the feeding is completed, only seven baskets full of fragments remained. Therefore, the actual increase of bread did not take place. The new nourishment in the form of the five stellar loaves with the wholeness of the forces of the Fishes only now does good for the hitherto unfed, or weakly fed, willing human being. With this, does the cognitional human being remain unfed? Do only five baskets full of fragments remain again? Here precisely the miracle of the increase of the bread sets in. The entire fullness of the heavenly forces will be given in the future to the one who christens their will.

In the first lecture of the cycle *The Apocalypse of St. John* (CW 104), Rudolf Steiner emphasizes the difference between the old initiation and the one to be brought by Christianity:

> While the earlier initiation is an initiation into the past, into primal wisdom, the Christian initiation uncovers the future to the one to be initiated. *This* is what is necessary, that the human being be initiated not only in regard to his wisdom, his feeling-thinking soul (*Gemüt*), but that he be initiated in regard to his will.

Christ himself placed the greatest value on the disciples' understanding of the difference between the two feedings and chastised them when he noticed their lack of understanding:

> Has your thinking and understanding still not awakened? Are your hearts still hardened? You have eyes and yet you do not see, and you have ears and yet you do not hear. Do you not remember when I broke the five loaves for the five thousand, how many baskets of crumbs were left for you? They answered: twelve. And when I broke the seven loaves for the four thousand,

how many baskets did you pick up? They said: seven. And he continued: Is your understanding still not awakened? (ch. 8, vers. 17 to 21 of the Gospel of Mark)

A geometrical form which represents the interplay of the numbers in the Feeding of the Five Thousand as in a symbol could be rightly called by Rudolf Steiner a "dodecahedral Formation of Love," a "Stone of Love," and could be used as a foundation stone for buildings where the sense of such a providing of nourishment becomes effective. The double dodecahedron was located exactly under the place of the First Goetheanum building, where in the separating plane between the two domes the lectern was positioned, behind which, in the small dome, Rudolf Steiner's mighty wooden sculpture of the Representative of Humanity should come to stand![69] It is obvious to assume that the event of the giving of sustinance also stood before his spirit with the coining of the expression "dodecahedral Formation of Love." In two of his Gospel cycles, he had already dealt with it in detail: in 1910 in the one held in Bern about the Gospel of Matthew, where he deals with the difference between the two acts of giving sustenance in the tenth lecture, and in the cycle about the Gospel of Mark, which was held in nearby Basel exactly one year before the laying of the foundation stone in Dornach. On September 20, the day of the laying of the foundation stone, Rudolf Steiner spoke in the sixth lecture about the behavior of the disciples towards these two acts.

Just as the Feeding of the Five Thousand can be connected with the pentagonal dodecahedron through the *number* ruling in it, so one may find from its *effect* a kind of continuation in the miracles of providing nourishment that the Grail gives to its guardians. Admittedly, here everything happens somewhat differently. Wolfram describes the Grail in his Parzival poem as a stone from which proceeds a stream of God's love, a stone that long ago was brought down to Earth by a host of angels. The name of the stone, in Wolfram's playful manner of dealing with names, is "Lapsit exillis," which can be interpreted as "lapis ex coelis" (Stone from the heavens) as well as "lapsit ex coelis" (It fell from the heavens). When Parzival enters the Grail Castle for the first time, having been shown the way by Anfortas in the guise of a *fisherman*, and the miracle of the feeding plays out there before his eyes, he perceives it in such a way that a hundred squires enter the hall and first receive *bread* from the Stone of Love in white cloths, which they distribute to the four hundred knights present. Here, the number of the those offering food—one hundred—and the number of those being fed—four hundred—join together to form the number *five hundred*. After the offerings of bread, the Grail then also gives in abundance various other, quite earthly-appearing delicacies. With the bread, neither a fivefoldness nor a twelvefoldness is spoken of.

Still, the twelvefoldness is interwoven as an inner figure of the whole poem, but it requires some effort to discover it. Rudolf Meyer has drawn attention to it in his book *The Grail and its Guardians*. In Wolfram's supplementary Titurel fragment, which consists of only two cantos, the second canto, whose title is "Gardevias" (Guard the way!), revolves around a rope twelve fathoms long, a "Bracken rope" (*Brackenseil*), which contains an inscription describing the path of the soul striving for perfected humanity according to that age. Twelve stations are to be passed through, each of which endows the sojourner with a new virtue, and at the end of which stands Love, in the medieval expression, *Minne*. Following Albrecht von Scharfenberg's elaboration of Wolfram's fragment of the "Younger Titurel," they are named:

> 1. Pure Manners, 2. Chastity, 3. Mildness, 4. Fidelity, 5. Measure in All Things, 6. Care (that is, Attentiveness), 7. Shame, 8. Modesty, 9. Stability (that is, Perseverance), 10. Humility, 11. Patience, 12. Minne (Love).

"Twelve flowers wind thee for a wreath when thou goest to the day of honor," says the rope's inscription. Wolfram had a clear mental picture of this twelve-membered path. For the way of his Parzival to the attainment of the dignity of the Grail kingship follows exactly the twelve stations. So, after all this, should the "dodecahedral Formation of Love," which was applied by Rudolf Steiner in rendering the foundation stone for the building of the Goetheanum, not also be brought into a connection with the Grail Mystery, especially since the place on Earth upon which this building was erected is not without relationship to the Grail territory? According to Rudolf Steiner's personal communications, the scene near Trevrizant's hermit cave, where Parzival

comes across Sigune, who holds her dead bridegroom Schionat-
ulander in her lap, takes place within the environs of the Goetheanum, at the grottoes of the Arlesheim Hermitage.

One of Rudolf Steiner's last lecture cycles before he took to
his sickbed, given in Torquay, August 11 through 22, 1924, on
Initiate Consciousness, sounds as a legacy with a consideration
of what can emerge from the forces of Christ in the sense of
spiritual nourishment. It may be primarily art through which the
heavenly can reveal itself in the earthly. For a long time now, for
centuries, an impulse has been developing in art that no longer
tends toward the sculptural-pictorial, as it used to, but rather toward the musical. This may be the artistic element of the future.
The Goetheanum building itself may also be considered predom-
inantly musical in its architecture, sculpture, and painting. In the
musical, the approach of the life-filled, spirit-life-filled figure of
Christ will one day be found. Here we pause and ask ourselves
whether it is not also the case that in music a twelvefoldness has
worked its way out of a fivefoldness. Indeed, it has! As is well
known, the course of development of music proceeds from the
pentatonic—a childhood stage for human musical creation—
via the formation of the seven-step ladder to a dodecatonic—a
twelve-step order of tones. Yet this occurs in such a way that,
to speak in the language of the Gospels, the five loaves do not
become twelve loaves in the sense of today's twelve-tonal music, but rather twelve baskets full of fragments. For the circle of
fifths of the twelve keys does not close, but gapes wide open by
the amount of the so-called Pythagorean comma, leading to the
fact that, geometrically speaking, when the twelve purely tuned
keys are transferred into a regular dodecagon enclosed by a circle, the neighborhood of each corner is swarming, as it were,
with pitch-degrees of the same tone notation. Their unification
with the corner's exact tone step can only be constrained by the
violent stroke of the evenly tempered tuning. More details about
this can be found in my book *Die Zahlengrundlagen der Musik
im Wandel der Zeiten* [the numerical foundations of music in the
flux of the times], part 2, chapters 3–5.

Copper was the metal used to make the pentagonal dodecahedron both in its double form for the Goetheanum and in its

*Fig. 29: The foundation stone laid on September 20, 1913.*
*[The "d" is missing from "Grundstein" (Foundation stone)].*

single form for the Waldorf School. It should not have been manufactured of any other metal. Copper is the metallic substance occurring on Earth which, in the present planetary stage of our solar system's development, originates from the effects of the planet Venus on our Earth planet, that planet of which the poets have sung as the star of love. Venus and Earth orbit the Sun in such a way that a full orbit of Venus around the Sun, its "sidereal" orbit, lasts about 225 days or seven and a half months, whereas a full orbit of the Earth around the Sun lasts 365 days. These two orbital periods mean that roughly every 584 days Venus is exactly between the Earth and the Sun; in astronomy, this period is called a synodic orbit of Venus, which refers to the geocentric orbital period of Venus around the Earth. With every such synodic orbit of Venus, as seen from Earth, a loop is inscribed in the sky. A next synodic orbit of Venus generates again a looping picture and so on. These successive loops, one on top of the other, which naturally adorn all of the twelve-sectioned zodiac, arrange themselves within it in consistent intervals in such a way that they divide it almost exactly into five equal regions. Thus, the poet's star of love conjures up in the zodiac the interplay of the two numbers 5 and 12, and indeed it takes 5 times 584 = 2920 days or almost 8 years exactly, until this plotting of a cosmic pentagon, whose corners are occupied by loops, has come to completion in the zodiac.

With this presentation, we have attempted to bring together some things to make the role of the pentagonal dodecahedron as foundation stone understandable. However, with this attempt one arrives at a boundary on the other side of which one can probably only begin to find real understanding. In this respect, the "Stone of Love" is not much different from the medieval "Stone of Wisdom" [The Philosopher's Stone], whose explanation as carbon refined to diamond is only an attempt to come close to an understanding. In parentheses: The Stone of Wisdom is not the Stone of Love, as wisdom does not yet enclose love in itself. Otherwise, there would be no difference between the two contrasting feedings of the Gospels, one of which is for wisdom and the other for love. When Rudolf Steiner considered the pentagonal dodecahedron to take on the function of the foundation stone for the Goetheanum, he acted out of an authority he received from beyond the threshold. From there he received the directive, from there came to him the essence of the dodecahedron as an "Imaginative" Formation of Love, as a World Dodecahedron, as a Human Dodecahedron. Yes, even more! In personal conversation he voiced that with the choice of the pentagonal dodecahedron as the form of the foundation stone and the suspended mounting of pyrite minerals within it, something significant had happened precisely for the holding force of the two domes of the building. In view of these indications, it is up to each of us, according to our strength, to make an effort to reach an understanding. If one does not do it, then one could experience, like at the time after the feeding was accomplished, what the disciples experienced, of whom it is said in the Gospel of Mark, chapter 6, verse 52:

Through the experience of the loaves, they were not
awakened to knowledge; their hearts were still entirely
hardened.

## All

The spirit spoke: Look up! It was in a dream.
I lifted up my gaze. In the illumined, cloudy space
I saw the Lord breaking bread for the twelve
and speaking expectant words of love.
Far above their heads he invited the Earth
with an all-embracing gesture.
The spirit spoke: Look up! A gossamer floating,
I saw, and the meal, already given to many,
There, spread under a thousand hands,
The table stood—but the ends faded
Into gray fogs—within, on pallid steps,
Sorrowful figures sat, uncalled.
The spirit spoke: Look up! The air bluing all around
An immeasurable meal, as far as I could see.
There, the wells of life sprang richly,
There, no bowl was stretched out in vain,
There, all the people lay upon full sheaves,
No place was empty and none should starve.

## *Alle*

*Es sprach der Geist: Sieh auf! Es war im Traume.*
*Ich hob den Blick. In lichtem Wolkenraume*
*Sah ich den Herrn das Brot den Zwölfen brechen*
*Und ahnungsvolle Liebesworte sprechen.*
*Weit über ihre Häupter lud die Erde*
*Er ein mit allumfassender Gebärde.*
*Es sprach der Geist: Sieh auf! Ein Linnen schweben*
*Sah ich und vielen schon das Mahl gegeben,*
*Da breiteten sich unter tausend Händen*
*Die Tische, doch verdämmerten die Enden*
*In grauen Nebel, drin auf bleichen Stufen*
*Kummergestalten saßen ungerufen.*
*Es sprach der Geist: Sieh auf! Die Luft umblaute*
*ein unermeßlich Mahl, soweit ich schaute.*
*Da sprangen reich die Brunnen auf des Lebens,*

*Da streckte keine Schale sich vergebens,*
*Da lag das ganze Volk auf vollen Garben,*
*Kein Platz war leer und keiner durfte darben.*

[Conrad Ferdinand Meyer]

Endnotes

69      According to Dr. Günther Wachsmuth's information in his book *The Life and Work of Rudolf Steiner*

# 4
# Rudolf Steiner's Buildings for the Mysteries

Essays by Erika von Baravalle

*Fig. 30: Painting by Karl Stockmeyer, Senior (undated).*
*Depiction of an esoteric lesson given by Rudolf Steiner for the*
*Francis von Assisi Lodge in the Model Building in Malsch.*

# The Model Building in Malsch

Within the entire universal work of Rudolf Steiner, the formatio of buildings holds special significance. Within seventeen years, he conceived and created three mystery temples, for which there also were foundation stones: an initiation temple (represented in the Model Building in Malsch and realized in the house for the Stuttgart Branch) and two buildings for theater and performance (the First and Second Goetheanum buildings in Dornach). With these buildings and further functional and residential buildings in the environs, he inaugurated a new, future-oriented building style.

The spatial design of the three Mystery buildings was quite different: as ground plans—for Malsch, a triaxial ellipsoid; for the First Goetheanum, two interlocking cylinders with hemispherical domes; for the Second Goetheanum, a trapezoid with an adjacent rectangle—all above which a variety of wall and roof forms can be found.

The Malsch model is often regarded as the precursor of the Goetheanum buildings. This is only partly true, since the physical form of each project is fundamentally different, as well as their exact purpose. In Malsch, we find a column-supported triaxial ellipsoid with an ambulatory; in Dornach, two likewise column-supported interlocking hemispherical domes; and, after the fire, a trapezoidal auditorium and a rectangular stage area, a very different kind of building but, like the old one, designed on the double-dome principle. The uniform ellipsoidal space of the initiation temple is strictly defined for esoteric work, whereas the Goetheanum buildings, with stages and auditoriums, await audiences. The first building [the Model Building in Malsch] has no specific exterior architecture, but was conceived as underground "hewn into the rock," i.e., to be kept hidden. In contrast, the two Goetheanum buildings were each erected widely visible on the Dornach hill, speaking to their surroundings through their organic forms. This briefly outlines Steiner's architectural spatial ideas.

Now, however, there are compositional elements of sculpture that connect the Malsch building with the First Goetheanum: the seven columns, whose capitals represent stages of metamorphosis of a fundamental motif. These were taken up again in the First Goetheanum, while the occult (apocalyptic) seals present in Malsch were left out. As early as 1911, Steiner newly conceived two heavily sculptured, high architrave rings for the project planned in Munich, which, in the First Goetheanum, with a scale of five meters [~16.4 feet] high—along with the metamorphoses of the building motif—were quite striking when one entered the double-domed building from the west. In Dornach, the eight tripartite colored windows and the painting of both cupolas were added. In the large and transformative stylistic step from the wooden building of the First Goetheanum to the concrete building of the Second Goetheanum, Steiner placed only two free-standing single columns on the south and north exterior (terrace) instead of the vault-bearing, free-standing ring of columns. For the interior, he planned a simplified architrave and two times seven half-pillars in the walls. This gave the moving architrave forms an explicit dominance.

Thus, one recognizes that the three Mystery buildings are connected by certain motifs, but also clearly emerge in their own character.

Let us now return to the fundamental motif for the Rosicrucian temple of initiation, the triaxial ellipsoid with the likewise ellipsoid-designed circumambulations. The question of the deeper meaning of the building design of a triaxial ellipsoid has not yet been fundamentally discussed by anyone.[70] When Steiner explained the building composition at the Munich Congress, he remarked in conclusion, "If the room should be completely furnished in the sense of the Rosicrucian worldview, then blue arches would still have to rise at the top."[71] From this it is clear that he already saw the vaulted-over building inwardly before

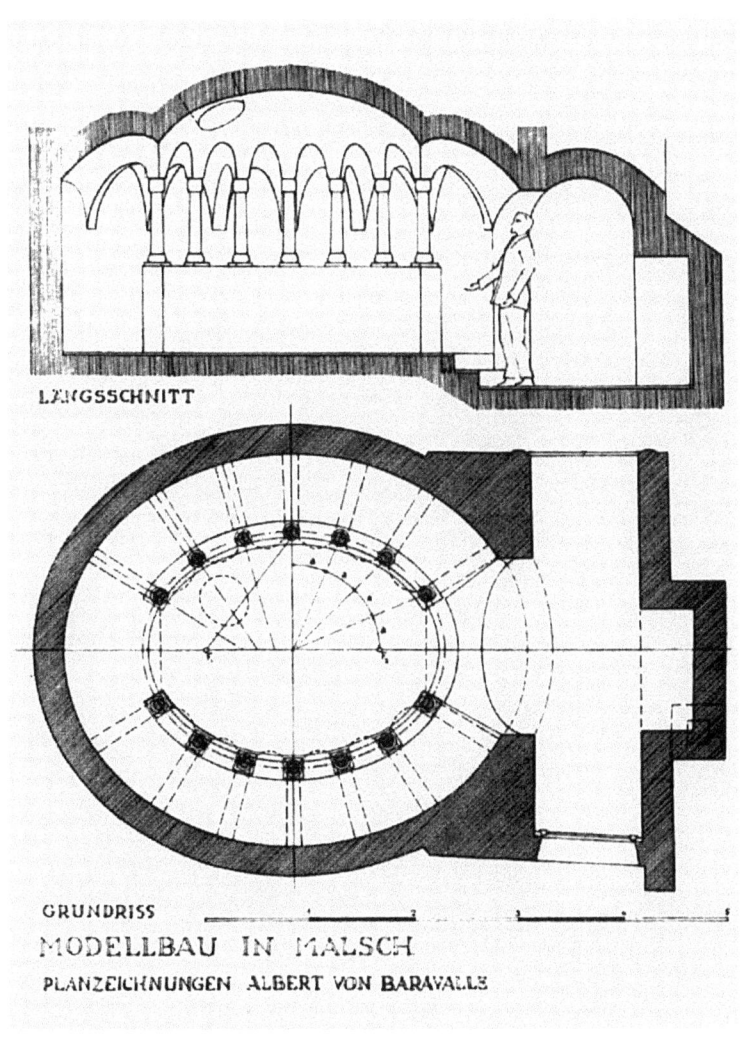

*Fig. 31: Ground plan and cross-section of the Model Building [in Malsch].*

him. Thus, in the summer of 1908, he was able to spontaneous-
ly answer Stockmeyer's question about the shape of the building—visibly pleased about it—and refer to a triaxial ellipsoid.
Whether Steiner told his esoteric student of the FM [Freemason-
ry] Lodge an occult point of view about it is unknown. Stockmeyer, like Steiner, was a mathematician familiar with the laws
of this geometric body and set about the demanding task full of
enthusiasm and a spirit of enterprise.

If one looks retrospectively for Steiner's motivation for
this construction, one finds an indirect indication given as an
answer in a question session [following a lecture] for mathematicians on April 7, 1921, in Dornach.[72] Steiner contrasted the
modern abstract, purely logical concept of space—with its three
equivalent axes x, y, z—with a concept of space in accordance
with reality:

> Instead, we must think that the space of the cosmos
> (*Weltenraum*) itself has a configuration which could
> also be pictured with a *triaxial ellipsoid* (emphasis Bar-
> avalle). And the arrangement of certain stars absolutely
> speaks to this. One usually calls our Milky Way system
> a lens and so forth. It is absolutely not possible to pic-
> ture it as a spherical surface.

So, it was the cosmic archetype of space that Steiner had concerned himself with at that time as a building idea for the Rosicrucian temple of initiation and which he wanted to imprint directly upon the Earth.

This was a deed that cannot be valued highly enough and
which is clearly confirmed in Steiner's address at the laying of
the foundation stone on April 5/6, 1909, in Malsch. Therein, he
says:

> In pain has our Mother Earth solidified. Our mission
> is to spiritualize her once again, to redeem her, by re-
> making her—through the power of our hands—into a
> spirit-filled work of art. May this stone be a first foun-
> dation stone for the redemption and transformation of
> our planet Earth; and may the power of this stone be
> multiplied a thousandfold.

The building has found only one successor to date, and

that is in Lower Austria, in a remote valley in the Wechsel Mountains, in the village of Mariensee near Aspang. The underground room is about twice as large as the Malsch model. It was built into the earth of a biodynamic farm there; thereby, it expresses the inner relationship to Steiner's building impulse, which only dimly still lives in the consciousness of farmers and builders—the building impulse as the older "brother" of the biodynamic way of farming.[73]

Already in 1905, Steiner had spoken in his Berlin lectures "On the Lost and Refound Temple" of the old Freemasonic ideal of transforming the whole Earth into a garment of God.[74] Now, in Malsch, he fulfilled a first act of consecration towards this goal, which, with its main motifs, resounds as a prelude to the laying of the foundation stones in Dornach in 1913 and 1923: Turning to all hierarchies and to the spirits of the cardinal directions, as well as speaking the concluding Rosicrucian verse.

Three names are bound together with the Model Building in Malsch, as it can be experienced to this day: Rudolf Steiner, Ernst August Karl Stockmeyer, and Albert von Baravalle. To the first, we owe the conception of the building; to the second, the architectural realization and the still-existing, [now] restored, northern row of columns; to the third, the entire remaining design and decor.

The result of Stockmeyer's work appears so clearly and concisely before the visitor today that a layperson would have no idea of the complexity of the working process. But this process turned out to be complicated and difficult, as Steiner had only sketched his ideas for him and had not shown him ways to realize them. Stockmeyer strove to bring Steiner's thoughts as completely as possible into manifestation, without mixing in his own ideas. He could not achieve this by mathematical means alone, but instead had to figure out many things with his ingenious architectural intuition.

The appreciation of an expert can be found in a letter of the Dornach architect Hermann Ranzenberger, who had participated in the construction of the First and Second Goetheanum.

> It is a thoroughly and completely worked through job.
> In spite of its crude state, one senses everywhere the
> disciplined scaffolding of force and spirit (*Kraft-Geist-*

*Gerüste*) of this cultic space of consecration. An ethe-
rically pure spirituality is visibly-invisibly intrinsically
omnipresent. The clear, matter-of-fact spirituality in
form is revealed, for example, in the arches rising—
asymmetrically counter to the columns—onto the enclosing wall. These are the best I have ever seen and
experienced in asymmetrical arches. How wonderful
is the—at first slow and then increasingly more in-
tense—inner tension of these arches according to the
measure of the stress, which reaches its maximum at
the apex and then, as if after a fulfilled performance,
sinks down to the columns with a small, almost vertical
line. How calmly, lightly, elegantly, as never before,
the asymmetrical arches grow out of the wall. Another
example of the lively moving and disciplined play of
forms is the view through or rather up to the beginnings
of the vault, to the transverse arches, and to the slightly
curved vault surfaces arising between them from the
entrance. There everything is "mathematically" enliv-
ened within itself. . . . Also, particularly impressive for
me was, for example, the sculptural, negatively effect-
ing force between the aforementioned asymmetrical
arches. These "vault caps" hit the mark, their hollow
form has strong force as a hollow space.[75]

Stockmeyer wrote back with pleasure and gave essential explanations.

You have immediately discovered that here the individual building elements are not put together, but rather
that they were produced by necessity from the unified
building idea, as they so arose. What you especially
emphasize—the asymmetrical arches between the wall
and the columns—could not have been formed in any
other way. They are the only thing—in the otherwise
so differently formed parts—that recurs in complete
sameness fourteen times. Their form, which you find so
beautiful, is given by the requirement to form the side
vaults all as ellipsoids (triaxial). This requirement of
Rudolf Steiner could now only be realized if the spaces, which should be covered by these ellipsoid cupolas, have symmetrical trapezoidal form (in the ground
plan). Then I could also achieve that these small el-

lipsoids should merge with perpendicular tangents into the column architrave and into the outer wall. There was one more requirement to fulfill, which I set for myself: namely, that the main axis of the ellipsoids (largest axes) should be tangents of the main vault, because they should—besides the column-wall arches—take the lateral thrust of the main vault. This thrust is therefore taken up by the small ellipsoids at the most favorable place true-to-perception (*empfindungsgemaß*); and the transverse arches still help with it, in that they brace themselves against the main vault with their (geometrical) main apex, which lies not above, but laterally. In fact, one senses these small ellipsoids, as you write, as a hollow form having a strong force.

In the years 1958–65, Albert von Baravalle renovated the building, which had already fallen into slight disrepair, and finished its design and décor. In doing so, he followed the Rosicrucian artistic ideal of not adding anything of his own to the spiritual truth of Rudolf Steiner's motifs.

*Fig. 32: The First Goetheanum from the southwest.*

*Fig. 33: West portal. Watercolor by Albert von Baravalle, 1938.*

Endnotes

70      Also in Erich Zimmer, *Der Modellbau von Malsch und das Erste Goetheanum* [The Model Building in Malsch and the First Goetheanum], the question is not asked directly.

71      Erich Zimmer, *Der Modellbau von Malsch und das Erste Goetheanum* [The Model Building in Malsch and the First Goetheanum]; Rudolf Steiner, *The Fourth Dimension*, question and answer session in Dornach, April 7, 1921, p. 138f.

72      Rudolf Steiner, *The Fourth Dimension*, question and answer session in Dornach, April 7, 1921,  CW 324a

73      See Werner Schäfer, "Der Säulenbau in Mariensee: Ein Entsehungsrückblick" *STIL* 22, no. 1 (Easter 2000): 14–20. [The building was conceived and realized by a small group inspired by the "cultural oasis" impulse given by Rudolf Steiner in Koberwitz during Pentecost (June 8) 1924:

Rudolf Steiner [was asked] what he foresaw would be Germany's future, and the latter replied: "The (factory) chimneys will topple and Germany will be reduced to an agrarian state." Then Rudolf Steiner said very seriously: "All will depend on forming islands of monastic seclusion in the countryside where German cultural and spiritual life can be cultivated. Foreign lands will send their sons and daughters there to be educated." After a pause he added: "And it will be a long way from one island to the next."

In Mariensee, during Holy Week (Mar. 31–Apr. 7) 1985, the group conceived of the idea to build an esoteric meeting room modeled on the Model Building in Malsch. By July 1985, they had all gathered together in the area where the building was to be erected to begin the planning stages. The laying of the foundation stone took place on Oct. 27, 1985, and preparatory work continued, with a break during the winter weather, and reconvening in April 1986. Major construction was completed by Christmas 1986 and throughout the following years the group's circumstances led to various changes. The interior work was completed during the 1990s and a building initiative and communications group was formed in Oct. 1999. From Oct.

26–28, 2018, a seminar was held for the 33rd anniversary of the Mariensee Building. Further updates were unavailable at the time of publication; cf. Edgar Spittler, "Über den Marienseer Bau" (About the Mariensee Building) *STIL* 40, no. 2 (St. John's Tide 2018): 46–48.]

74      Rudolf Steiner, "Concerning the Lost Temple and How It Is to Be Restored," *The Temple Legend*, lectures in Berlin on May 15, 22, 29, & June 5, 1905, CW 93.

75      *Occult Seals and Columns* CW 284.

# The House of the Word

When it [the soul] begins to experience what is in the
forms of the building, then, before this receptive soul,
the form will immediately disappear—and through
what the form is, through the *speech of the form*, will
be found the path of the soul out into the spiritual....

Rudolf Steiner, *Architecture as Peacework*

A s with natural organisms, all the details of buildings conceived in a Goetheanistic, organic way are related to each
other and to the work as a whole. Steiner occasionally points
out that if the smallest detail is changed, everything must be
changed.

## *The Organic Art of Building*

Probably the best-known principle according to which Steiner
created visible relationships of form is the law of metamorphosis discovered by Goethe in the plant world. Steiner developed
it as early as 1907 for a series of columns in seven stages, and
thereby introduced something entirely new into the history of
architecture. Within the First Goetheanum, in the large cupola
space, he then presented the forms for the first time to the general public and added a second series of six steps in the small
cupola space. He also designed corresponding pedestal motifs
for both series and a five-meter [~16.4 feet] high architrave that
dominates in both spaces. Thereby, he gave the interior of the
Mystery building a multifaceted sculptural imprint.

*Fig. 34: Cloakroom windows in the North.*

## The Building Motif

For the outer wall of the large-domed room, which had a pure-ly geometric shape (a dome-covered cylinder), he conceived a fundamental signature motif that spoke to visitors as a sculptural relief above all the portals and windows on the terrace floor. During a tour, one was already confronted with it 29 times on the outside. There were five different variations in addition to the two additional ones on the inside. These form-relationships are more easily recognizable than the stages of transformation of the metamorphosis series.

Even from a distance, the motifs stand out. One was encour-aged to first walk along the building from the west to the side-wing. What could one experience there?

In the west, above the main portal of the entrance, the five-limbed form appears especially striking. Embedded between two stately pilaster capitals and an equally mighty canopied vault, a kind of hieroglyph commandingly confronts us: above,

222

*Fig. 35: South portal.*

two wing-like structures; below, a carved central motif; and, on either side of it, two compacted, strongly convex elements, divided into five geometric surfaces. This portal does not offer an inviting gesture; it is weathered by the earnestness of the time. From the hill it looks far into the landscape. What speaks to the observer with such unyielding sternness? What enigmatic word does it conceal?

In a further step, one discovers the same form, only flatter, above the windows like an echo—not so forceful, but clearly perceptible. On each of the side-wings, we find a group of eight slender cloakroom windows where the motif appears quite elongated. We experience a completely different variant above the side-portals. The motif greets us more delicately than in the west, the wings are slimmer and longer, and the compacted forms have been transformed into radial elements spread out at the sides. This gesture has a friendly effect; it is auspiciously inviting. And so we now turn to the other motifs within. The form above the stage ramp greets us with wide, gentle wings. In the very east, where Rudolf Steiner's sculptural group should stand, the seventh variant beams at us: a five-pointed star with a pentagon in the center [Fig. 38].

*Fig. 36: Rose window in the south, on the sides. Drafts by
Rudolf Steiner.*

## The House of the Word

We look around and catch sight of the row of colored windows.
Immediately in the south, with the first one, a rose-colored window, our presentiment is confirmed: The building motif is a cipher for the human being. Steiner characterizes it by a face that
reveals itself to the viewer of the west portal after it rises from
its reclining position and takes a lyre in its hand, as a sign of the
unfolding of its artistic forces [Fig. 36].

   With the building motif, Steiner has thus implemented the
Delphic inscription in a sculptural form, from which we hear
the word of the threshold: "O Man, know yourself!" In the east,

*Fig. 37: Drawing by Friedrich Bergmann. View from the stage towards the west.*

the pentagram variant reminds us of the human form, the entelechy, which is one day to be developed through the power of the Christ into the tenth hierarchy.

This path of evolution is depicted by the continuous bands of the architrave that unfold from the threefold arch motif above the western entrance to the hall on both sides. The first half is designed as more concave, the second as more convex. Rudolf Steiner thus expressed the course of human history: Up until the Mystery of Golgotha, human beings were guided by divine powers, but since then they have had to find the way by their own efforts, in the sense of Paul's word: "Not I, but the Christ in me."

If we go up the central aisle of the Great Hall to the west entrance under the organ loft, we experience the unique total-work-of-art as a harmony of all forms and colors. Turning around and

*Fig. 38: View from the auditorium to the small cupola room
[towards the east].*

looking eastward, in the two building motif variations already described, we hear again the admonition, "O Man, know yourself!" but now alternating with a second call, "O Man, evolve yourself!" Like a mighty chorus to a great orchestral symphony, this resounds from the architraves and the series of columns.

And now we first understand what role the building motif has to play in this building: It is always surrounded by the play of forces of the supporting pillars and the vaults resting on them. With a schematic drawing, Steiner explained the fundamental

*Fig. 39: Fourth through seventh columns with architrave in the large cupola room.*

static principle of architecture: It is "the divine" that creates balance between the polarities of Lucifer and Ahriman [Fig. 40].[76] From the west portal outside to the small cupola inside, we repeatedly encounter the primal motif like a kind of "leaf" in the Goetheanum organism, which finally reveals its compositional secret through Rudolf Steiner's monumental wooden sculpture, "The Group": The building motif is The Group, and The Group is the whole building, through which the Christ speaks.

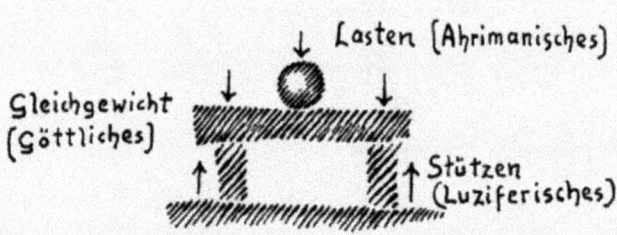

*Fig. 40: In the field of tension of loads and carrying.*
*[See Fig. 19]*

Endnotes

76      See Rudolf Steiner, *Art as Seen in the Light of Mystery Wisdom*, lecture in Dornach on January 2, 1915,  CW 275.

# The Michael Building:
## The Spatial Concept of the Second Goetheanum

Architecture is the art of space, the creative circumventing of dimensions and proportions. The concept arises from the soul-spiritual and physical function and seeks its form of spatial limitation and spatial division from the scale of possibilities. Only when the building stands 1:1 upon the Earth can one actually speak of architecture. If it is a great work of art, then it has its absolute mass, into which sculptural and pictorial elements are incorporated. The spatial gestalt is primary. With the words "building concept" (*Baugedanke*), Rudolf Steiner refers to the total-work-of-art (*Gesamtkunstwerk*), while with the term "spatial concept" (*Raumgedanke*) he refers to the building structure as such.

In both of the Goetheanum buildings, we have as a collaborative function the new, open Mysteries. Their esoteric core was at first still connected to old traditions. In 1924, after the Christmas Conference, Rudolf Steiner gave this work a completely new path. This significant metamorphosis is also expressed in the spatial concept of the Second Goetheanum. While the first building, with its two hemispherical domes, links on to traditional building forms, the spatial design of the second is something fully new and unique in the world to this day.

Rudolf Steiner held many lectures and talks to illustrate the concept behind the First Goetheanum and occasionally wrote about it. From this emerges a multi-layered picture of this incomparable total-work-of-art. In addition, he outlined the idea of the building in a short, pithy formulation: "House of the Word." Everyone could understand this in their own way. On June 17, 1914, he spoke of the emerging forms inside as the "larynxes

*Fig. 41: Albert von Baravalle: Reconstruction model 1:100 of the First Goetheanum (1937).*

*Fig. 42: Rudolf Steiner: Model for the Second Goetheanum (March 1924).*

of the gods."[77] That was a more esoteric aspect to it. And on September 20, 1914, in a commemorative address for the laying of the foundation stone in 1913, he pointed to the final mystery: "The Christ will speak, he who seeks an expression, a revelation through the Word of the higher hierarchies . . . . And this building is to be the mouth!"[78]

In March 1924, he created the model of the *Second Goetheanum*. He was no longer able to hold special lectures about it, only occasionally giving indications, such as in the Karma Lecture of April 27, with the auspicious concluding remark about the "forms awakening an envisoning of karma" (*Karma-Schauen erweckende Formen*) of the planned second building. On October 25/26 and November 1, 1924, essays appeared in the two Basel newspapers with which he introduced the Second Goetheanum to a broad public. He wrote them from his sickbed. Thus they have a character of a bequest, like his oral specifications to the leading architect Ernst Aisenpreis.[79]

What points of view can be found in the essays mentioned? First of all: the necessity that the building forms stand newly harmonized with anthroposophical wisdom. This resulted in the very individual Goetheanum style, whose forms, however, also depend on the material: concrete instead of, as previously, wood. As a special characteristic of the second building, Rudolf Steiner emphasizes the correspondence with the formation of the surrounding Jura landscape and explains the simple but grand building gesture with the indication:

> . . . [There are] essentially straight lines and flat surfaces [for enclosing walls and roofing], which in their angular inclinations close together to form the totality of the building concept. Only towards and in the portals do the line and surface forms become somewhat smaller and more manifold in their membering.

In such a way, Rudolf Steiner conceived this building as a counterpart to the first, where not only on the inside but also on the outside a variety of individual forms occupied the observer's gaze. With the transformation of that variety into the very strictest simplicity, he at the same time completed the last step of his organic building style, in which the additive principle of earlier building styles is completely overcome.

*Fig. 43: Albert von Baravalle: Northeast view of the Goetheanum following Rudolf Steiner's model.*

At various points in these essays, Rudolf Steiner discusses the requisite close relationship between interior and exterior design and brings together "the bold forming of the west front" with the ground plan. Anyone who studies these comments carefully can see that the author always had a totality in mind and not just the exterior architecture shown in the model, which had to be completed first as the basis for the building permit. In the last paragraph of the article for the *Basler Nachrichten* (Basel News), he emphasizes the monument character of the building: "Out of the idea (*Idee des Baues*) for this building, the concept arose whereby something of the character of a monument evolved. This [idea] is to create an image, one that is artistically and completely faithful to the truth (*ein künstlerisch völlig wahrheitsgetreues Abbild*) of what is worked out inwardly through spirit-cognition. Here Rudolf Steiner certainly has in mind the School of Spiritual Science with its sections. The fact that this is not only esoteric but at the same time thought to be effective far out into the world is expressed in the mighty dimensions and the overall gestalt of the building. Thus, he can assure in conclusion: "The opinion is present with the builder that something will be created which the general, unbiased taste, knowing or wanting to know nothing of anthroposophy, can definitely go along with." How does this building speak to human beings? In earlier times, when one walked along the road from Arlesheim towards the Dornach hill, one could see the building all the time. Like a rocky peak, it greeted you from the crest of the hill. Today there are only a few places with such a free view. For people who love mountain hiking, this presented a familiar atmosphere and incentive to climb.

If one observes the building from the north or south, a slowly rising and cascading building gesture appears, which is related to the structure of the mountain ridges in the surrounding area and harmoniously embeds itself in the landscape uphill, while downhill it speaks majestically over the edge of the hill into the round of the further range of hills. If one imagines into the roof silhouette the unfortunately missing ledge between the auditorium and the stage wing, the gesture appears even more powerful and expressive.

If one approaches the building in full from the northwest and looks up at the moving forms, one can experience the impulsive force of the striking lines rising up and swinging over to the entry. In certain aerial views or on Rudolf Steiner's model, the building with its side-wings rising slant-wise to the west can remind one of the gesture of an eagle that has just settled or even risen into the air.

Finally, if one steps up from the western end of the hill—not far from House Duldeck, at the beginning of the wide road leading to the front of the building, which with the flanking stones along the pathway reminds one of a "sacred road" from antiquity—the following picture presents itself:

Before us, a gigantic building rises to the heavens. Surprisingly, there is nothing oppressive about the mighty concrete masses. An inviting and at the same time protective gesture comes towards the observer. Austere, but not threatening; mysterious, but not enigmatic—the building begins to speak to the newcomer. There is no rejection by the front: the gaze can roam unimpeded from fillet to fillet along the flanks of the structure to the side-wings and glide just as freely up over the terrace, entry

*Fig. 44: Photo: Erika von Baravalle.*

porch, window arches, front roof-edge, and central section to the highest visible point of the roof. The soul of the observer is expanded and uplifted.

Thus, the building makes itself accessible to the calmly sensing eye like an essential counterpart. This is made possible by a simple geometric figure that is hidden not only in the ground plan, but also in a slanting line leading diagonally upwards and backwards: a trapezoid opening towards the east. Astonished, the observer divines something of this mystery. After countless, ever-new encounters and intervening experiences inside the Great Hall, the knowledge may at some time flash like lightning: Yes, the idea of this building was born from *The Philosophy of Freedom*; here it stands for us as a building concept manifested in stone, stone-made (*steinerner*) building thought!

The book, published in 1894, could also be called a commemorative publication (*Festschrift*) for the beginning of the new Michael Age. It took Rudolf Steiner thirty years to inscribe the fundamental idea as a spatial structure also into the physical body of the Earth. A festive mood came over Ita Wegman as she remembered the three days from March 10–12, 1924, when she was able to witness the creation of the building model under Rudolf Steiner's hands. On the date of May 3, 1925, she reported in the newssheet about it.

> It was only after the Christmas Conference that Rudolf Steiner was able to work intensively on the new concert for the building. This new Goetheanum had to be brought together with the Michael impulses; it had to be a Michael Castle (Michaelsburg), where the students of Michael could find each other and come together in order to hear the messages of Michael. It had to be castle-like, in order to be able to withstand the impact of adversarial powers; to be built of firm material, artistic and beautiful, but strong and strict in its forms and lines. It had to be carried out at the behest of the Archangel Michael, given by him to his helpers, standing under him, in the spiritual world. The time for this had to be awaited. In the spiritual world, the new Goetheanum had to appear; only then was it possible to bring it down to the physical plane. This, Rudolf Steiner did for us. This ceremonious moment came, as I said, after the Christmas Conference—unforgettable for those who were able to witness it.
>
> When the point in time came, the master put on his white smock, ordered the prepared clay, and began to sculpt the model of the new Goetheanum. He worked feverishly, essentially without resting. I was allowed to be present, to witness with astonishment, to experience with holy awe, how the model came into being. In three days it was finished and then stood there, unique in its strict, powerful, and yet so beautiful forms. From the model, we should now erect the new Goetheanum on the Dornach hill, a building for the anthroposophy of the present and the future! Anthroposophy with its friends and adversaries needs a construction that does justice to both, a building in which, in its inner spatiality, one can devote oneself to art and can hear the word that anthroposophy wishes to proclaim, and which shows on the outside in its form and in its resistant material that it will remain steadfast and protective.
>
> Michael's Castle, new Goetheanum!

Delighted, the master stood next to his model. When this model was then carried away from the studio to the Glass House for the preparation of the plans, he said to me: "It caused a sensation when the model was carried from the studio to its second workstation, the Glass House." Yes, how can it cause anything but a sensation when, right in front of people's eyes, wonders occur! May we all help that this Second Goetheanum—prepared with so much love, with so much effort, yes, even perhaps with the sacrifice of his health—can be erected, in all its grandeur and glory, in honor of its great master Rudolf Steiner.[80]

With this report, Ita Wegman has lifted the veil that was woven around the secret of Rudolf Steiner's idea for the building up until his death: "Michael's Castle," that is the core thought of the Second Goetheanum. Is it not immediately evident? The Goetheanum building belongs, together with the Karma Lectures and the School of Spiritual Science, to the three great, mutually dependent Michael-gifts that flowed out of the Christmas Conference. If Rudolf Steiner had been able to open the erected building, he probably would have spoken about it. Inconceivably, Ita Wegman's report has not been taken up earnestly to this day [2013]. It was completely lost in the turmoil of the Society's history, in the course of which she and her friends were banished from "Michael's Castle." Therein lies a double tragedy, the extent of which is now becoming known.

With the spatial form for the Second Goetheanum, Rudolf Steiner wrote a threefold message into the Earth: Philosophy of Freedom, karma research, and the Michael School. Filled with cares about the construction of the building, he crossed the threshold of death. Still on the last afternoon of his life he asked his doctor, Ita Wegman, if everything was ready in the studio, so that he could make the interior model. This was no longer possible, but he had already given the most important details beforehand. They have the character of a bequest.

On May 5, 1918, he had spoken in Munich about the intimate relationship between clairvoyant research and the architectural act of creation and described the process thus:

238

. . . A mental picture, which is actually thinking in forms that directly, by thinking, could represent forms of force-distribution in space, dimensional relationships in space . . . . An objective thinking . . . which cannot but let its content pass over into spatial forms, into moving spatial forms, into forms that are stretching, overarching, bending-upon-themselves; in which the will flowing in the world is expressed . . . . So, the seer has to develop gifts which point to what quivers and shudders through the great World Building. And that—which he as a seer thus sees through and lives through—lives on unconsciously in the architect and carver, permeates their creative work, in that they fashion artistically.[81]

From these words, pictures can arise in us that remind us of the expressive power of a Michelangelo when he brought the spirit of the creator into appearance on the Sistine ceiling: stormily roaring along with lordly gaze and gesture, creating Sun and Moon.

The conception of the Second Goetheanum certainly also had a dramatic character. What a creative struggle must have taken place to restrain such widely stretched polarities of form into such a harmonious balance? Only with the Sun-force of Michael, the great inspirer, could this ingenious process succeed. With the shaping of this thought into space, Rudolf Steiner has given humanity a building of the highest order.

Thus, we also learn to understand why, since 1914/15, during lectures and guided tours of the First Goetheanum, he repeatedly remarked that this was only an imperfect first beginning and that he would design the building quite differently if he could do it again. For a long time, the seed of the second building lay dormant in him, which we can see in the building elements of the Boiler House (*Heizhaus*, lit. "Heating House"), House Duldeck, and in the pathway lights.

The spiritually inspired idea of the Second Goetheanum, which stands incomparably as a grown, organic whole, was "brought down" from spiritual spheres of space. It is to this— not only to the connection with the earthly environment—that Rudolf Steiner ultimately points in his essay for the *Basler Nachrichten* (Basel News) with the words: "With concrete, forms

*Fig. 45: Second Goetheanum. Partial view, soon after removal
of scaffolding. Photo: Rietmann, 1928.*

had to be sought in which space, out of its own nature, unfolds
the formation that can take up anthroposophical work."

Spatial forms are what it came down to. Generously moving lines and surfaces that seamlessly, i.e.—organically—merge
together with one another. He achieved this new creation by
dispensing with all chracteristic presentations and sculpturally
chiseled individual elements. Monumental, bold forms emerged,
which are only possible in concrete.

A view into the spiritual workshop of the master builder may
clarify for us the transformation of the building and its concept
in space: Put together from eight parts, the first building crowned
the Dornach hill with its two domes, the cylinder of the auditorium, the building wing enclosing the stage, the three entry

porches, and the terrace base. In the second, even taller building, we can count eleven building appendages, ten of which are bound with each other in such a way that they appear as a unit: three-part roof, audience and stage wing, entry, two side wings, and two free-standing columns. Only the terrace base of the whole building is clearly set off. The remaining parts merge into one another.

The impression of an inseparable organic whole is brought about above all by the ingenious "grasp" of drawing upwards from the roof surfaces of the side wings slant-wise to the trapezoidal center of the main roof, so that they lie like a transverse band over the longitudinally running parts of the building (cf. Fig. 51). That therewith, not only a cross (which is also predisposed in the building) appears, but that the "eagle wing" impression can emerge, is due to a threefold slanting—westward and upward as well as at the side edges—of this roof part. The composition of the whole of the roof surfaces is so multilayered in relation to each other and to the building structure that one reaches a limit when trying to comprehend the process of creation. One experiences the absolute necessity in the interplay of all components, and one senses: Such a thing as this could never emerge from any kind of mental weighing—therein lies a secret of inspiration.

We can now observe the building from another aspect and approach it with the question: What has actually become of the building motif, which on the outside and inside of the first building the observer so often encounters as a sign-like relief? In long studies, it can reveal itself as a cipher for the human being, from which the Mystery cry, "O Man, know yourself!" resounds to us. Rudolf Steiner described it on January 1, 1924, by drawing a metamorphosis for the new building on the chalkboard, but then did not manifest it in his model in this way. Did he drop this significant motif altogether? Albert von Baravalle answered this question in an essay in *Das Goetheanum* of March 23, 1952, after he had already designed three models as fictitious intermediate metamorphoses in 1935. He shows how the building motif was not lost, but rather transformed into architectural forms.

*Fig. 46: Albert von Baravalle: Southern view of the Second Goetheanum according to Rudolf Steiner's model.*

In this way, we can trace and get to know the secret of the composition of the roof surfaces described above: It is the transformed building motif that speaks from the roof surfaces above the west wing to the vault of the heavens and turns a second time to human eyes, westward far out into the landscape, as the surrounding form of the red window. According to Rudolf Steiner's intention of exterior and interior correspondences in the building, it should also resound to the visitors as a negative of the form of the roof high above from the ceiling of the [Great] Hall. Only in this way would it receive its full meaning. According to a statement of November 1, 1924, in the essay for the Basel *National-Zeitung*:

> Surface and line designs, angular designs, etc. are to be held in such a way that what is shaped and membered in the interior presses into the exterior forms and thereby reveals itself.

The building motif metamorphosis is an example of the simplification of which Rudolf Steiner speaks again and again. In a tremendous melting-down process, Twenty-Nine sculptural reliefs on the outer wall have become two architectural forms, bringing the same thing to expression. Thus can we learn to read the second building like the first one. It is only a different form of writing. Rudolf Steiner calls it a new style, which he inaugurated with the concrete building of the Second Goetheanum and its earlier born "child," the Eurythmeum ([today] Rudolf Steiner Halde).

Let us bring before us the exterior architecture of the auditorium [of the Second Goetheanum]. In addition to simplification, we find an inversion of inside and outside. First of all, the two free-standing columns stand out, each supporting a roof tip in the north and south. They have neither a pedestal nor a detached capital, but their somewhat broadened head merges directly into the architrave band leading over to the side wing. (At the Eurythmeum, similar columns are placed like guards in front of the internal working space.) Instead of seven columns inside the large cupola space, we have one—the central one—outside on both sides. And instead of the pillars for the wall on the outside of the first building, Rudolf Steiner specified the "supports," the girders, anchored deep down in the second building, which were already structurally calculated during his lifetime. They were to partition the inner wall instead of free-standing columns.

Let us now observe the architrave zone outside! West of the column, which 'I'-like from above is footed upon the terrace floor, we find under the indented curved narrow roof edge a fillet, but from the column on the broad architrave band. This reminds us of the upper part of the architrave in the large cupola space and, with its polar concave-convex, points to the inside-out principle in the development of humanity: Before the Turning Point of Time, human beings were guided by divine beings (inworking from outside: concave principle); with the I-leadership (middle column), they must carry out their development themselves, from within themselves (unfolding from within: convex principle). Whoever is familiar with these ideas finds them not only inside but already outside in the second building, and can hear from it the second important mystery call: O Man, evolve yourself!

In this way, the principle of simplification arises—out of the appropriate material, which Rudolf Steiner decisively emphasized—not in an impoverishment of the variety of forms of the first building, but rather in a powerful concentration, as an enhancement. In this, his mastery reveals itself particularly clearly, and we comprehend why he occasionally indicated how at the end-point of an evolution, what appears is not the most complicated form but rather a simplified one.

This applies not only to the seven stages of the planetary seals and capital forms, but also to the step-wise manifestation of three completely different spatial thoughts, which he developed in the small span of seventeen years, from 1907–24: Seedlike, in the triaxial ellipsoid of the Rosicrucian temple of initiation [Model Building in Malsch], the spiritually inspired idea was there as a fundamental composition in the double cupola of the First Goetheanum, it came to flowery unfolding in the fundamental design of the Second Goetheanum, composed of trapezoid and rectangle, it appears—despite the differentiation of the building structure—drawn together as ripe fruit. The decisive factor is the transposition of the designing from out of the realm of sculptural small forms into the realm of architectural forms— from which emerges the contemporary gesture of generosity as a contribution to the social order of the world.

The concept for the building of the Second Goetheanum building, like the first, reveals the being "Anthroposophy," but in a new style whose "modernity"—which Rudolf Steiner had long striven for—has been proven. It still arouses growing interest in the lay and professional world. The spatial design of the Second Goetheanum breathes breadth, sublimity, boldness, and liberation, but also unconditional austerity and equilibrium: truly a Michael building![82]

Endnotes

77    *Ways to a New Style in Architecture,* 3rd edition, 1982, p. 118-120.

78    See in this volume Rudolf Steiner, "The Longing of the Soul for the Spirit".

79    More details in Erika von Baravalle, "Zum zwölften Todestag des Architekten Albert von Baravalle" [On the twelfth anniversary of the death of the architect Albert von Baravalle] *STIL* June 1995, p. 29 as well as Easter 1955, p. 33

80    Ita Wegman, "The Old Goetheanum and the New (May 3, 1925)" in *Esoteric Studies*, 22–24

81    New edition with photos of the models in *STIL*, St. John's Tide, 1995.

82    Supplementary remarks can be found in my essay on the creation of the model of the Second Goetheanum; cf. Erika von Baravalle, "Vor 66 Jahren entstand das Modell des Zweiten Goetheanums" [66 years ago, there arose the model of the Second Goetheanum], *Nachrichten für Mitglieder* (News for members) 67, no. 12 (March 18, 1990): 53–55; Erika von Baravalle, "Zum zwölften Todestag des Architekten Albert von Baravalle" [On the twelfth anniversary of the death of the architect Albert von Baravalle], *STIL* 17, no. 2 (St. John's Tide, 1995): 21–29.

# Forms that Awaken an Envisioning of Karma

Rudolf Steiner spoke again and again about the First Goethe-anum, above all about the enigmatic carved forms inside. He was also able to use these to explain his organic building principles, which had not yet been realized in the spatial form of the building. His lectures were not addressed to professionals, as were, for example, the courses for doctors or educators. There were several reasons for this. On the one hand, the buildings erected by the Anthroposophical Society were to be used and cared for responsibly by the entire membership and, after all, the members were always ready to take on the role of building any further buildings; in this way, Rudolf Steiner gave them for the understanding of all. On the other hand, his buildings were especially important to him as so-called "experiential forms" or "forms of experience" (*Erlebensformen*), which he consciously and willingly juxtaposed with the "intellectual forms" or "forms of understanding" (*Verstandesformen*) of his spiritual-scientific works as a different revelation of the same wisdoms (*Weisheiten*) opened up through a conscious schooling of the sense organs.

Already in his address at the foundation of the Building Association (*Bauverein*) on December 12, 1911, he had shown how in every great cultural epoch a unique style of building arose, through which the message of the epoch was literally inscribed on the Earth. It was a primordial law that to all Mystery schools there also belonged a special building impulse. Thus reads the beginning of his first Christmas mantra in 1906:

See the sun
At the midnight hour.
Build with stones
In the lifeless ground . . . .

*Die Sonne schaue*
*Um mitternächtige Stunde.*
*Mit Steinen baue*
*im leblosen Grunde . . . .*[83]

Incessantly, Rudolf Steiner urged his students to study the motifs of the First Goetheanum: "To read the building, that is what matters"—not in a way that speculates intellectually, but rather "feeling artistically into the forms."

Steiner could not hold any lectures about the Second Goetheanum because he fell ill and died before it was built. However, a year earlier, from March 10–12, 1924, he had created a large exterior model which he himself shaped in wax in the span of three days, from which the plans for the building application were drawn.

Besides this, in the fall of 1924, he also wrote two essays from his sickbed for both Basel newspapers, from which his valuation of the project as a continuation of his impulses becomes clear.

Occasionally, he spoke briefly about the planned building, for example at the end of his last course away from Switzerland in Torquay [England], where he marked the fundamental principle of both buildings as musical and therefore so little understood by people.

## *The lecture of April 27, 1924*[84]

Already once before, on April 27, 1924, at the end of a Karma Lecture, he also spoke about both buildings. He depicted the architectural forms of all earlier such Mystery buildings as forms that awaken an envisioning of karma and that absolutely must re-emerge into cultural life, and brought up the fire of the First Goetheanum as a symptom of the influence of the adversarial powers against karma research. Then he continued: "But let us hope that in the near future, in the same place, forms that

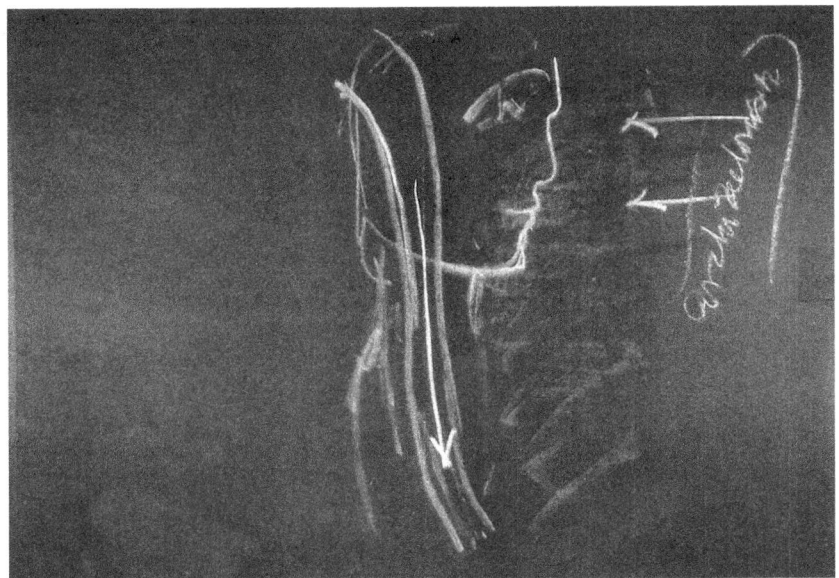

*Fig. 47: Re-encounter with ourselves. Rudolf Steiner's
blackboard drawing of April 27, 1924.
From: Wandtafelzeichnungen zum Vortragswerk 16
(Blackboard drawings from lecture work), 37; [cf. Karmic
Relationships, vol. 2, p. 84.]*

awaken karma-vision will stand before us again."[85] This referred
to the preliminary work for the building to be built in concrete,
the model of which had already been completed.

It was in the days when the drawings of the building application plans were completed. All the people present in Dornach
would have known that. They followed every step towards the
realization of the building with excitement. In a closing remark,
Rudolf Steiner briefly explained why he was depicting this significant function of architecture on this particular evening. He
wanted to entrust his words not only to the circle of Dornach
members, but also to many friends from outside who had stayed
from the Easter conference, so that they could carry this hopeful
announcement into the world.

Let us clearly bring before us Rudolf Steiner's presentation:
First of all, we are pointed towards a fact that is probably astonishing for some people of today: that an endless gaze into nature
does not fully satisfy the human being, but rather leads one to
a "soul emaciation for the world of the senses." Yes, it finally

comes to organic "injuries," against which we need a "healing remedy." The healing remedy is something one had in former times in the human-appropriate way of building temples and churches, which could "absorb" the gaze of the observer in the right way.

The presence of such architecture in the landscape is therefore the first prerequisite for such an awakening for the envisioning of karma. However, it is not enough that a person only sees the buildings and perhaps zealously adores them. A second component must be added on, in that the observer develops a certain soul configuration. Through a striving for true self-knowledge, they should penetrate deeply into their own being with the help of exercises to develop Imagination, such as those offered by the cultus of earlier cultural epochs. In this way, an interplay between the architecture standing outside in the world and one's own soul could arise, in an *in-between realm*, in which the contours of certain shapes then appeared.

It is this third factor that matters. Out of the living ground of spiritual memories, there arise essential pictures that touch us in a unique way. In Steiner's generously sketched chalkboard drawing, the *"field of the middle"* is marked by sweeps of meandering orange-colored chalk, slightly playing over the profile of the human face [Fig. 47 (light shadings between face and two arrows)]. Its rounded forms have a childlike, devotional character. From the encountered architecture, two red-yellow arrows point to the area of the eye and the mouth. From behind the head, a long tube, drawn in blue, open on both sides, extends deep down into the chest area. In its center, a long yellow arrow indicates the direction of self-discovery. The picture—unlike the schematic sketch in the volume on karma—stimulates a vivid imagination of the mystical happening, a re-encounter with ourselves in earlier incarnations.

In a singular way in the context of his life's work, Rudolf Steiner has thus here discussed the process of a vision of karma arising. Only with this can we appreciate the grand dimension of significance of the two Goetheanum buildings. Steiner clearly speaks of exterior architecture as it appears in the landscape as something that catches the eye. One can now ask which aspects of the two Goetheanum buildings fulfill this condition.

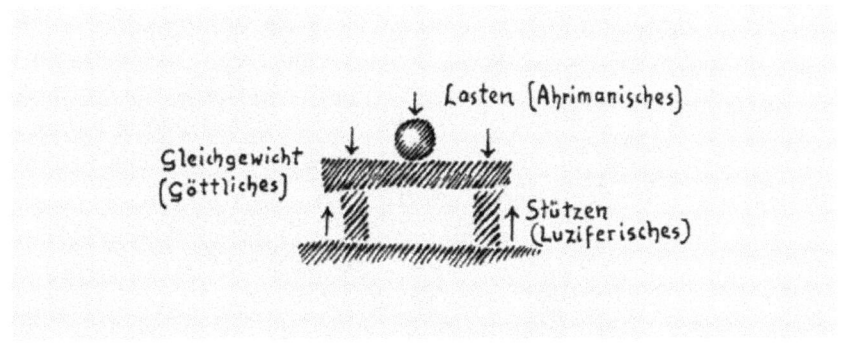

*Fig. 48: Diagram of the supporting and loading forces. [From: Art as Seen in the Light of Mystery Wisdom, lecture in Dornach on Jan. 2, 1915, p. 119.] [See Fig. 19]*

## The First Goetheanum

The First Goetheanum did not yet have organic architectural forms, but it did have many sculptural elements, mostly reliefs and mainly in the interior. The spatial structure had as its fundamental motif a circle, a purely geometric form that expressed the character of a building. The core of the building consisted of two interlocking cylinders of different sizes with corresponding hemispherical domes. Looking back on earlier buildings, Steiner pointed to "the evenness of the carrying and the forces of stress", an experience of the fundamental static law of all architecture, which he also emphasized again and again in his lectures on architecture. On January 2, 1915, he recommended to his listeners to "crawl into" these fundamental elements and drew a diagram on the blackboard [Fig. 48] in which we can easily recognize an archetype of his sculptural Christ-group.[86] He based all the variants of the portals and windows in the area of the large cupola on this structure. Between the supporting half-pilasters and the load-bearing upper section, he inserted a motif that speaks and contains the inscription above the entrance to the temple of Apollo at Delphi. This is clear from the presentation of the southern rose window. [The motif] "sounds" to the

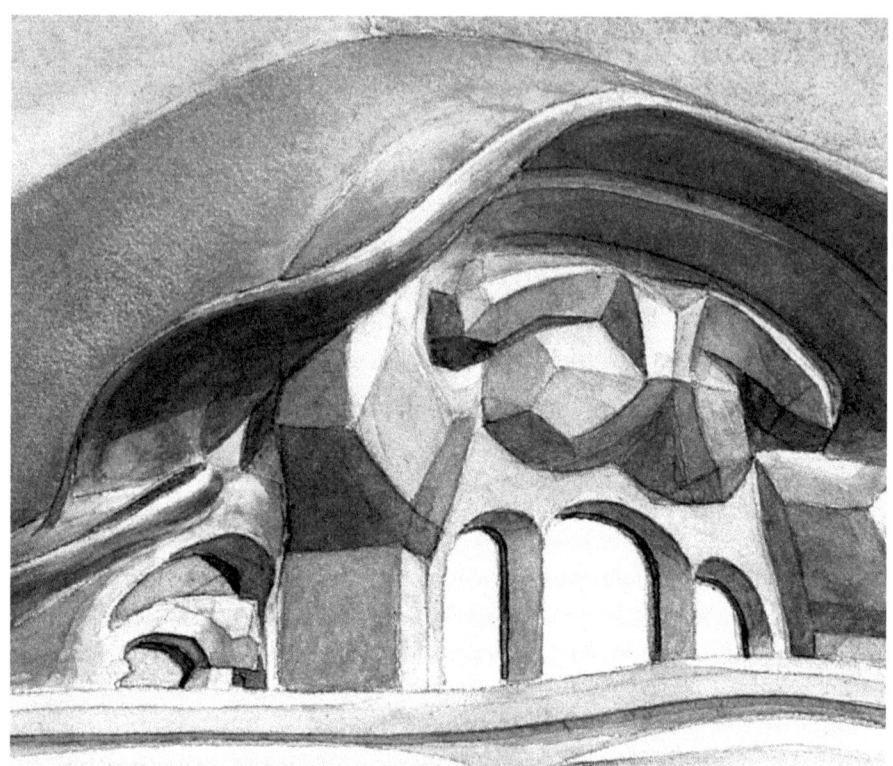

*Fig. 49: View from below towards the west portal of the First Goetheanum.*

observer in different variants: Twenty-Nine times outside, and then in two further variants on the inside above the proscenium and at the very east of the stage, where the wooden sculpture (the "Group") was to stand and could have revealed itself to the observer as the "Representative of Humanity."

In the most impressionable design above the west portal, the motif with an austere guardian gesture can also be surmised in its ability to awaken an envisioning of karma, when the observer carries out the cognitive process presented in the southern rose window: "I behold the building (*Ich schaue den Bau*)—The world builds (*Die Welt baut*)—And the building becomes the Human Being (*Und der Bau wird Mensch*)." One can remember mythological events in the history of humankind and find oneself reflected back in the various building motifs.

The building motif above the west portal speaks thus:

I am the Sphinx of Oedipus,
who barred for him the way
until the riddle's solving word
from his lips she heard.
I am the picture of the threshold's guardian
with admonishing earnest greeting.
If you remain silent, so I become for you
the countenance of Medusa.
I am the inscription which, once grand,
was to be read in Delphi;
Apollo's wisdom opened to those
who sought his divine being.
They step onward and find themselves
in the motif's mirror,
Grasp me in the transformation
as the World-Becoming seal:
O Man, O Man, know YOURSELF!

*Ich bin die Sphinx des Ödipus,*
*Die ihm den Weg verwehrte,*
*Bis sie des Rätsels Lösungswort*
*Von seinen Lippen hörte.*
*Ich bin des Schwellenhüters Bild*
*Zu mahnend ernstem Gruße.*
*Verharrst du stumm, so werd' ich dir*
*Zum Antlitz der Meduse.*
*Ich bin die Inschrift, die einst groß*
*In Delphi war zu lesen,*
*Apollons Weisheit dem erschloss,*
*Der sucht' sein göttlich Wesen.*
*Er schreite fort und finde sich*
*In der Motive Spiegel,*
*Begreif in der Verwandlung mich*
*Als Weltenwerdens Siegel:*
*O Mensch, o Mensch, erkenne DICH!*

— Erika von Baravalle

# The Second Goetheanum

Anyone who has recognized the significance of the building motif for the first building will also understand why Rudolf Steiner had to proceed from this motif with the conception of the second building, which—together with the double-dome principle already presented on January 4, 1915, as the fundamental structure of all his buildings—constitutes the most important element of the exterior architecture. It had taken him a year to formally transform it into concrete material before he was able to draw the motif on the blackboard at the end of the Christmas meeting. And then, after the creation of the model inspired by Michael, it was not—as announced—to be found again above all the portals and windows of the west wing. What had happened?

The architect Albert von Baravalle had discovered it as a powerfully sealing roofing form over the west wing and in 1935 designed plasticine models as intermediate stages for understanding the process of transformation from a signature relief into the architectural large-scale form.[87] With a stylistically giant step, Steiner had also given the spatial form of the building an organic character. Thus, the Delphic motif now speaks to the air beings and gods and can only reveal itself to the human eye in an airplane or as a model. For trained eyes, however, it can also be recognized around the large, red, west window. The motif "O Man, know yourself!" which introduces every lesson in the First Class of the School of Michael, already resounded through an entire scene in the first Mystery Drama.

That the building motif has the function of awakingening the envisioning of karma is clear from a verse by Rudolf Steiner for Ita Wegman, illustrated in the fourth volume of the biography by Emanuel Zeylmans van Emmichoven. Next to the drawing of a building motif variant are the handwritten words:

> Forget not this sign
> It will open up for you
> The spiritual gate
> To your right
> old-experienced
> soul companions. —

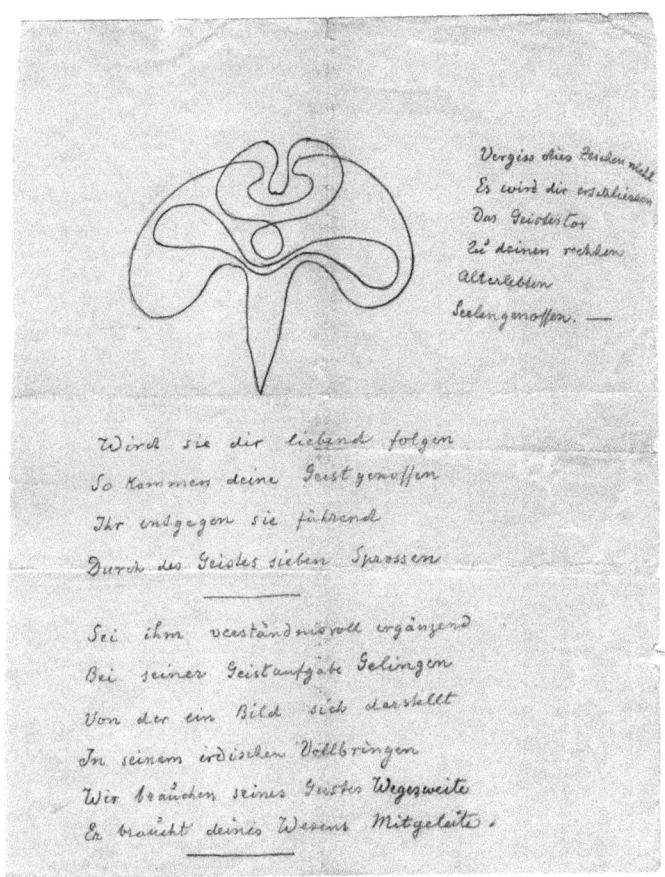

*Fig. 50: Rudolf Steiner: Drawing of a building motif variant and part of a verse for Ita Wegman. © Ita Wegman Archive, Arlesheim; [cf. J. E. Zeylmans van Emmichoven, Who was Ita Wegman, vol. 4, pp. 228–231.]*

*Vergiss dies Zeichen nicht*
*Es wird dir erschließen*
*Das Geistestor*
*Zu deinen rechten*
*Alterlebten*
*Seelengenossen.—*[88]

These words were written in March 1924, the month of the creation of the building model, which Ita Wegman was the only person to witness.[89]

255

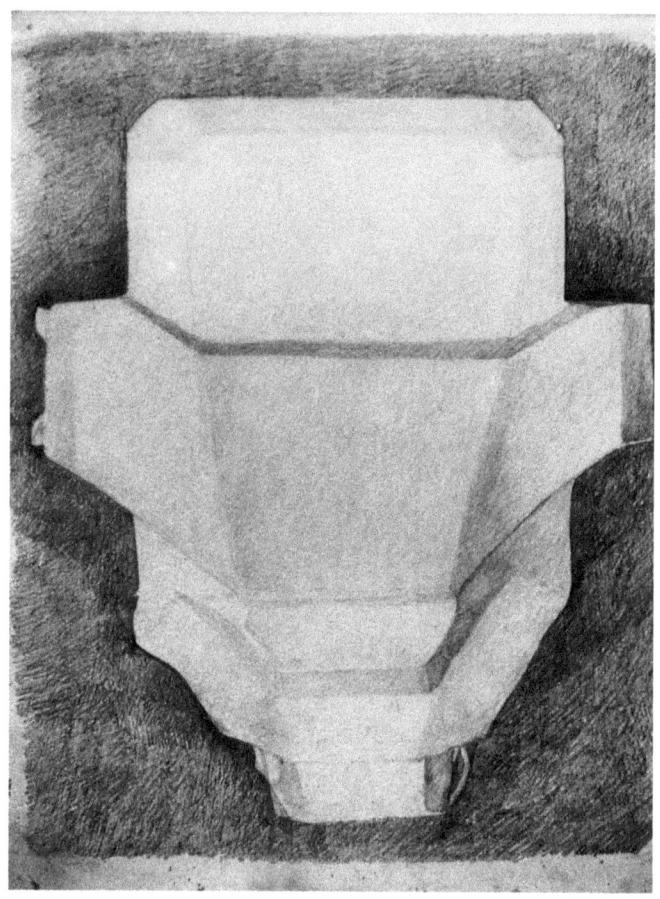

*Fig. 51: Roof-top view of Steiner's model.*

There are still many other ways of experiencing the Michael building that can be connected with the function to awaken karma-vision: the construction of the presentation of the whole of spiritual science, *The Philosophy of Freedom*, The Group (whose principle of balance can be experienced in many places of the building), and the social "awakening to the other." All these motifs have already been discussed in my earlier essays.[90]

At certain times, from the west, the entire building appears as the building motif: through light and shadow, the forms around the upper window are chiseled out in a crystal-clear way, flanked

*Fig. 52: The Second Goetheanum from the west: good visibility of the building motif.*

on both sides by three vertical support-elements, each with inviting fillets and vaulted by the protective, shimmering roof surfaces, slightly cambered on the sides. With its broadly supported side-wings, this Michaelic building of the future breathes breadth of spirit and invites all human beings to participate in an envisioning.

Endnotes

83      Rudolf Steiner, "Behold the sun," *Truth-Wrought Words*, 28–29; CW 40.

84      Rudolf Steiner, *Karmic Relationships*, vol. 2, lecture in Dornach on April 27, 1924, CW 236

85      Unfortunately, this weighty sentence has remained unnoticed in various presentations up until today, so that when one speaks of the forms that awaken karma-vision, one is usually referring to the First Goetheanum only.

86      Rudolf Steiner, *Art as Seen in the Light of Mystery Wisdom*, CW 275.

87      Albert von Baravalle, "Das Baumotiv des II. Goetheanum" (The building motif of the 2nd Goetheanum), *STIL* 17, no. 2 (St. John's Tide, 1995): 34–37.

88      J. E. Zeylmans van Emmichoven, *Who was Ita Wegman*, vol. 4, pp. 228–231.

89      Ita Wegman, *An die Freunde. Aufsatze und Berichte aus den Jahren 1925–1927*; "The Old Goetheanum and the New Goetheanum."

90      Erika von Baravalle, "Vor 66 Jahren entstand das Modell des Zweiten Goetheanums" [66 years ago, there arose the model of the Second Goetheanum], *Nachrichten für Mitglieder* (News for members) 67, no. 12 (March 18, 1990): 53–55.

# 5.
# Rudolf Steiner's Addresses Regarding the Laying of the Foundation Stone

RUDOLF STEINER

# Address Given during the Act of Consecration
# September 20, 1913

W̶e begin our work. — (Turning to the [west, north, east, and south], and, for each direction, calling out a name:)

You Seraphim, you Cherubim, you who lead the world, and you, who like streaks of lightning, take up the sheaths of the Cherubim through the spiritual streams, wedding them to the creative existence of the world, you high Thrones, you we call as protectors of our activity; and you, you Wisdoms (*Weisheiten*), who are all that is present in human beings prior to any manifestation of their being, and you, you Keepers (*Bewahrer*) of the eternal world-forces, and you, you Formers of our existence, who set the pattern of all being into the streams of existence: You we call as the protectors of our activities. And you, you Personalities of this spiritual stream, and you helpers, Archangeloi and Angeloi, who are for the Earth the messengers of the spiritual life of human beings, we call you all to be the protectors and steerers of this action of ours. We are calling on you to come down onto the Human Soul, which we want to consecrate, insofar as it is up to us. We take a step towards the Human Soul that we want to consecrate for the work, which, according to our best knowledge of the time, is to be of service to it.

As a symbol of the Human Soul, which consecrates itself to our great work, we have formed this stone. It is for us a symbol (*Sinnbild*) in its double twelve-memberedness of the striving Human Soul, placed as microcosm into the macrocosm. Anthropos, the Human Being, as derived from the essential-beingnesses (*Wesenheiten*) of the divine-spiritual hierarchies. In such a way, this, our cornerstone (*Eckstein*), is the symbol of our own soul, which we integrate into what we have recognized as the right spiritual striving for the present time. So, we will place this stone, which is formed according to the world-pictures of the Human Soul, into the kingdom of the elements. Within this stone, two rocks are to be found, taken from the condensed kingdom of the elements, which best express how the macrocosmic forces collaborate in the condensed kingdom of the elements. This twelve-memberedness we will sink as the genuine sign of the Human Soul into the place above which will rise what is to become for us like a sign of our working, if we understand it rightly, my dear theosophical friends, on this evening. And with this stone we want to sink into the Earth that which lies within our stone through which we have avowed as recognition of the authenticity of our spiritual life.

This certificate that within our stone will be sunk down, bears the inscription:

*In the Name* of the Seraphim, the Cherubim, the Thrones, the Wisdoms, the Movers (*Beweger*), the Formers, the Personalities (the Archai), the Archangeloi, the Angeloi! There lives, as microcosm in the macrocosm, the human being, *Anthropos*, also represented here as a twice twelve-membered image, symbol of the spiritual world. And within this symbol the verse of Rosicrucianism, well known to you, my dear friends, expresses the sense of our striving: (*E.D.N. I.C.M. P.S.S.R.*) *Ex Deo nascimur. In Christo morimur. Per spiritum sanctum revivescimus.*

As a formulation of our vow (*Angelobeformel*)—let us understand ourselves rightly—it appears on this stone, which, as a *cornerstone* (*Eckstein*), is an expression of the one who wants to seek themselves in the Spirit, who wants to feel himself in the World Soul, who has a presentiment of himself in the World-I: the Human Being. This stone we sink into the condensed kingdom of the elements, this symbol of the force for which we are striving through 3, 5, 7, 12, laid by the Johannes Building Association in Dornach on the twentieth day of September 1880 after the Mystery of Golgotha, that is, 1913 after the birth of Christ, when Mercurius as the evening star stood in the Scales.

Architect:
Carl Schmid-Curtius

As the Administrative Board of the Johannes Building Association (*Johannesbau-Verein*):

[Sophie] Stinde
[Emil] Grosheintz
[Hermann] Linde
[Felix] Peipers
[Pauline Countess von] Kalckreuth
[Carl] Unger
[Emilie Baroness von] Gumppenberg
Mrs. [Lucie] Bürgi
Mrs. [Maria] Schieb
Mrs. [Marie] Hirter-Weber

As the Central Executive Council of the Anthroposophical Society:
[Marie] von Sivers
[Carl] Unger

and Dr. Steiner,
as the spiritual leader of the activity.

This document is incorporated into the symbol of the Human Soul, and then into the condensed kingdom of the elements. — (The document is incorporated into the copperplate container, and this is then soldered.)

The stone, as the symbol of our souls, is sunk into the condensed kingdom of the elements. — (The stone is carried by Dr. Peipers, held by [four] men on long straps, and brought to the place where it shall rest. It is placed in such a way that the larger dodecahedron lies to the east, and the smaller one to the west, that is, converse to the building, whose larger dome is aligned toward the west and whose smaller one is aligned toward the east.)

The stone as symbol (*Sinnbild*) of our soul is sunk into the Earth; it may be taken as a true embodiment of spiritual truth, landmark of the striving towards knowledge, towards love, towards strong action, of the symbol of humankind. It shall be a sign of our souls, so that to us sounds forth evermore from the deepest sense of the World Word: *Ex Deo nascimur. In Christo morimur. Per spiritum sanctum reviviscimus.*

There, out of the symbol of the human soul shall emerge a sign of the human soul. Into the sign of the human soul, I consecrate you with the first blows, those which shall be made on this our building of truth (*Wahrbau*).—(3, 5, 7 blows on the small, 12 blows on the large dodecahedron.)—The stone has thereby become a sign from the symbol. And now, we want to entrust it to the kingdom of the condensed elements, to the Earth, into which our soul has been sunk, to develop in the evolution of humankind that which is the Earth's mission. So the stone, from the sign, now becomes the sheathed one (*zum Verhüllten*), by our entrusting it to the Earth. The human soul rises up threefold to the three mysteries of existence: Symbols are they first, signs are they then, whilst the soul reads the eternal World Word; still yet, the deepest depths of the World Mysteries—they become livingly bonded with the soul when this soul is able to give itself the sheath from the kingdom of the hierarchies. —So be sheathed! Become a sheathed one out of the symbol and the sign, so that you may be a firm cornerstone of our striving, of our searching, as we have recognized it to be right in the evolution of humankind. Thus, we want to make the stone, which is the sign of our soul, into the sheathed one.

RUDOLF STEINER

# Address Given to Those Gathered around the Top of the Earthen Pit, after the Laying of the Foundation Stone
# September 20, 1913

My dear Sisters and Brothers!
Let us rightly understand ourselves today on this festive evening. Let us understand that this act in a certain sense signifies a vow for our soul. Our striving has brought it about that here, in this place, from which we can see far out to the four elementary directions of the heavenly rose (*Himmelsrose*), we may erect this true embodiment of spiritual truth (*Wahrzeichen*) of the spiritual life of modern times. Let us understand that we, on today's date, feeling our souls bonded with what we have symbolically placed within the Earth—that we wed ourselves to this spiritual evolutionary stream of humanity which we have recognized as right. Let us try, my dear sisters and brothers, to take this vow of our souls: that we want to look away at this moment from all the pettiness of life, from all that bonds us, must necessarily bond us as human beings with the life of the everyday. Let us try at this moment to awaken in ourselves thoughts of bonding the human soul with the striving of the Turning Point of Time. Let us try for a moment to think that by doing what we today have vowed to do, we must carry the consciousness within us to look out into the far, far cycles of time in order to become aware of how the mission—of which this building should become a true embodiment of spiritual truth—will join the great mission of humanity on this our Earth planet. Not in pride and arrogance, but in humility, devotion, and willingness to sacrifice, let us try to guide our souls up to the great plans, the great goals of human activity on Earth. Let us try to place ourselves in the position in which we actually should be and must be if we rightly understand this moment.

Let us try to think how the great announcement and message—the eternal Gospel of divine-spiritual life—once reached our Earth evolution; how it reached the Earth when the divine spirits themselves were still the great teachers of humanity. Let us try, my dear sisters and brothers, to put ourselves back into those divine times of the Earth from which a last longing, a very last memory still dawns upon us, when we hear from the ancient Greek lands something with the last tones of Mystery wisdom—and at the same time with the first philosophical tones—the great Plato, proclaiming the eternal Ideas and the eternal sheath of the world. And let us try to grasp that what has passed over our Earth evolution since then, has passed over with luciferic and ahrimanic influences. Let us try to make clear how the interrelationship of the divine world-existence with the will, with the feeling, and with the divine-spiritual cognition, has yielded up the human soul.

Let us try at this moment to feel deep, deep in our souls, what in the lands in the east, west, south, north, *those* human souls out there feel today—those whom we may recognize as the best, but who do not go beyond what we can express with the words: an indeterminate, insufficient longing and hoping for the spirit. Look around you, my dear sisters and brothers, and see how this indeterminate longing, this indeterminate hope in the spirit prevails in today's humanity!

Feel, listening, here at the foundation stone of our true embodiment of spiritual truth, how there is present in the indeterminate longing and hope of humankind for the spirit, an audible cry for that answer—for that answer which can be given where spiritual science prevails with its Gospel of the announcement of the spirit. Try to inscribe into your souls the greatness of the moment we are passing through this evening. If we can hear the longing call of humankind for the spirit and want to erect the building of truth (*Wahrbau*) from which is to be proclaimed more and more the message of the spirit—if we feel this in the life of the everyday world, then we rightly understand ourselves on this evening. Then we know, not in arrogance and not in an overestimation of our striving, but in humility, in devotion, and in willingness to sacrifice, that we must be, in our humble striving, those who will continue the  spiritual work which has been initiated in the Occident in the course of advancing human development—but which ultimately must lead through the necessary counter-stream of the ahrimanic forces; so that today, humanity stands at a point where souls would have to wither and become sclerotic if that cry of longing for the spirit were not answered. Let us, my dear sisters and brothers, feel these fears! This is how it must be if we continue to struggle in that great spiritual struggle—which is a struggle—glowing-through with the fire of love; in that great spiritual struggle of which we may be those who will continue that which was led by our ancestors when they deflected the ahrimanic onslaught of the Moors over yonder.

We stand, led by karma, at this moment, in the place through which important spiritual streams have passed: Let us feel within ourselves on this evening the seriousness of the situation! Once, humankind had reached the end-point of the striving for personality. In the fullness of this earthly personality, when the old heirloom from the divine leadership of the primal beginning of Earth evolution had withered away, the World Word appeared over yonder in the East:

> In the Primal Beginning was the Word
> And the Word was with God
> And a God was the Word.

> *Im Urbeginne war das Wort*
> *Und das Wort war bei Gott*
> *Und ein Gott war das Wort.*

And the Word appeared to human souls and spoke to human souls: Fill Earth evolution with the meaning (*Sinn*) of the Earth. Now, the Word itself has passed over into the Earth aura, has been taken up by the spiritual aura of the Earth.

Fourfold has the World Word been proclaimed through the centuries, which are soon to become two millennia. Thus, the World Light has illumined within the Earth evolution.

Ahriman sank ever deeper and must sink deeper still. Let us feel ourselves surrounded by human souls in which there resounds the cry of longing for the spirit. But let us feel, my dear sisters and brothers, how these human souls would have to remain with the general cry of longing because Ahriman, the dark

Ahriman, spreads chaos over the aspired-to spiritual knowledge of the worlds of the higher hierarchies. Feel that the possibility is at hand in our time to add to the fourfold proclaimed spiritual word that other one which I can also only present in symbols.

From the east, it came over—the Light and the Word of the proclamation. From out of the east, it went over to the west, proclaimed fourfold in the Four Gospels, awaiting that from the west would come the mirror, which will add *knowledge* (*Erkenntnis*) to what is still *proclamation* (*Verkündigung*) in the fourfold -pronounced World Word. Deeply moved are our hearts and souls when we hear the Sermon on the Mount, which was spoken when the times of maturation of the human personality were fulfilled; when the old light of the spirit had disappeared and the new spiritual light appeared. The new spiritual light has appeared! But since it appeared, it went through the centuries of human evolution from the east to the west, waiting for the understanding of the words which once sounded in the Sermon on the Mount into human hearts. From the depths of our world evolution, there resounds that primeval prayer which was spoken as the proclamation of the World Word—since fulfilled by the Mystery of Golgotha. And there sounded deeply the eternal prayer, which was to announce to the microcosm in the deepest recesses of the soul—out of the innermost essence of the human heart—the secret of existence. It was to resound in what has been proclaimed to us as the Lord's Prayer, when it resounded from the east to the west. But so waiting, this World Word restrained itself—and at that time sank into the microcosm—so that one day it might sound together with the Fifth Gospel; the souls of human beings had to further ripen in order to understand what from the West, as the most ancient, as the macrocosmic Gospel, as an echo, is now to sound, encountering the Gospel of the East.

If we meet the present moment with understanding, then we will also have an understanding that to the Four Gospels a Fifth can be added. So, this evening, in addition to the microcosmic secrets, may the words sound forth expressing the secrets of the macrocosm. As the first part of the Fifth Gospel shall sound here the most ancient Macrocosmic World-Prayer, which is bonded with the Moon and Jupiter, just as the Four Gospels are bonded with the Earth:

AUM, Amen!
The evils are working,
Witness to a loosening egoity
Selfhood's debt from others incurred
Experienced in the daily bread
As Heaven's will no longer prevails,
For human beings have been separated from your kingdom
And forgotten Your names
You Fathers in the heavens.

*AUM, Amen!*
*Es walten die Übel,*
*Zeugen sich lösender Ichheit*
*Von andern erschuldete Selbstheitsschuld,*
*Erlebet im täglichen Brote,*
*In dem nicht waltet der Himmel Wille,*
*Da der Mensch sich schied von Eurem Reich*
*Und vergaß Euren Namen,*
*Ihr Väter in den Himmeln.*

The Lord's Prayer had been given as the prayer of humanity. The microcosmic Lord's Prayer, which was proclaimed from the east to the west, is now encountered by the sounding of the most ancient macrocosmic prayer. So it sounds again when—rightly understood by human souls—it sounds out into the world expanses and is given back with the words which have been imprinted from out of the macrocosm. Let us take it with us—the Macrocosmic Lord's Prayer—feeling that with it we begin to gain understanding for the Gospel of Knowledge (*Erkenntnis*): The Fifth Gospel. Let us carry home from this important moment with earnestness and dignity in our soul—our will; let us carry home the certainty that all the wisdom for which the human soul is seeking—if the seeking is genuine—is a counter-stream of the cosmic wisdom; and all human love—rooted in the selfless love of the soul—is fructified from the love that is prevailing in human evolution.

Throughout all times on Earth and into all human souls—out of the strong human will that is filled with the meaning of the Earth—through the cosmic force, there works a strengthening, which humanity, indeterminately directing its gaze toward a spirit, craves for today. A spirit whom it hopes for, but does not want to recognize; for Ahriman has sunk an unconscious horror into the human soul wherever the spirit is spoken of today. Let us feel this, my dear sisters and brothers, at this moment. If you feel this, so will you be able to ready yourselves for your spiritual work, and as those who can reveal spiritual light "then also to bear witness with the force of thinking; when over fully awakened spiritual vision, dark Ahriman—dampening wisdom—wants to spread the darkness of chaos." My sisters and brothers, fill up your souls with the longing for real spirit *knowledge* (*Erkenntnis*), for true human *love*, for strong *willing*. And try within yourselves to stir up that spirit who can trust the speech of the World Word, which stands facing us out of world distances and out of the widths of space, sounding into our souls. This is what the one who has grasped the meaning of existence must really feel this evening: Human souls are at a limit of their striving. Feel in humility—not in pride—in devotion and willingness to sacrifice—not in overestimating yourselves—what is to become of that which is the true embodiment of the spirit (*Wahrzeichen*) for which we have laid the foundation stone today. Feel the significance of the knowledge, which becomes significant because we are able to know: In our time, in the widths of space, the Sheath of Spirit Beings (*die Hülle der geistigen Wesenheiten*) must be penetrated, when the Spirit Beings come to speak to us of the meaning of existence (*Sinn des Daseins*). All and everywhere in the periphery, human souls will have to take up and absorb the meaning of existence. Hear how in the diverse places of spirit, where spiritual science, religion, and art are spoken of and enacted in accord with their true meaning; hear how the striving forces of souls are becoming ever more sclerotic; feel that you should learn to fertilize these souls, these striving forces of the soul, out of spirit Imaginations, Inspirations, and Intuitions. Feel what one will find who will rightly hear the tone of creative spirituality.

Those who, in addition to the old Lord's Prayer, will learn to understand the sense of the prayer of the Fifth Gospel—they will be able to fundamentally recognize this meaning out of our turning point of time.

If we will learn to understand the sense of these words, so will we seek to take up the seeds that must blossom if Earth evolution is not to wither, if it should continue to fruit and flourish; so that the Earth—through human will—can thereby achieve the goal set for it from the primal beginning.

So, feel on this evening that the wisdom and the sense of the new knowledge, the new love, and the new potent force must become alive in human souls. The souls that will work in the blossom and the fruit of future evolutions of the Earth will have to become those who understand what we today, for the first time, want to incorporate into our souls: the macrocosmic, further-resounding voice of the most ancient eternal prayer:

> AUM, Amen!
> The evils are working,
> Witness to a loosening egoity,
> Selfhood's debt from others incurred,
> Experienced in the daily bread,
> As heaven's will no longer prevails,
> For human beings have been separated from your kingdom
> And forgotten Your names,
> You Fathers in the heavens.

So we now depart—taking with us in our souls the consciousness of the significance of the earnestness and dignity of the act we have carried out—the consciousness of this evening that shall remain . . . igniting in us the striving for knowledge of a new revelation given to humanity, for which the human soul thirsts; from which it will drink, but only when it will fearlessly gain faith and trust in that which can proclaim the science of the spirit, which in turn shall unite what for a while must pass separated through the evolution of humankind: religion, art, and science. Let us take this, my sisters and brothers, with us, as something of a commemoration of this collaboratively celebrated hour that we no longer may forget.

RUDOLF STEINER

# The Longing of the Soul for the Spirit:
# A Sign of the Times
# Commemorative Address on September 20, 1914

Today, I would like to remember *Christian Morgenstern* in a way connected with the manner in which he approached this spiritual movement of ours from his own spiritual life that he had lived through before he joined our stream.[91] In a certain respect, this way of Christian Morgenstern is only an individual case, a representative case for impulses, for forces and elements which can be felt in the whole of modern spiritual life and which were hovering before my soul at the time when we laid the foundation stone for our building one year ago today. Around the place where our foundation stone was laid, I had to point out, at that time, how something was to be done, how something was to be established with this building; something which meets the longings, the spiritual hopes of individual human beings in the present; and something which will do this more and more in the future. It had to be emphasized that unconsciously hovering within souls is the longing for the spiritual life contained in our spiritual stream. Souls long for this spiritual life, only they do not know it. And something would like to be given (so it was emphasized) [for these souls], not out of the arbitrariness of a human being or a society, but out of the signs of the times, out of what the times are driving towards, what the souls of the times are striving for—mostly unconsciously, perhaps—souls who for this or that reason are very much opposed to the form in which the more recent spiritual life, the new spiritual stream, must initially make its entry into world history.

When I had to finish the second volume of my *Riddles of Philosophy*, there was a question: whether—since for nearly thirteen years our spiritual stream had existed (even in public

275

life)—the last chapter should contain a reference to our anthroposophy. Of course, only a part of the rich content that has passed through our souls for so many years could be indicated on the few sheets that could be dedicated to actual spiritual science. Naturally, the question had to arise before me: What is the most important thing that must enter first into modern human souls? The most important thing that must enter is the knowledge that there is a spiritual life that exists and weaves in the human being—independent of the human body—and that this spiritual life is the same that unfolds from embodiment to embodiment in repeated earthly lives. Leaving aside all the other things that have passed through our souls, these two truths are those which, one might say, still enter into modern spiritual life as something quite foreign. To the materialistic sense, they appear foolish and fantastic, as a contradiction to the entire scientific spirit of these new times. This is how they appear to the materialistic sense. But they are taken in with long drafts by the soul which has really participated in the longings and hopes, in the forces and impulses of the modern spiritual life—that soul which has rejoiced at the return of spiritual proclamation, and which has been sick in regard to the spiritual life of our time, at the impossibility of extracting from the outer life something which justifies speaking of a spiritual world in spite of all modern science.

One might say, such a concern remains only for a while hovering in the spiritual atmosphere—only for a while; but then comes the age when such a concern penetrates into the sphere of everyday life itself. And here is the point where the concern of our spiritual movement announces itself directly as that which must become—in the most intimate sense of the word—a concern of the heart of humanity. Today, one can still speak as if our spiritual movement addresses only individual souls who are interested in it; as if it were only for those souls who can feel what must enter into modern spiritual life. But already the times are before us when souls will become atrophied, for the spiritual atmosphere under the influences of materialism does not give any life-forces to these souls. You, my dear friends, you have all reached the time at which—because so much is still left behind from the more or less spiritual impulses of a more spiritual past—your souls are not yet so atrophied; your souls are still looking for the breadths of the spirit; but you do not know the desolation that will already occur in the next generation if the impulse of spiritual culture does not flow into humankind. Those who are young children today will go towards a life that will incessantly ask them the question—not theoretically, but in life itself: For what do we live? For what, this barren existence? And standing horrifically before our souls in the future: the pale faces of those who are young children today—distorted by the needs and worries of life—for whom nothing can shine through material life to give comfort to the soul in the face of that desolation, which is all that can take hold in the life of human beings while materialism alone exists. Then, my dear friends, comes that great compassion, that all-inclusive empathy, which swells in the soul; that sympathy with those who will come—and who will only be able to find the Earth worth living on if that which spiritual science is able to give is prepared in the spiritual atmosphere of this, our Earth. O, the proclamations of the past: they were strong and powerful; in them pulsated that spiritual life which today in outer life can still sustain those people who do not want to receive into consciousness the news of the spiritual world. But we live in the age in which this will pass away, in which this comes to an end. It is for the *future* that we want to create the forms that compose our building.

Truly, we see them—the longings and hopes that have been spoken of—if only we just look into the souls of modern human beings. I said that one of the most important things that humankind must first understand is the teaching of repeated earthly lives. A time will come when the person who does not know about repeated earthly lives, who has not heard anything about them, will stand before life as before a wasteland. In individual souls who are connected with the whole of modern spiritual life, the idea arose; it arose, as it were, in such a way that—if one wants to describe how it appeared—one has to say that there are souls who ask themselves: How do we get along in life, when we look around and are confronted with such peculiar phenomena? How do we manage? Then such souls, standing just so in the modern spiritual life, come and say to themselves: Oh, in my phantasy, at least, I must envision something of an idea of immortality, which at first is quite remote from the materialistic consciousness of the time! This idea of immortality sometimes meets us in remarkable places of modern spiritual life. I would like to point to such a place as a symptom. On another occasion I have pointed out in the case of the same modern personality that this idea of immortality does appear in him—but you will see in the very first sentence in what way it appears!

Herman Grimm, the distinguished exponent of the arts in recent times—a personality with whom I was given the opportunity to speak many a word—once wrote the following words (one would like to say, strangely enough) in an essay which actually spoke of a completely different subject:[92]

> It is possible to conceive of a condition where the spirit of a human being, detached from the bodily bonds, hovers over the Earth like a mere mirror of events.

(Now right away comes, one would like to say, the hesitation!)

> I'm not stating an article of faith here; it's just a phantasy.

(But this phantasy is necessary. . . .)

> Let us suppose that for some human beings, immortality would take shape in such a way that they would float over the Earth, unconstrained by what used to blind them, and all the destinies of the Earth and of human beings, since the birth of the planet, would be revealed to them. The past would be to them a fabric of harmonious beauty. Every thought of every heart would be a necessary part of it; every deed that we call good or that we condemn—the falling of a tree leaf and the collapse of whole cities under which the ground begins to move—everything would have equal rank among the incidents; because it was the same single force that moved everything.
>
> Now suddenly—let us dream on—

(Herman Grimm does not dare to grasp the thought as a reality. . . .)

> this spirit, which so freely looked over things, would perhaps be forced to be bound again to the body of a mortal human being. If the highest talents of every kind

were bestowed on this human being, then would it nevertheless be the case that only just the memory of the
previous state is possible?

(The idea of reincarnation! . . . Now he unfolds the thought:
how the soul—which he has only thought hovering above the
Earth in a disembodied state—would have to return again into
an earthly body.)

> They would be born in a certain age. They would have
> a father and mother, a homeland, a class, a heart that
> loves and hates, vanities, pains, joy, displeasure, de-
> spair, delight—when, even in a moment, would they
> be capable of the free lucidity that was once their el-
> ement? They would begin to doubt whether they had
> ever really enjoyed freedom; and soon the memory
> of it would reside hidden deep in their soul, pressed
> into a dim foreboding. Whereas they otherwise had the
> hearts of human beings before their eyes like a glass
> beehive—where they saw thoughts flying in and out
> and working—they now must merely guess at them
> like secret mysteries.[93]

(And so on.)

These are such passages, my dear friends, wherein we are
confronted with the modern human longing for what we want,
and what, in the form that it must first appear before humanity,
seems so improbable to this humanity.

Our building and our work on it are, as it were, the vow that
we want to work devotedly to study the longings and hopes of
modern human beings in order to find from the spiritual world
what can meet these longings, these hopes. This is what I had to
say when one year ago the foundation stone was laid.[94]

I would also like to mention another passage from Herman
Grimm. Human beings today consider the history of the past, the
historical life and development, purely according to the course
of the external facts; and, more and more, materialism has led
to this historical life and development being considered in this
way. Yes, if one puts what is called history today next to what
we try to describe as successive lives in the post-Atlantean time,
then it becomes understandable how little can be understood today of what we say—also concerning historical matters—of that

which must come and for which our building should be a true embodiment of the spirit. But the longing for it is present, the deep longing![95] A little-known essay by Herman Grimm contains words that are particularly valuable to me because they basically reflect a conversation I once had with him in Weimar.[96] Herman Grimm says there that an expansion of the concept of history is imminent.

> Today a world-historic upheaval is taking place before our eyes, such as has never been experienced in any epoch of history, as far as we are able to survey it. The peoples of Europe are suddenly demanding to be on their own. The mutual influence of the races on each other is to be denied altogether in theory, and reduced to a minimum in practice. This new conception is not the fruit of a doctrine instituted by the educated, but of a natural instinct, quaking the different peoples to their depths. It does not emerge in the individuals, but it moves the masses. . . .
>
> Something has secretly ripened, and the last events are the storm that shakes it from the tree. There is a universal law according to which great masses of people repel and attract each other in connection with their ability to bring about general spiritual progress, either by joining together or by separating themselves. . . .
>
> What we now generally call "history" is the lore of the coexistence of those peoples who have held the peninsula of Europe, adjoining Asia to the West, in the course of the last three or four thousand years.[97]

Herman Grimm once said, in view of *history*, that he foresees a time in which all those who are regarded as the most outstanding of the nineteenth century will no longer be regarded as such, but will rather become entirely other people who will emerge from the dark twilight of time. History has been prepared in such a way that, as it has evolved in the course of time, a transformation of the human soul is necessary for an evaluation [of history] today, a transformation down to the deepest roots of [the soul's] life. I have emphasized this viewpoint again and again, but it cannot be said often enough.[98]

Yes, my dear friends, out of the offerings of modern spiritual life, without our spiritual science, it is impossible to achieve that which is longed for. People are striving for a new history—for a new view of historical development—which is characterized by the words I have just read out. But this longing cannot be fulfilled anywhere because the elements, the forces, the impulses for it are missing. One would like to say: As a longing that is present, present in the best of our time, we strive for the fulfillment of this longing.

But the connection of this longing with what we are striving for in all modesty goes particularly deep for me when I consider how art itself has taken this course through humanity; when I consider how this art took its starting point from the spiritual revelations that came down to human beings in the primitive culture of peoples, from the spiritual fathers themselves; how then that which lay in the primitive culture of peoples was fertilized by the Christ impulse; how this Christ impulse also made its way into the artistic forms, but how we then came to a dead point—to that dead point precisely of the artistic development upon which humanity now stands. With pain I have immersed myself in the life of those artists who tried to find from the bottom of their hearts what will bring spirit again to modern art. The life of serious artists has become tragic, and it is tragic even in the face of world history, because there is a search for something that can also go into the forms, and because only that which comes from a real, actual grasp of the spiritual world can speak to this search. How human longing finds itself—just as it is rooted in the deeper sensations of those who suffer from modern culture—how it finds itself harmoniously together with what our spiritual movement is able to give! We must think back to the Stuttgart cycle *At the Gates of Theosophy*, where I spoke of the Christian Initiation and gave the Washing of the Feet as the first stage.

Many years lie behind us now, when out of the spirit was spoken how the plant must bow to the stone, how it owes to it the ground of existence; likewise, the animal bows to the plant, and the human being to the animal, up to the hierarchies of the spirits. This also lived as a longing in Christian Morgenstern; it united harmoniously with what was thus spoken; and we hear resounding again that which was given to that longing, what spiritual science was able to give to such longing; we hear it resounding again in the poem which we have also heard today—"The Washing of the Feet": "I thank you, you silent stone."

It gives me a picture of the way in which the longing of the finest human beings in this modern age will grow together with what spiritual science has to give us. These longings will flow into the mental pictures, into the ideas, into the whole intellectual life. But as I said, it has been in pain that I have looked at those artists who were searching for content for their art. Carstens stands before my eyes, Overbeck, Cornelius: they tried to bring the Christ impulse into their art—all in vain. Just study a life as tragic as that of Cornelius, with whom Herman Grimm was so close. In the form that Christianity had taken, he sought to find the living life of Christ—in the form that it could penetrate his soul to then flow out into his art. But he lived within the dead point. One can look at modern architecture: we walk through—not the artistically created—but rather through the preserved, prepared herbarium of old art styles. Only the living connection with the Christ impulse will be able to infuse life into these art forms. But precisely that part of the Christ impulse which is living—that which penetrates into the forms—from what has flowed into human beings through the Mystery of Golgotha. For the forms do not come to life by merely speaking of Him [Christ]—without whom human life is also dead in art.

What we were able to create, both with our spiritual movement and with our building, is nothing more than a beginning; the very first beginning of a building style which one day is to come, which one day must come. But it is precisely this that we are trying to do with our spiritual movement: to take up the impulse of the Mystery of Golgotha into our souls; to absorb it completely; and to absorb it in the way in which a humanity of the future will need it. In this context, I must also remember words that yet again Herman Grimm wrote in an essay, in which he divides humankind's evolution in a certain way (I mentioned this already in the Hague Cycle,[99] namely that he distinguishes three millennia: one before the Mystery of Golgotha, then the millennium of the Mystery of Golgotha, and one after). I would like to specifically call before your souls today words with which Herman Grimm characterizes the second millennium, because, again, these words reveal something of the longings of modern human beings. They are words which can penetrate deeply into the soul, if you look directly at what is living in the hopes of modern times and which essentially can be made fertile only by spiritual science.

The second millennium: Christ is here before our eyes in two forms. First of all, as the creeds of the religions have him appear:

> Christ must not, as a historical personality, stand in a series with other great men. He towers above them and is surrounded with a semblance of untouchability. Many, therefore, treat the great phenomena of history apart from Christ in a special way. They take Christ's relation to everything else for granted. But we cannot evade him, for example, as too exalted, since he himself and personalities connected with him meet us at every turn; and since also the overpowering spiritual authorities living before Christ—I mention Socrates or Plato—can only be understood in comparison with him today.
>
> A man of high rank, who venerated Ranke, is said to have demanded from him that Christ should be introduced into the "history of the world" as the initiator of all human destinies. This demand (it is reported) caused fierce inner struggles in scholars, but ultimately it was rejected, with the notion that the already existing explanation was sufficient. Christ faces us in world history in a double form: as the founder of Christianity, and as the superhuman, all-capable Son of God, as the Church teaches. I hold this dual figure of Christ to be a historically unworkable one. We have not to explain Christ, but to accept him and the effect of his teaching as fact. Christ's works are to be included in the account of the course of world events. In the history of Roman politics, the birth and transformation of the Earth by Christ belongs as an event of world-shaping power, and is not to be relegated to Church history as a special chapter. The teachings of Christ have been effective from the time of Christ's appearance. Not only did Titus destroy Jerusalem on their account, but they are also to blame for the fact that from Augustus' reign onwards, Latin and Greek poetry and fine arts moved downwards from the heights, because their innermost lifeblood was missing from then on. The attempts to

represent Christ as the most beautiful, divine human being soon began, until these attempts reach their highest expression in Raphael's paintings. This took many centuries; but the direction towards this goal is recognizable. Raphael's significance will not be measured by any other view of history, while at the same time no one who understands modern history in this way would be compelled—either as writer or as reader—to confess or even hint at their own thoughts about Christ, if they do not want to. For to dismiss these things in us stands with us alone as a human right. Scholars whose work has consisted in the study of Greek history have, to the widest extent, regarded it with such enthusiasm that zealots might accuse them of pagan beliefs. Nothing would be more unjust. The development of the Greek mind is as beautiful and worth knowing as that of the whole world that touches us, or that of a flower, or that of any law in the field of chemistry.

If we look for the reason why Ranke could have been in doubt for a while as to whether or not the double historical figure of Christ should be retained, then it is perhaps also here a matter of special inclinations which are observable in every historian. . . . He lifts us then easily to a height, but this height is not the highest. . . . One would have to find out what he intentionally left unmentioned in his history of the popes. . . . Perhaps he let himself be flattered by those who wanted to rise on account of him, but he renounced praise that was bought, and loved quiet, untrodden paths on which he met no one. If such a man, growing old, embraces everything that has happened, his worldview is of lasting value. But it does not reveal the future. . . .

New world relationships, we feel, are forming. Nothing has yet remained spiritually untouched by them. A veil already covers the nineteenth century: something that forms a perceptible partition between us and the nearest past. Again and again the question resounds in secret and aloud: Where do we want to go; where must we go? In all areas of human existence, this uncertainty prevails. It generates strange new contemplations. Reformations are taking place before our eyes.[100]

Think, my dear friends: a human being who strives to find

spiritual life in the life of humankind, to whom even the Christ hovers before his eyes in double form, but who does not want to speak of the form which is not the simply human one! Because Herman Grimm says further:

> I believe that for the history of the future, the beginnings of the community founded by [the Christ]—as the real vitality of humanity's history—points to the Christ as a historically established power of the highest rank. . . .
>
> The history of Christ, the growing authority of his thought, and general political progress, make up an intertwined fabric. Raphael's inner urge to portray Christ himself and his experiences sprang not from chance, but from the nature of his Italian nationality. . . .
>
> We see that the most widespread book today, translated into all the languages of the world—the New Testament—is compatible with other books of national origin. These other books are recognized, at the same time as the Gospels, as the source of our spiritual elevation and formation—although there seems to be an unbridgeable gap between them and the Gospels. These other books, in contrast to the doubtful authors of the Gospels, have definite authors, who live on at the same time as their works. The most distinguished of them were poets; others were visual artists; next to them are the philosophers who observed nature; and the end of the line is formed by statesmen and generals. These men of the highest national rank rule over the peoples (*Völkern*), back to their most distant past, and their relationship to the character of the people and to the doctrines of international Christianity determines everywhere today the present and the future. A wonderful contrast.
>
> Christ knows only the undistinguished humanity for whose redemption He sacrificed Himself. . . .
>
> The most powerful men known to the millennia of human history have been five poets living before and after Christ: David, Homer, Dante, Shakespeare, Goethe. An Oriental, a Greek, an Italian, and two Teutons. Very different in their careers and in their poetic power, but similar in the scope of the still increasing impact of their works. They are also alike in that we penetrate

their souls most deeply. For these five we know best out of all human beings of earlier life. Yes, one could say, we know them alone. For Christ, we do not know. Him we marvel at.[101]

But where is the possibility to present the Christ in a new form to humankind?—in such a way that it will no longer be necessary to say: "These five we know best out of all human beings of earlier life. Yes, one could say, we know them alone. For Christ, we do not know. Him we marvel at."

If humankind will once decide to receive the spiritual-scientific form of the Christ into their hearts, then the epoch will have come for which human beings long; because they cannot yet see the form which the Christ must take if he is to correspond to their longings.[102] If one enters the path which leads to spiritual science, then one will find the possibility to speak about the Christ in such a way that, through this, life, content, and security will again enter into the souls of human beings—that security which is at the same time the security of peace itself. For is it not like a question which is asked but still stands there without an answer when Herman Grimm says that he believes: for the history of the future, the forming of the first Christian community, as the real vitality of humanity's history, points to the Christ as a historically established power of the highest rank?

Spiritual science is the answer to such questions; the answer that must be given today. Because just with reference to the contemplation of Christ, humankind has arrived here at a dead point. Truly, it is what Herman Grimm feels, who had only the questions but not the answer!

One will have to hold back the answer as long as it is not firmly founded in the manner of spiritual science.

But how is it still, my dear friends, with the placement of this form of Christ in the culture of the present? How far away is that which is pulsating through the souls of today from that which we must seek as this form of Christ! Yes, rather, one must say that that of which Herman Grimm spoke as being unpleasant regarding the biographers of Christ is confronting us more and more. Because it has become more and more bleak as to how human beings of the present try to understand the Christ merely out of the knowledge given by outer cultural life. The tones with which the Christ was characterized in past centuries are worn out and can no longer live in the modern soul. For this very purpose, new tones, new ways are needed. Therefore, we see how the representations of Christ become more and more bleak, when these representations of Christ cannot draw from that which spiritual science intends to make accessible to humankind. As they approach the present, they become more and more bleak. And we have experienced the bleakest—I would like to say—in a portrayal of Christ in a very bad drama of a grand prince, which represents a blasphemy on everything that has happened through and around Christ, and which so rightly proves the base level of the portrayals of what has happened through the Christ. How our spiritual life, according to the means of the present, ends up in the impossible: this is shown precisely by this abominable Christ drama, which, in its entire spirit, is actually an anti-Christ drama. But out of the spiritual life of the present, longings develop which are a good soil and become more and more a good soil, out of which can sprout what we strive to put into it as seeds—in this soil full of hopes and longings, in this soil, within which must transform into certainties the hopes and longings of those who today already live as young children but would be condemned to live unhappily if spiritual science does not come among humankind.[103]

Everywhere we see these longings; we see them also as the ground from which the unfortunate Christ drama sprouted, of which I have spoken. We also see the longing for the understanding of this Christ impulse—but we also see, so to speak, the lack of understanding that is brought to this true longing for true understanding. There was something quite strange for me, I must confess, when I read the words which Solovyov had written. I discovered them only recently; they made a special impression on me—you can guess why! The most diverse attacks have come from this or that side in recent times—Jesuit, I was called from one side; Jew, in another place—because of this, I had to have my baptismal certificate photographed. Well, my dear friends, that doesn't matter; these are the necessary side-effects of being forced to say—even if only with stammering words—what humanity needs. But also, those others, who speak of the longings for a right understanding of Christ, have been able to report on a remarkable insight that was presented to them. Hence, the words of Solovyov, spoken in 1886:

> I am literally persecuted; my writings are banned because they are said to be harmful to Russia and Orthodoxy. Today, I am supposed to be a Jesuit, tomorrow a Jew, etc., so that one must be prepared for everything.[104]

My dear friends, some of what is to be said as that which meets the deepest but also the most necessary longings and hopes of life—some of it is already harmful! And one is of the opinion that it must not be allowed! Only when the people of the present time come to regard the painful events of the present as a trial and let themselves be led to a spiritual life in the sense that I was allowed to suggest yesterday will they learn to see the necessity of these present painful events and judge them differently from their immediate impressions. Yes, my dear friends, with human beings who speak like Solovyov it will always be possible to communicate; one will find the way to them beyond all national differences. But it is not I, it is Solovyov—a member of the Russian people of whom I spoke yesterday—the same Solovyov who spoke words on behalf of those who are so intimately connected with what depresses us so painfully today—it is he who characterizes this clique with the words:

> Our governmental, ecclesiastical, and literary scoundrels are so brazen, and the public is so foolish, that one must be prepared for everything. . . .
> All my writings, not only the new ones, but also the reprints, are *absolutely* banned.

"Our governmental scoundrels are so brazen . . ."—of course, he speaks of those who have "absolutely banned" *his* writings.

My dear friends: Today, as we stand once again before the unfinished building for which we laid the foundation stone a year ago, let us take within ourselves the vow that we want to hold faithfully to what spiritual science can give us. Let us consciously take in the understanding that spiritual science can meet the longings and hopes, the needs of humanity. Let us take in this consciousness that spiritual science will make it possible for humanity—in such a way that even free spirits like Herman Grimm did not dare to speak—to speak as it is necessary to about the

Christ impulse—especially under the impression of the painful events of today. And let us take into ourselves the consciousness that if we learn to speak properly about the *Christ*, we will learn to speak properly about the *history of humankind*. For the Christ does not belong to *one* people; the Christ belongs to all human beings. The Christ did not speak to the members of *one* people: You are my brother . . . . He spoke it to all of the members of humanity. We then find the way to every human being and to those peaceful choirs of all higher hierarchies—and we find the way to the Christ.

This, my dear friends, must also be a foundation stone which we want to lay in our heart, upon which we want to build the invisible building for which the visible building is the outer symbolum (*Symbolum*). May this outer symbolum, in a primitive, elementary way, fulfill at least in part that which we tried to call for from the world powers a year ago! May it be fulfilled for our salvation that in these forms one sees how the spirit—which has communicated itself to the Earth through the Mystery of Golgotha—flows through our forms, seizes the forms, penetrates them with the Christ impulse; so that permeating the soul is the consciousness that is expressed in the words which are still not understood deeply enough: Not I, the Christ in me! May this building (even if it represents only imperfectly what is wanted), may it also gain for human beings, at least in a small measure, what it wants—to make the impression on those human souls who enter it: Not I, not my personal self is that which makes an impression on the eye through the external forms—but rather the *Christ* will speak; He who seeks an expression, a revelation through the Word of the higher hierarchies . . . . And this building is to be "the mouth"!

May then the souls, finding themselves in the spirit of this building, feel somewhat pervaded by a similar inner sensation (*Empfindung*), which can be called: *inner sensation of the connection of the individual human soul with the Earth's soul* . . . . and pervaded by the sensation of how this soul of the Earth lives today, how it has lived since the beginning of the Earth, how it lives in all souls! May this soul then feel like a spirit by the mouth of God; may this soul speak like Christian Morgenstern:

The animal, the plant, these beings had

still the un-human patience of the Earth;
there was a year, what today is yet a second.
Now nothing proceeds fast enough for her.
The human being began its impatient becoming.
She feels: "Now, finally, has the great hour come:
for this have I cultivated myself over millennia.
Now I no longer need to save my body,
now I will soon hang as a spirit at the mouth of God."

*Das Tier, die Pflanze, diese Wesen hatten*
*noch die un-menschliche Geduld der Erde;*
*da war ein Jahr, was heut nur noch Sekunde.*
*Jetzt geht ihr nichts mehr rasch genug von statten.*
*Der Mensch begann sein ungeduldig Werde.*
*Sie spürt: "Jetzt endlich kam die große Stunde:*
*auf die ich mich gezüchtet Jahrmillionen.*
*Jetzt brauch ich meinen Leib nicht mehr zu schonen,*
*jetzt häng ich bald als Geist an Gottes Munde."*

May such inner sensations be able to enter the souls of more and more people as they live into our building's forms! That is what our building is for. It should never be claimed that it presents what it should be—not even with a small degree of perfection does it present itself so. In the highest imperfection it presents what it can prefigure for the hopes and longings of more recent times. But even if we never presume to speak of the hour of the laying of the foundation stone as the great hour of world existence, but rather want to speak of it as the small hour of world existence—even if we say that we may contribute only a little, something modest to evolution, to the great tasks of humanity—we still want to sense the great tasks of existence to which, even if with modest means, we are to dedicate that which, one year ago, we laid with the foundation stone.

Endnotes

91      See Rudolf Steiner: *Christian Morgenstern, der Sieg des Lebens über den Tod* [Christian Morgenstern, the victory of life over death], edited by Marie Steiner (Dornach: Philosophisch-Anthroposophicher Verlag, 1935).

92      Herman Grimm, "Frederick the Great and Macaulay," in *Literature*, 137f.

93      See also Rudolf Steiner, "The Relativity of Knowledge and Spiritual Cosmology," in *Dying Earth and Living Cosmos*, lecture in Berlin on Apr. 1, 1918.

94      Rudolf Steiner, "Building Forms as Culture- and World-Sensing Thoughts." CW 181.

95      Rudolf Steiner, *Architecture as Peacework*.

96      Rudolf Steiner, *Initiation, Eternity and the Passing Moment*, lecture in Munich on Aug. 25, 1912, CW 138.

97      Cf. Hermann Grimm, "Voltaire and Frederick the Great," in *Literature*, 121f. In [a lecture given a few weeks later in Dornach, on Oct. 7, titled,] "Times of Expectation," Dr. Steiner says:

> For Herman Grimm, "history" was not an enumeration of what is usually recorded as history. He wanted that this history could be for him an evolution of the spiritual forces—but, for this, he could only rise up to the level where history was for him a development of the capacity of phantasy. The fact that there are Imaginations in humanity which unconsciously flow into humanity in order to be implemented through human activity; that history is based on Inspiration and Intuition—this could not dawn on him. To him, history was a work of phantasy by the peoples (*Völker*). He could only come to the point of peeling away Maya by means of what he called the works of phantasy by the peoples (*Völker*)—and he could not come to what must present itself to the human spirit if this spirit wills to find the ascent from the physical world into the spiritual world. Only later will one really understand what it meant for the nineteenth century when Herman Grimm says: Of what special interest can it be for us how history has given Julius Caesar back to us! Julius Caesar—thought Herman Grimm—interests me much more, as he is

presented by Shakespeare. This is more true than all that a historian of today writes about him. Again and again, he pointed out how much he liked to read Tacitus because he is a person who knows how to enliven through the soul what he has to depict, to transform it into the spiritual. And so, out of such preconditions, such a wonderful thought arose as the one that Herman Grimm wrote down in the nineties and which is written in his book on Homer—a thought that really stands there like an expectation of what should come as a pronouncement from the hierarchies.

Rudolf Steiner, *Inner Reading and Inner Hearing*, lecture in Dornach on Oct. 7, 1914, CW 156.

98      See also Rudolf Steiner, *The Karma of Materialism*, lecture in Berlin on Sept. 18, 1917; Rudolf Steiner, *Initiation, Eternity and the Passing Moment*, lecture in Munich on Aug. 25, 1912. CW 176 and CW 138.

99      Rudolf Steiner, *The Effects of Esoteric Development*, lecture in the Hague on Mar. 28, 1913, CW138:

100      Herman Grimm, "Raphael als Weltmacht", 467– 471.

101      Ibid., 458.

102      Cf. Rudolf Steiner on Hermann Grimm in *Building Stones for an Understanding of the Mystery of Golgotha*, lecture in Berlin on Apr. 14, 1917, CW 175, p. 205f.

103      Cf. Rudolf Steiner, *Et Incarnatus Est*, lecture in Basel on Dec. 23, 1917, CW 180.

104      Letter from Vladimir Solovyov to Faivel Meir Bentsilovich Getz, December 1886, in *The Burning Bush*, translated from the Russian by Gregory Yuri Glazov, 406–407:

You, probably, know that I am now enduring a direct persecution. Every composition of mine, not only a new one, but also a reprint of an old one, is unconditionally forbidden. The Ober-Procurator of the Synod P(obedonosts)ev told one of my friends that every activity of mine is harmful to Russia and Orthodoxy and, consequently, cannot be tolerated. And in order to justify this decision, various fables are invented and disseminated about me. Today I have become a Jesuit, while tomorrow, perhaps, I'll be circumcised; at present I serve the pope and Bishop Strossmayer, while tomorrow I will probably serve the Alliance Israélite and the Rothschilds. Our state, church, and literary swindlers are so shameless and the public so stupid, that anything can be expected.

# Architectural Forms as Culture and World-Sensing Thoughts Commemorative Address on September 20, 1916

Today three years have passed since we gathered on this hill—since a number of our friends gathered here to lay the foundation stone of this building. This building is to be a true embodiment of the spirit (*Wahrzeichen*, lit. "true sign") for those spiritual impulses which are breaking into the new development of culture—those impulses that have become an absolute necessity in the new development of culture; a necessity because the insight into the world that humankind needs for its very existence can only be hoped for from these impulses; because the loving, human understanding necessary for human life can only be hoped for through these impulses. At that time, we began that festive event with the feeling of experiencing an important moment of that spiritual development which, for a longer or shorter period of time, we have sheltered in our hearts, in our forces of conviction. At that time, everything went through our thoughts that the human heart may feel of the ascending development of humanity. We did not think at that time about what—although foreseeable—need not always be considered on account of that mysterious force which thoughts harbor; we did not think of that sorrowful, painful time which, meanwhile, has broken in upon European humanity. It still lay in the future—even if in a near future—this experience which belongs, in any case, to the most painful that earthly humanity could have lived through. No matter how painful all else that they have had to experience has been, this experience which, in the meantime, has swept over the ground of Europe—this experience belongs to that which could severely depress one who lacks the power of inwardly rising-up from out of the deepest consciousness of the weaving and working of the spiritual world.

Now, after three years of work on our building, it really does not seem to be a time to celebrate joyful festivities. One would really have to be untrue to one's own heart in a certain way if one only wanted to let a festive mood arise. And so, we will have to leave that which can be a festive mood to another time, and we will do better today if we take more to heart—in a few thoughts that are reminiscent of what has already been said here from this very place—the ideals: those precisely which, in a way, historically stood within our movement; those that filled us when we set about realizing this building.

This thought has proceeded out of the devotional character that many souls, or at least a number of souls, have had throughout the years in which, one might say, our movement has been nurtured in its journey. The longing for our movement to build a place of its own arose in a mature soul most luminously, most energetically—in the soul of our unforgettable Miss Sophie Stinde in Munich—and coinciding later with what arose as a necessity for the performances of our Mystery Plays and such as was connected with them. Thus, the thought was first directed to building a place for our movement and for that which spiritually flows through our movement. And from this thought was born the other: in this very place itself, to realize our spiritual movement; that is, to build this place in such a way that in its forms, in its whole being itself, a representation of our spiritual movement could stand outwardly visible before the world. For this purpose, however, the building in question had to be placed in a living, productive way not only in the modern spiritual life alone, but it—the building—had to be placed in the midst of all the necessities, all the emerging necessities of the modern spiritual life. What was to be created was not just some, so to speak, indifferent building for our souls; rather, a cultural thought had to be manifested through our building itself. Then the question could come before the soul: What does this modern spiritual culture itself require as an architectural concept of modern culture? Then one could not get along without the knowledge that all really fruitful architectural concepts—like all fruitful artistic impulses in general—were connected with the spiritual movements of the corresponding ages, with the emerging spiritual movements of the corresponding ages. One cannot think of

Greek architecture without having the feeling that the forms of this architecture are themselves like Greek cultural thoughts—crystallized, poured into form, brought to life in form. Whoever delves into this Greek style of building will find that what has been achieved in this style, in this pure architectural style, corresponds to the sensitivity felt in the worldview of Hellenism, corresponds to what the Greek felt as an answer to their tremendous question of humanity: Which forces are there, working from out of the Earth-being, that carry the human essence in order that it is harmoniously placed, as human essence, upon this Earth? When one sees the ancient Greeks (by recreating them in the spirit) wandering over the Greek landscape with their particular world-perceptions, in their way of looking at the world with its essence, then one feels how in these Greeks—more or less unconsciously—something lived that could spring up directly from the Earth's forces of gravity, to then place them on Earth in correspondence with how they felt as earthly human beings between birth and death. The recapitulation of this feeling lives in the beautiful measurements, in the wonderful statics of Greek architecture—it lives in that inner coherence of Greek architecture, which makes the form of this architecture appear as if it had grown out of the mysterious gravitational and static forces of the Earth's body itself—out of those forces which in their inner, proportional harmony at the same time weave and flow through what the Greek tragedians, what Homer, what Greek sculpture, what also Greek philosophy, created. A great artistic stream can only come from an emphatic worldview. The Greeks wanted to live in the *spirit of the Earth*. Out of the spirit of the Earth they created their architectural statics.

As we let our view glide over the centuries, we again find—allowing for the imprecision necessary for such a survey—we again see how, under the influence of the Mystery of Golgotha and under the impulses which have impelled a part of the Earth's humanity to the understanding of this Mystery of Golgotha, new architectural forms develop. We see how the human being has also discovered, in regards to their sensitivity, that they are not only standing within their being—which runs its course between birth and death, in earthly and spiritual activity—but also that from above, the World Soul penetrates and spiritualizes everything that human beings can do to affect the Earth. And we see an outer embodiment of what medieval humanity received from above, from the *heavenly spirit*, just as the Greek received their impulses from the earthly spirit; we thus see medieval architecture emerging. Medieval architecture, in turn, is spiritualized, interwoven, and permeated by the energetic, mighty stream of the worldview that goes through the world in an enlightening way. We would have to mention many things if we wanted to show how the Christian spirit lives in art; we would have to cite many things to show how the Christian spirit lives in pre-Raphaelic art, in the art of Raphael, in the art of Leonardo and Michelangelo, how the Christian spirit lives in the Gothic as that which strives heavenwards—many things to mention, if we wanted to describe all the impulses that were so powerfully expressed in the characteristics of the design (*Gestalt*), where one tried to express the working and speaking of the soul inspired by the heavenly spirit, which then found its highest development in Dürer, in Holbein. For the same impulse that lives in Gothic architecture lives in Dürer, lives in Holbein.

With this, however, we have already come up, as it were, in a great overview (which of course must necessarily be imprecise) to the most recent times. And there the human spirit is, as it were, brought to a halt: when the misery of the Thirty Years' War passes over Europe, over Central Europe in particular, which was preceded by a wonderful uplifting of hearts to freedom in such movements as those of Zwingli, Hus, and the like. One then sees—originally without this idea, in order that it can be more fully understood, but then in such a way that the following becomes clear: This whole misery of the Thirty Years' War was fomented and stirred up by a spirit which already had in itself much of the later Jesuit spirit. And we see coming up under the influence of this apparently spirit-nurturing impulse the very forces which poured materialism over Europe. We see arising a time in which a worldview emerges that, according to the inner sensations of human beings, wants to go only to the material, but cannot grasp the material because it does not want to grasp the spirit in matter. We see across Europe a worldview that does not want to let freedom unfold; because it more and more wants to squeeze everything that strives for freedom into rigid, blind obedience. We see how the human-all-too-human pours into that which flows through history as spirit. And under this influence we see the impossibility of directly realizing forms in art from out of that which lives spiritually.

And at first, one could say, there emerges the spiritual baroque stylet, which is by all means a faithful expression of the more modern times, but shows in itself how what lives in human thoughts, in human sensations, expresses itself in a subjective-willful way in the artistic form, in the artistic works in general. No longer do we see how the soul feels urged to witness secrets of Earth-statics, of Earth-heaviness, as it did when it built Greek temples; no longer do we see the soul expressing directly that which it witnesses when it immerses itself in heavenly heights, as it did then when it created the Gothic, when Dürer adapted his so very expressive figures to the inner experiences that saturated his great soul. *More often* we see how attempts are made, everywhere where architectural thoughts should be, to impose instead the thoughts of the human intellect, that which is permeated with human-all-too-human sensations. We see how all kinds of figures are inserted into the columns, into the arrangements of the supports—things which do not have a structural effect; which arise from human intention; which have only a decorative effect; which do not know how to separate the sculptural thought, the painterly thought, from the architectural thought; and which, in turn, do not know how to combine—because they do not know how to purely separate—these different kinds of motifs. We see how an affected inwardness is used to carry a religious worldview that is no longer filled with true inwardness. We enter many a church building whose columns we no longer understand because those that built them have not studied the objective conditions of the world; because the columns were supposed to express something that had already fled from the artist's direct elemental force on account of the worldview they held. One walks through porticoes in which columns have forms that are not architectural, but are picturesque; niches are delimited by columns in a picturesque way. But a sense of mystery should speak out from such niches; a sense of mystery should show how these columns carry what they have to carry. We see human figures of saints placed in the most impossible places, not arising from an immediate architectural necessity, which lets the sculpture arise in the right place and lets the painting arise in the right place from out of the architecture. We see how something works in art that no longer directly serves the worldview; we see the materialistic worldview coming forward, but it is powerless to create a real art form that is appropriate for it.

And then the way was not far which led to the degenerations of the baroque style—that style which is interesting and full of significance because it shows how the more modern times want to live, turning itself away from the spirit; how it, however, cannot find any original artistic thought, but only the everyday thoughts with which one is filled, and can more or less only express itself inartistically. This becomes especially clear when the baroque style, one could say, is snatched from the Jesuits by Louis XIV and implemented into the secular. However, humankind never remained unaware that what should be an art that gives testimony to a significant event—a monument—should not be without connection with the highest and greatest that humankind can find when it immerses itself in the universe. But, into the modern human-all-too-human, like a crash, something mixed in there which, in a somewhat rigid, in a somewhat academic form (as we would say today), asserted itself like a renewal of the ancient art in the middle of the baroque style; so we often see, one could say, a baroque way mixed with the ancient. So that we see, especially in the art that is linked to the name of Louis XIV, how stiffly classical forms outwardly conceal all-too-human baroque forms inside, through which the human spirit does not want to somehow find admission to any world secrets—even if they are obvious—but through which it only wants to perpetuate its whims, its everyday feelings and sensations, in the forms that appear to it all around on the outer surfaces.

And so, we see how buildings come into being—for certain reasons, I do not want to name individual buildings, because they are not yet judged in the right way even by the present time, and therefore the judgment would not be understood—how buildings come into being that are virtually human whimsies cast into forms . . . judged from the innermost artistic need. We see how the baroque Voltairism of thought reappears in countless places in the baroque shaping of artistic form. But not in the way Greek or Gothic forms are adapted to the innermost essence of the human worldview and world perception, but in the way a superficial exterior is an imitation of what the human being experiences in their inner being.

And then, when we direct our view further over the development of human art, we experience how in the eighteenth century human longing goes back to revive the Greeks, to revive the Greek perception, the Greek sense of art. We see how such a spirit as Winckelmann seeks a truly religious consecration in understanding again the Greek spirit, the Greek spirit of art. We then see how, under these impulses of Winckelmann, the nineteenth century strives to recreate artistic forms that were there in the Greek spirit. But the worldview of materialism had never been able to gain the force—the inner force that is needed to think, to feel, to inwardly perceive strongly enough what is thought, felt, and perceived—so that it pours out, as if of itself, into its own forms, as was the case with Hellenism, as it was with the Gothics. And so, in the nineteenth century, we see that wonderful yet essentially strange external striving of an Overbeck, of a Cornelius, to create forms, to create artistic designs, but without the mighty, streaming, permeating impulse of a worldview. Old motifs, old worldviews are sought; old ideas are revived.

Architecture especially suffered from this powerlessness of modern materialistic thinking. Beautiful, splendidly beautiful things in the renewal of the Renaissance, in the renewal of antiquity, have been produced by the architects of the nineteenth century. But everything stands, I would like to say, under the impulse that has just been indicated. Study such a wonderful revival of the Renaissance as that by Gottfried Semper (you can study it at the *Polytechnikum* in Zurich) and you will see how impossible it is for the architectural thoughts to somehow grasp what should be expressed through architectural thoughts.

And so, we see that time approaching when architecture—even though it has a certain greatness because it has studied and expressed ancient forms in a wonderful way—nevertheless shows itself to be powerless in the face of the higher developmental impulses of humanity. We see how Greek forms are built up, as it were, like an outer shell around those corporate bodies which, in reality, basically only disfigure that which they themselves do not know, as, for instance, many a modern architect has done when they have developed Greek forms like shells over modern parliaments. Or we can see how deeply architects influenced by the Gothic style, who with their hearts and souls are quite distant from the old Catholicism, build up the Gothic like an outer shell around what should happen in the Gothic building—a building, however, which they are completely distant from with their own feeling, with their own sensibility. And so we stand before such buildings with a finer perception for art in that we feel they are erected by human beings who, with their hearts, with their sensations toward the offering of the Mass that is to be performed therein, stand quite distant from all that is happening there.

How different are the effects of the buildings that were built by those who were still in sympathy with the old Christian feelings—those feelings which were felt in the times when the host was lifted up for consecration with other inner sensations than in modern times; how different are those buildings which have an effect like an embodied mysticism in contrast to the cold life of the present, if one looks for this life in the overall context of the spiritual and social life of humankind; how different in the case of the buildings in whose stone composition nothing has poured out of what is supposed to take place in it as holy activity and as feelings trembling through the human soul! And so, one often has the feeling towards this art that one has—if one really looks at works of art with interest—when an atheist paints a Madonna!

Only from this perception could the impulse arise for the cultural thinking that was necessary for our building. The old impulses, as we know, can no longer be brought to the liveliness that enables them to come alive in the forms. What is created in the old forms will only be antiquated. But we may believe that our spiritual science has such a strong inner force that from out of itself it can give birth to forms; and those forms of which it may be believed that they emerge through an inner, living process from our spiritual-scientific worldview—those wanted to be realized in our building. And that connection should show itself again which must exist between art and worldview, and which can always be expressed only by the fact that a Madonna can only be painted by one who carries an impulse from inner sensations of encountering the Madonna in their soul. Modern human beings will not carry this impulse in their souls in such a way that they can make artistic forms out of it in truth. *New impulses* must come into humanity through spiritual science, if humanity does not want to lead itself ad absurdum. Therefore, the beginning must be made with new artistic forms, which arise from out of themselves through a new worldview. Whoever, therefore, wants to understand what the building—whose foundation stone we laid three years ago—wants to represent, must understand this from the living comprehension of our spiritual-scientific worldview, must understand how that which is intended as a beginning flows out of that *synthesis between the understanding of heaven and the understanding of Earth* which we call the spiritual-scientific worldview, just as Greek architecture came out of the earthly outlook of Hellenism, just as Gothic grew out of the heavenly outlook of medieval Christianity. We would be foolish if we wanted to believe that with a first stroke, we would at once entirely achieve what is acceptable, not to say perfect, in the higher sense. Imperfect things can of course only be achieved for the first beginning. And we will never be able to think otherwise than to admit to ourselves that what we have begun is quite imperfect; a first, a very first beginning for forms which must arise, which will perhaps be in many, many respects very, very different from what has been attained with our building. But, one can already see in the building that with it is sought a living, growing forth of artistic forms from the impulse, from the inner sensation which pulsates through our worldview. Hence, since so much is different, those who are of the type who never want to tolerate anything new, just cannot understand—understandably cannot understand—this which is so different from what was perceived in the previous forms, in the previous way of sculpture, in the previous way of painting. Only when we see in this modest way what is imperfect, an imperfect beginning in our building, will we have the right feeling—a feeling which one can have precisely for the beginnings of a development, because in the beginnings of a development one can feel that something quite different can still be created out of the imperfect beginning, which wants to give nothing more than a stimulus.

For three years now, work has been done on the building; and those whose hearts are connected with what is intended by the building will now be filled with a true feeling of gratitude towards all those who have made sacrifices for what was to happen—sacrifices in this or that form—who have further contributed their labor; and many beautiful, glorious forces of such work have flowed into that which lies before us on this Dornach hill. And even if these three years have brought difficult feelings and inner sensations into our movement, we can still say: However things may develop, whatever may flow out of the karma of our movement—that which was possible to be felt in connection with what has been done, this is just such a feeling that flows deeply from the essence of our movement, which can really be counted among the most beautiful fruits of modern perception. We saw many a metamorphosis of this perception; we saw, for example, some people, such as our unforgettable Miss Stinde, whose whole heart and soul hung on the fact that this building was to be erected in Munich; we saw her, in a devoted way, change her perceptions in order to witness the transformation brought about by karma. Only the future will be able to teach us whether the resolutions made at that time for this transformation were absolutely correct, when the facts will reveal how the present culture receives that which is the anthroposophical movement. Many of the things that could have been expected have indeed failed to materialize; and it would seem like foolish boasting today if even just a few of the things that could rightly be described as having failed to materialize were to be reiterated.

The building was there. It also showed in external forms that a certain movement is there. One can see for oneself in the list of our movement's literature, in the many languages of the present educated world—one can see how often the opportunity was given to understand our movement, how much opportunity was given to relate what arose on the Dornach hill to certain necessities of our cultural movement. One could have expected, especially in the present time (which imposes such a heavy trial on humankind), that judgments would have been asserted that may have shown understanding for the deeper cultural significance of this spiritual-scientific direction, especially in view of this heavy time of suffering. As for voices of this kind: one may say that there was not even one which came from the outside during the difficult, sorrowful time of war; there were only a few isolated ones which came from within the Anthroposophical Society itself, and which naturally, due to the fact that the outside world showed so little understanding for the movement, had to fade away in the wind.

And so, today, when we want to look back, so to speak, on the impulses that inspired us three years ago, we can again only inwardly avow: to will to remain faithful to this impulse; to will to seek understanding for what this spiritual-scientific worldview, with all that is connected with it, should be for developing humanity.

From outside of Europe, from far away Asia, judgements are coming which are, in a certain respect, more correct in the assessment of the European world situation than all of what is sweeping through Europe. But just such judgments show that the renewal of Europe is possible only through the spiritual-scientific worldview. May the understanding for it really come. We suffer from the karma of thoughtlessness, that thoughtlessness which is at the same time brutal, because everywhere it likes to trample upon that which merely anticipates the spiritual necessities that lie at the foundation of our development in this time. Remarkable, remarkable: The longings (I have said it many times), they come to life everywhere—those longings which do not understand themselves—because they do not know where to go; and because they cannot find the way through the brutality of the time to that which should, as a worldview, have our building as a true embodiment of spiritual truth. They who observe just a bit of the times find many, many signs of the time; but only signs of longings. There is, one might say, a strange old fellow, a simple journeyman who, however, by what he has become, is a living witness in opposition to the nonsensical judgment of recent times which says that spiritual science could only be something for educated people and not for the simple souls. This is a nonsensical judgment; for it is precisely the simplest souls who feel in themselves those longings which can really be satisfied when they are not held back from their longings by the so-called brutal education of the time. What longings breathe in words such as these of a simple journeyman, who has read some books, has looked around in what one wishes for and can long for in the present, and who expresses himself in the following lines:

> Into the dream and spirit sphere,
> It appears, I am pulled,
> And each wave whispers
> To me, many a strange secret.
> And the sounds of life surge
> Out of the bosom of Nature;
> Misty shrouds, see I, fall
> From the world secrets' eternal trail.

> *In die Traum- und Geistersphäre*
> *Scheint es, bin ich eingezogen,*
> *Und es flüstern jene Wogen*
> *Mir manch fremd Geheimnis zu.*
> *Und des Lebens Töne wallen*
> *Aus dem Busen der Natur,*
> *Nebelhüllen seh' ich fallen*
> *Von des Weltgeheimnis ew'ger Spur.*

One is only able to come to the point of encountering such longings and finding the way to human hearts! We can look from this simple journeyman—who is actually a strange old fellow, as I said—who tried to get through from cognizing to beholding; we can look to the man whom I have already mentioned,[105] to Christian von Ehrenfels, a professor at Prague University of whom I have said that in his *Kosmogonie* [Cosmogony] he tries to get an idea from imagining backwards, where we see longing inclined towards the way which is to be reached, to be striven for, precisely through the spiritual deepening in such a manner as viewing events in reverse. The darkness of the present so-called philosophy, of course, lets such spirits see only in a limited way, but sometimes lets a yearning sprout up in them—though the stultifying education of the time holds them back from the understanding of spiritual science. And so, it remains as their experience. But such experiences as these are sometimes quite remarkable. And this *Kosmogonie* of Christian von Ehrenfels— it ends in a remarkable way. He sought in his own way, this professor, to look upon the world and the course of the world; he sought to make clear to himself the needs of the present from the course of history; and what does he say at the end?

In this sense, and from this perspective, I have tried to understand human history, and have arrived at the following conclusion—which, however, I can only communicate now without the armament of scientific arguments as a mere expectant anticipation:

In God, with the elevation of the human intellect (and probably with similar processes on other heavenly bodies), self-consciousness is awakened and a phase of the internalization of His working begun.

In and with the human being, God is looking for a leading idea, which would be able to guide His hitherto instinctive designing (*Gestalten*) into channels of purposeful consciousness.

This idea has not yet been found.

Think: such a human being calls, of course, the most nearby spirit that he can still surmise—his God—as the more recent time does in general. But he has understood from history that he lives in a time in which this spirit standing next to him has something planned for humankind, that he stands at a decisive turning point. So that he says to himself: In God himself a phase of the internalization of his work has begun . . . . That, he still feels. "In and with the human being," he continues, "God is looking for a leading idea." As a human being he does not feel powerfully enough, is not thinking strongly enough towards leading ideas, guiding aims; but he suspects a God who is looking for leading ideas, "which would be able to guide His hitherto instinctive designing" (the designing of God), "into channels of purposeful consciousness. This idea has not yet been found." With this, the book closes: So, may it be then that a God who hovers somewhere finds a leading idea out of the instinctive will. Thus concludes a philosophical book written in the immediate present.

Wherever we look—the two examples I have given, that of a journeyman and that of a university professor, they could be multiplied a hundredfold, a thousandfold—it would become apparent everywhere how such a deep longing exists that is to be fulfilled by what is to be expressed through our building. When one realizes how this building had to be held at a distance from everything conventional, and how only that which flows out of the spiritual-scientific worldview as an impulse of inner sensation and perception (*Empfindungsimpuls*) should be embodied in it in this way, when one realizes how we had to keep a distance from that outer symbolization on the other side, if we understand how we had to keep a distance from that which occurs everywhere in outwardly dull occult societies and societies striving for occultism, if we understand how truth had to be sought in the idea for the building between the conventional and the stale symbolism of the more recent times—then we will also discover, from this building-monument, what fruitful seeds and productive impulses want to be present in spiritual science.

If we take up such a will, such a feeling into our soul for all that the future may bring, then the building will be able to be for us—even already as it is today after three years—what we perceived as a beginning when we laid the foundation stone three years ago, full as we were with our spiritual-scientific ideals. Let us feel this especially in the midst of the time in which quite different impulses lead themselves ad absurdum; let us try to feel how the one is connected with the other: One will see that one *can* feel it, when one *wills* to. However, much of this feeling has not yet been truly realized. But in many of our souls there lives an honest, genuine will; and this honest, genuine will— if it is true to itself—will add understanding to the honesty of the will; and then—in all our souls—the other foundation stone will be able to form. This other foundation stone would like to carry spiritually into the world, in various and manifold ways, that which we ourselves wanted to establish, for the sake of our ideal, upon the physical foundation stone which, three years ago, we sacredly entrusted to the Earth, here on this hill.

Endnotes
105
 Rudolf Steiner, *The Riddle of Humanity*, lecture in Dornach on Aug. 13, 1916, CW 170.

# Abbreviations:

*Nachrichten für Mitglieder* = *Das Goetheanum: Was in der Anthroposophischen Gesellschaft
vorgeht? Nachrichten für deren
Mitglieder.* [The Goetheanum:
What is going on in the Anthroposophical Society? News for
the members.] Members supplement in the weekly journal.

*M.A.DE.* = *Mitteilungen aus der anthroposophischen Arbeit in Deutschland*
[Communications from the anthroposophical work in Germa-
ny]

*Since 2003 supplement in *An-
throposophie: Vierteljahrschrift
zur anthroposophischen Arbeit
in Deutschland* [Anthroposophy:
Quarterly on anthroposophical
work in Germany]

*STIL* = *STIL: Goetheanistisches Bilden
und Bauen* [STYLE: Goetheanistic forming and building]

# First Publication of Essays

Erika von Baravalle:

- **On the Mystery of the Laying of the Foundation Stone**:
  "Vom Mysterium der Grundsteinlegung: Zum 90. Jahrestag der Grundsteinlegung des ersten Goetheanumbaues am 20. September 1913, *Nachrichten für Mitglieder* [News for members] 80, no. 38 (Sept. 21, 2003).

- **"It Will Be Ensheathed!" Rudolf Steiner's Address, Given during the Act of Consecration**:
  "'Er werde verhüllt!' Zu Vorgang und Wortlaut des Grundsteinlegungsakts für das Erste Goetheanum" ['It will be ensheathed!], *Nachrichten für Mitglieder* [News for members] 81, no. 38 (Sept. 19, 2003): 1–3. The original stenographic report on Steiner's address was made by Rudolf Hahn and was given to Marie Steiner by Mrs. Hahn.

- **The Dornach Hill as the Center of the Anthroposophical Movement**:
  "Der Dornacher Hügel als Zentrum der anthroposophischen Bewegung: Fortsetzung der Betrachtungen zur Grundsteinlegung 1913, *Nachrichten für Mitglieder* [News for members] .

- **The Composition of the Foundation Stone**:
  "Zur Komposition des Grundsteins." First published in the original German edition of the present book, 2013.

- **The Relationship of the Foundation Stone to the Second Goetheanum Building**:
  "Der Grundstein in seiner Beziehung zum Zweiten Goetheanum-Bau." First published in the original German edition of the present book, 2013.

- **The Model Building in Malsch**:
  "Der Rosenkreuzer-Initiationstempel, dargestellt im Modelbau von Malsch", *STIL* 29, no. 2 (St. John's Tide, 2007).

- **The House of the Word**:
  "'Haus des Wortes.' Bauformen als Schule der Be-
  gegnung IV: Das Erste Goetheanum.", *Nachrichten für
  Mitglieder* [News for members] 84, no. 37 (Sept. 14,
  2007).

- **The Michael Building: The Spatial Concept in the
  Second Goetheanum**:
  "Der Michaelsbau: Zum Raumgedanken des Zweiten
  Goetheanum," *M.A.DE.* 50, no. 197 (Michaelmas,
  1996).

- **Forms That awaken an Envisioning of Karma**
  "Karma-Schauen erweckende Bauformen," *Nachrichten für Mitglieder* [News for members] 87, no. 20 (May
  14, 2010).

Max Benzinger:

- **An Eyewitness Report of the Laying of the Foundation Stone**:
  "Ein Augenzeuge der Grundsteinlegung berichtet: Aus
  einer Niederschrift von Max Benzinger", *M.A.DE.* 17,
  no. 65 (Michaelmas, 1963).

Ernst Bindel:

- **The Symbolic Significance of the Pentagonal Do-
  decahedron as the Foundation Stone of Spiritually
  Significant Buildings**:
  "Die sinnbildliche Bedeutung des Pentagon-Dode-
  kaeders als Grundstein geistig bedeutsamer Bauten,
  *M.A.DE.* 10, no. 38 (Christmas, 1956).

Walther Bühler:

- **"When Mercurius Stood in the Scales." The Cosmological Aspect of the Laying of the Foundation
  Stone**:
  "'Da Mercurius in der Waage stand': Der kosmolo-
  gische Aspekt der Grundsteinlegung," *M.A.DE.* 7, no.

25 (Michaelmas, 1953)

Fritz Götte:

- **The Human Soul's "Cry of Longing for the Spirit"**:
  "Der Menschenseele 'Sehnsuchtsschrei nach dem Geiste': Zur Ansprache vom 20. September 1913", *M.A.DE.* 17, no. 65 (Michaelmas, 1963).

- **Macrocosmic World-Prayer, the Lord's Prayer, and the Foundation Stone**:
  "Makrokosmisches Weltengebet, Vaterunser und der Grundstein," *M.A.DE.* 10, no. 38 (Christmas, 1956).

- **From the Laying of the Foundation Stone in 1913 to the Laying of the Foundation Stone in 1923. Part I**:
  "Von der Grundsteinlegung 1913 zur Grundsteinlegung 1923, Teil I: Bis zum 20. September 1913,"*M.A.DE.* 7, no. 25 (Michaelmas, 1953).

- **From the Laying of the Foundation Stone in 1913 to the Laying of the Foundation Stone in 1923. Part II**:
  "Von der Grundsteinlegung 1913 zur Grundsteinlegung 1923, Teil II," *M.A.DE.* 7, no. 26 (Christmas, 1953).

Nelly Grosheintz-Laval:

- **Memories in Commemoration of the Ceremony of the Laying of the Foundation Stone of the First Goetheanum**: "Erinnerungen im Gedenken an die Feier der Grundsteinlegung zum Ersten Goetheanum," *M.A.DE.* 7, no. 25 (Michaelmas, 1953).

Heinz Müller:

- **Memories of the Fire of the Old Goetheanum on New Year's Eve 1922/23**: "Erinnerungen an den Brand des alten Goetheanums in der Silvesternacht 1922/23." (Gesprochen bei der 30 Jahres-Erinnerungsfeier 1952 in Stuttgart) , *M.A.DE.* 7, no. 26 (Christmas, 1953).

Wilhelm Schrack:

– **Letter to Jürgen von Grone**: "Eine Erinnerung aus der Zeit vor der Grundsteinlegung 1913," *M.A.DE.* 7, no. 26 (Christmas, 1953).

Rudolf Steiner:

– **Address Given during the Act of Consecration, September 20, 1913**:
Rudolf Grosse, *Die Weihnachtstagung als Zeitenwende* (Dornach: Philosophisch-Anthroposophischer Verlag, 1976).

– **Address Given to Those Gathered around the Top of the Earthen Pit, after the Sinking of the Foundation Stone, September 20, 1913**:
"Grundsteinlegung des Goetheanum-Baues am 20. September 1913. Die Ansprache Rudolf Steiners auf dem Dornacher Hügel," *M.A.DE.* 17, no. 65 (Michaelmas, 1963).

– **The Longing of the Soul for the Spirit: A Sign of the Times. Commemorative Address on September 20, 1914**:
*Die Sehnsucht der Seelen nach Geist: Ein Zeichen der Zeit. Worte Rudolf Steiners am ersten Jahrestag der Grundstein-Legung des Goetheanum in Dornach am 20. September 1914*, edited by Marie Steiner (Dornach: Philosophisch-Anthroposophicher Verlag, 1938).

**Architectual Forms as Culture and World-Sensing Thoughts. Commemorative Address on September 20, 1916**:
*Bauformen als Kultur- und Weltempfindungsgedanken. Worte Rudolf Steiners am 3. Jahrestag der Grundstein-legung des ersten Goetheanum in Dornach am 20. September 1916*, edited by Marie Steiner (Dornach: Philosophisch-Anthroposophicher Verlag, 1934).

Elisabeth Vreede:

– **"When Mercurius Stood in the Scales." The Stellar Script**:
"'Da Merkurius in der Wage stand.' Die Sternenschrift," *Rundschreiben der Mathematisch-Astronomischen Sektion* [Circular letters of the Mathematical-Astronomical Section] 2, no. 1 (September, 1928).

# About the Authors

## Erika von Baravalle

December 18, 1928, in Heidelberg, Germany; † June 5, 2016, in Dornach, Switzerland. 1949–64 studies in music education, German, and German literature; final examinations for conservatory and university, student teacher with degree. Further studies in classical archaeology and educational science. Upper school teacher at the *Freie Waldorfschule* (Free Waldorf School) in Tübingen, Germany. 1964, marriage to Albert von Baravalle, Dornach. 1968–89, public high school teacher of German and music in Basel. Since 1965, artistic and scientific research on the fundamental principles and background of Rudolf Steiner's building impulse and the unfolding of the Goetheanum building thought; with numerous lectures, courses, and essays. 1977, organization of the first casting of Baravalle's 1:100 reconstruction model of the exterior architecture of the First Goetheanum. In the following years, she was able to send over 40 casts to anthroposophical centers. [Until her death in 2016], supervising, archiving, exhibition, and publication of the architectural and artistic work of Albert von Baravalle

## Max Benzinger

1877; † February 2, 1949, in Stuttgart, Germany. Locksmith, activist of the threefolding movement, therapist. In Munich, took care of Christian Morgenstern when seriously ill. Made the Goetheanum's copper foundation stone for Rudolf Steiner, also a large wooden model of the building. In Dornach, he collaborated in the construction of the Goetheanum. In Stuttgart, he was involved in the activities for the social threefolding movement.

## Ernst Bindel

August 6, 1890, in Magdeburg, Germany; † November 16, 1974, in Stuttgart, Germany. Waldorf teacher, mathematician, physicist, and writer. He was the last Stuttgart Waldorf teacher hired by Rudolf Steiner in 1925. In 1921, he became a member of the Anthroposophical Society. He studied Richard Wagner's music at an early age and was able to attend the Bayreuth Festival in 1911. During the years when the Waldorf School was closed, he again worked at upper-level secondary schools and after World War II became a major collaborator in the reconstruction of the Stuttgart School, in which he continued to work after his retirement until shortly before his death. Selected works:

"Die Ergänzung Schopenhauers durch Wagner" [The supplementation of Schopenhauer by Wagner] and "Tristan und Isolde" [Tristan and Isolde] *Bayreuther Blätter* [Bayreuth papers] 37, no. 1–3, 4–6 (1914): 5, 73;

*Die ägyptischen Pyramiden als Zeugen vergangener Mysterienweisheit: Zugleich eine allgemein-verständliche Einführung in die Symbolik von Zahlen und Figuren* [The Egyptian Pyramids as witnesses of past Mystery wisdom: Together with a generally understandable introduction to the symbolism of numbers and figures], 4th edn. (Stuttgart: Freies Geistesleben, 1975);

*Die geistigen Grundlagen der Zahlen: Die Zahl im Spiegel der Kulturen. Elemente einer spirituellen Geometrie und Arithmetik* [The spiritual foundations of numbers: Number in the mirror of cultures. Elements of a spiritual geometry and arithmetic], new edn. (Stuttgart: Freies Geistesleben, 2022);

*Die Zahlengrundlagen der Musik im Wandel der Zeiten* [The numerical foundations of music in the flux of the times], 2nd edn. (Stuttgart: Freies Geistesleben, 1985);

*Pythagoras: Leben und Lehre in Wirklichkeit und Legende* [Pythagoras: Life and teaching in reality and legend] (Stuttgart: Freies Geistesleben, 1962).

## Walther Bühler

April 2, 1913, in Homburg (Saarland), Germany; † October 14, 1995, in Unterlengenhardt, Germany. Physician, cosmologist, versatile researcher, speaker, writer. Friendships during years of study with Gisbert Husemann and Walter Holzapfel. Dissertation on "Mondenwirksamkeit in der Nativität" (*Lunar effects on nativity*). Attended Ita Wegman's medical courses in Arlesheim. Employment at the *Physiologischen Institut* (Physiological Institute) in Heidelberg, Germany. Marriage to Oskar Schmiedel's daughter Gunda. Work at the "Burghalde" sanatorium in Unterlengenhardt, Germany. 1957, founded the *Para-*

*celsus Krankenhaus* (Paracelsus Hospital) in Unterlengenhardt. Lectured widely and published a variety of writings.

Selected works:

*Metamorphoses of Light: Lightning, Rainbows, and the Northern Lights. A Spiritual-Scientific Study.* Translated from the German by David F. Luborsky (Forest Row, East Sussex: Temple Lodge, 2015);

*Living with Your Body: Health, Illness, and Understanding the Human Being.* Translated from the German by L. Maloney (Forest Row, East Sussex: Rudolf Steiner Press, repr. 2013);

*Why Is Easter a Movable Feast? The Spiritual Significance of the Changing Date of Easter.* Translated from the German by Catherine de Bruyne, abridged edn. (Floris Books, 2017);

*Die Sonne als Weltenherz* [The Sun as the cosmic heart of the world] (Stuttgart: Freies Geistesleben, 1966);

*Der Stern der Weisen: Vom Rhythmus der grossen Konjunktion Saturn-Jupiter* (The Star of the Wise: On the rhythm of the great Saturn-Jupiter conjunction) (Stuttgart: Freies Geistesleben, 1983).

## Fritz Götte

August 31, 1901, in Jena, Germany; † April 28, 1989 in Au near Freiburg im Breisgau, Germany. Businessman, editor. Employee and later director of Weleda in Schwäbisch Gmünd, Germany, until 1951. Editor of *M.A.DE.* for many years. Fought uncompromisingly and successfully for the existence of Weleda against the Nazis. In 1947, co-founder of the publishing house *Freies Geistesleben* (Free Spiritual Life). Worked intensively after the war to rebuild the Anthroposophical Society and to bring together the various karmic streams.

Selected works:

*Cultura. Zehn Essays* [Culture: Ten essays] (Stuttgart: Freies Geistesleben, 1952);

*Die gesellschaftliche Arbeit im Zeitalter des Industrialismus* [Social work in the age of industrialism]. Edited by Institut für soziale Gegenwartsfragen (Institute for Contemporary Social Issues). *Sozialwissenschaftliches Studienmaterial VI* [Social Science Study Material VI]. (Freiburg: unknown publisher, 1976).

## Nelly Grosheintz[-Laval]

March 5, 1875, in Saint-Imier, Switzerland; † January 28, 1955, in Dornach, Switzerland. Wife of the Basel dentist Emil Grosheintz and sister-in-law of Oscar Grosheintz who lived in Bern, Switzerland. Together with her husband, she gave Rudolf Steiner the land of the Dornach hill for the building of the Goetheanum in 1913. (Dec. 1914: Maid of Honor at Rudolf Steiner and Marie von Sivers' wedding.) As the owner of House Duldeck, which Rudolf Steiner designed and placed right on top of the Mystery hill, she asked him to make three significant changes to his project: enlarge the narrow corner reinforcements on the Goetheanum side into round "meditation rooms"; introduce the balcony there and on the valley side; and expand the attic for guest rooms. In the lower central room, there was a long table in the middle where the parents dined with their two sons and many guests.

## Heinz Müller

December 25, 1899, in Gehren (Thuringia), Germany; † November 26, 1968, in Hamburg, Germany. Waldorf teacher, lecturer, co-worker at the research center of the Union of Independent Waldorf Schools, student of mathematics and physics. "Member" of the German youth group, Wandervogel. Participation in the East-West Congress in Vienna in 1922. Invitation from Rudolf Steiner to a speech course in Dornach in the summer of that year as his personal guest. Co-initiator of the Pedagogical Youth Course in 1922. Participation in the Christmas Course in 1922. Experienced the fire from its beginning. Accompanied Rudolf Steiner to the newly founded Waldorf School in Hamburg, where he worked for the rest of his life. Participation in the Christmas Conference in 1923. Special artistic method as class teacher with performances of self-written plays (e.g., "Julian Apostata" [Julian the Apostate]).

Selected Works:

*Spuren auf dem Weg: Erinnerungen* [Traces along the way: Memories], 4th edn. (Stuttgart: J.Ch. Mellinger, 1983);

*Report Verses in Rudolf Steiner's Art of Education: Healing Forces in Words and Their Rhythms*. Translated from the German by Jesse Darrell, 2nd edn. (Great Britain: Floris Books, 2013).

## Elisabeth Vreede

July 16, 1879, in The Hague, Netherlands; † August 31, 1943, in Ascona, Switzerland. Mathematician, astronomer, member of the founding Executive Council (*Vorstand*) of the General Anthroposophical Society, leader of the Mathematical-Astronomical Section at the Goetheanum. Came from a theosophical home. First encounter with Rudolf Steiner in 1903 in London. One of Rudolf Steiner's early collaborators, first in Berlin, and, since 1910, put all her forces at the disposal of the anthroposophical movement. 1914, collaboration on the Goetheanum building. From 1918, built up library and archives at the Goetheanum with her own funds. 1920, moved to Arlesheim. Participation in the Hague Course for Higher Education (*Haager Hochschulkurs*) in 1922. Section circular letters (*Rundschreiben*) since 1927; star calendar since 1929. Many lectures and essays. Supported young mathematicians such as Hermann von Baravalle, Ernst Bindel, and George Adams.

Selected works:

"Die Berechtigung der Mathematik in der Astronomie und ihre Grenzen" [The justification of mathematics in astronomy and its limits] *Anthroposophische Hochschulkurse* [Anthroposophical courses of higher education], 135–164, lectures from Dornach on October 13 & 14, 1920.

*Mathesis: Beiträge zur Weiterbildung der Mathematik und verwandter Gebiete im Sinne der Geisteswissenschaft* [Mathesis: Contributions to the further education of mathematics and related fields in the sense of spiritual science]. Edited by Elizabeth Vreede. Mathematisch-Astronomischen Sektion der Freien Hochschule für Geisteswissenschaft am Goetheanum (Mathematical-Astronomical Section of the Free School of Spiritual Science at the Goetheanum) (Stuttgart: Orient-Occident, 1931);

*The Constellation at the Time of Christ's Birth* (Arlesheim: unknown publisher, 1937).

*Astronomy and Spiritual Science: The Astronomical Letters of Elisabeth Vreede*. Translated from the German by Ronald Koetzsch and Anne Riegel (Great Barrington, MA: SteinerBooks, 2007).